DOCTOR WHO

VOLUME 3: SKY JACKS!

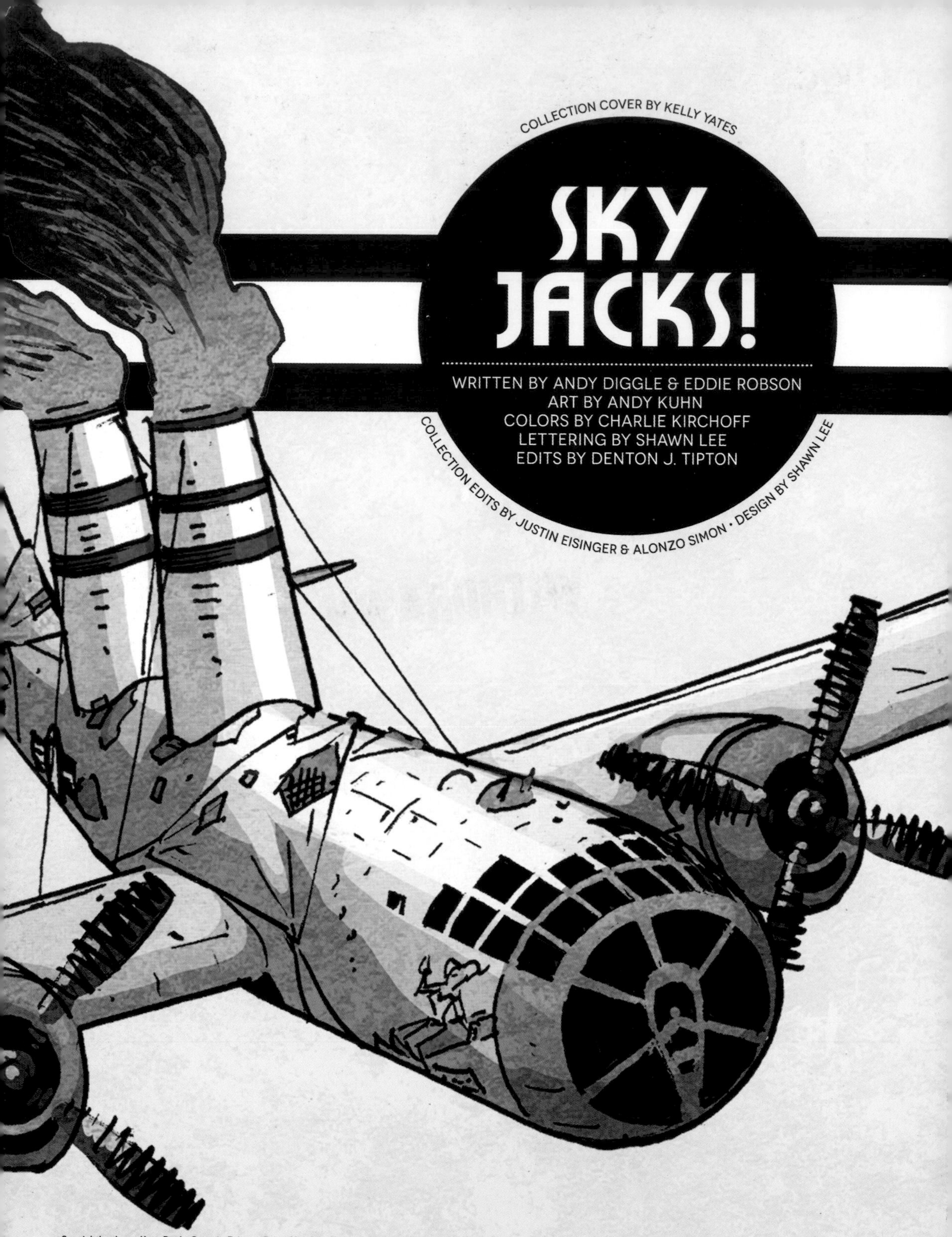

COLLECTION COVER BY KELLY YATES

SKY JACKS!

WRITTEN BY ANDY DIGGLE & EDDIE ROBSON
ART BY ANDY KUHN
COLORS BY CHARLIE KIRCHOFF
LETTERING BY SHAWN LEE
EDITS BY DENTON J. TIPTON

COLLECTION EDITS BY JUSTIN EISINGER & ALONZO SIMON · DESIGN BY SHAWN LEE

Special thanks to Kate Bush, Georgie Britton, Brian Minchin, Richard Cookson, Matt Nichols, and Ed Casey at BBC Worldwide for their invaluable assistance.

IDW founded by Ted Adams, Alex Garner, Kris Oprisko, and Robbie Robbins

ISBN: 978-1-61377-791-6

16 15 14 13 1 2 3 4

IDW

Ted Adams, CEO & Publisher
Greg Goldstein, President & COO
Robbie Robbins, EVP/Sr. Graphic Artist
Chris Ryall, Chief Creative Officer/Editor-in-Chief
Matthew Ruzicka, CPA, Chief Financial Officer
Alan Payne, VP of Sales
Dirk Wood, VP of Marketing
Lorelei Bunjes, VP of Digital Services

Originally published as DOCTOR WHO VOLUME 3 issues #9–12 and DOCTOR WHO SPECIAL 2012.

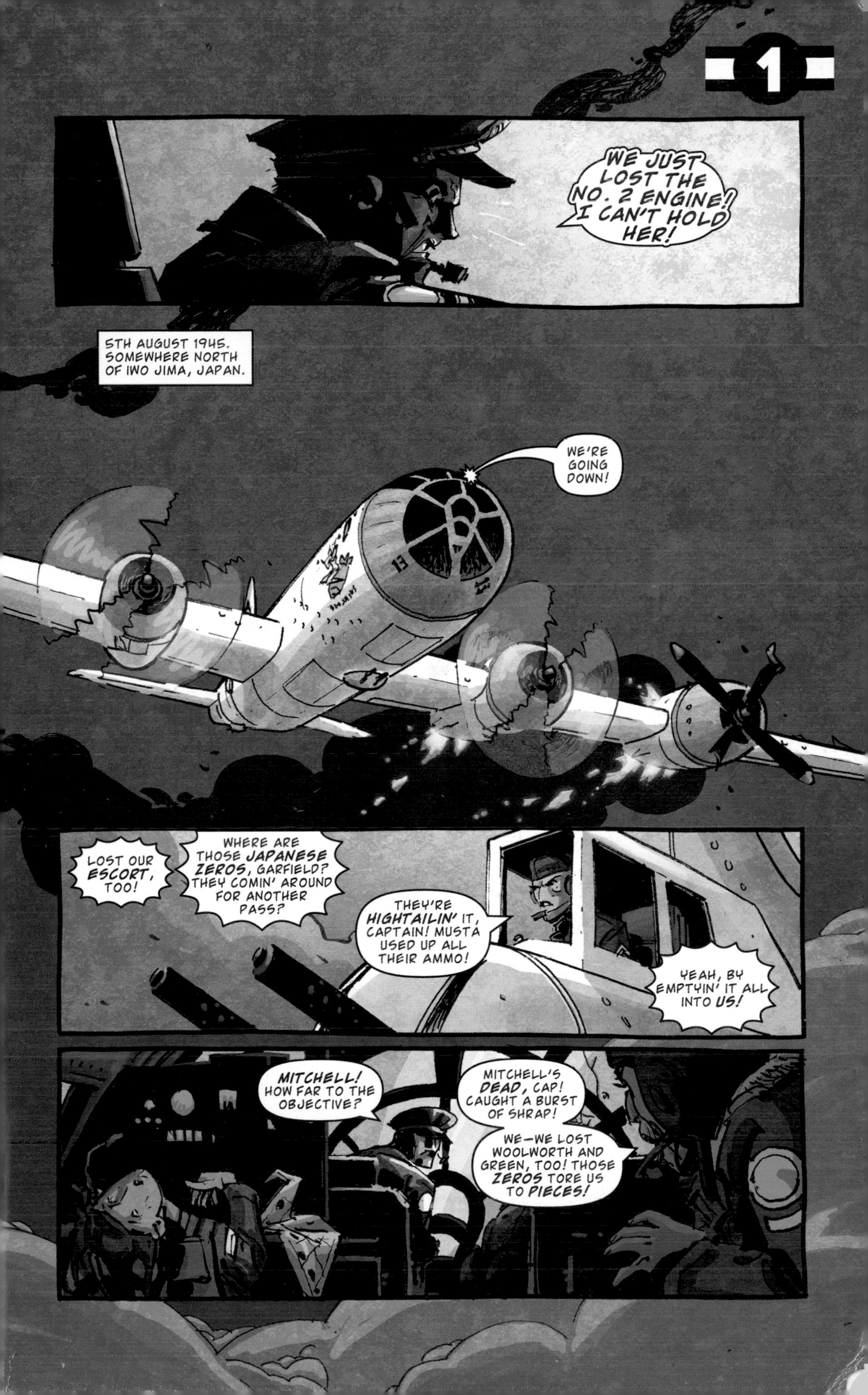
1
WE JUST LOST THE NO. 2 ENGINE! I CAN'T HOLD HER!
5TH AUGUST 1945. SOMEWHERE NORTH OF IWO JIMA, JAPAN.
WE'RE GOING DOWN!
LOST OUR ESCORT, TOO!
WHERE ARE THOSE JAPANESE ZEROS, GARFIELD? THEY COMIN' AROUND FOR ANOTHER PASS?
THEY'RE HIGHTAILIN' IT, CAPTAIN! MUSTA USED UP ALL THEIR AMMO!
YEAH, BY EMPTYIN' IT ALL INTO US!
MITCHELL! HOW FAR TO THE OBJECTIVE?
MITCHELL'S DEAD, CAP! CAUGHT A BURST OF SHRAP!
WE—WE LOST WOOLWORTH AND GREEN, TOO! THOSE ZEROS TORE US TO PIECES!

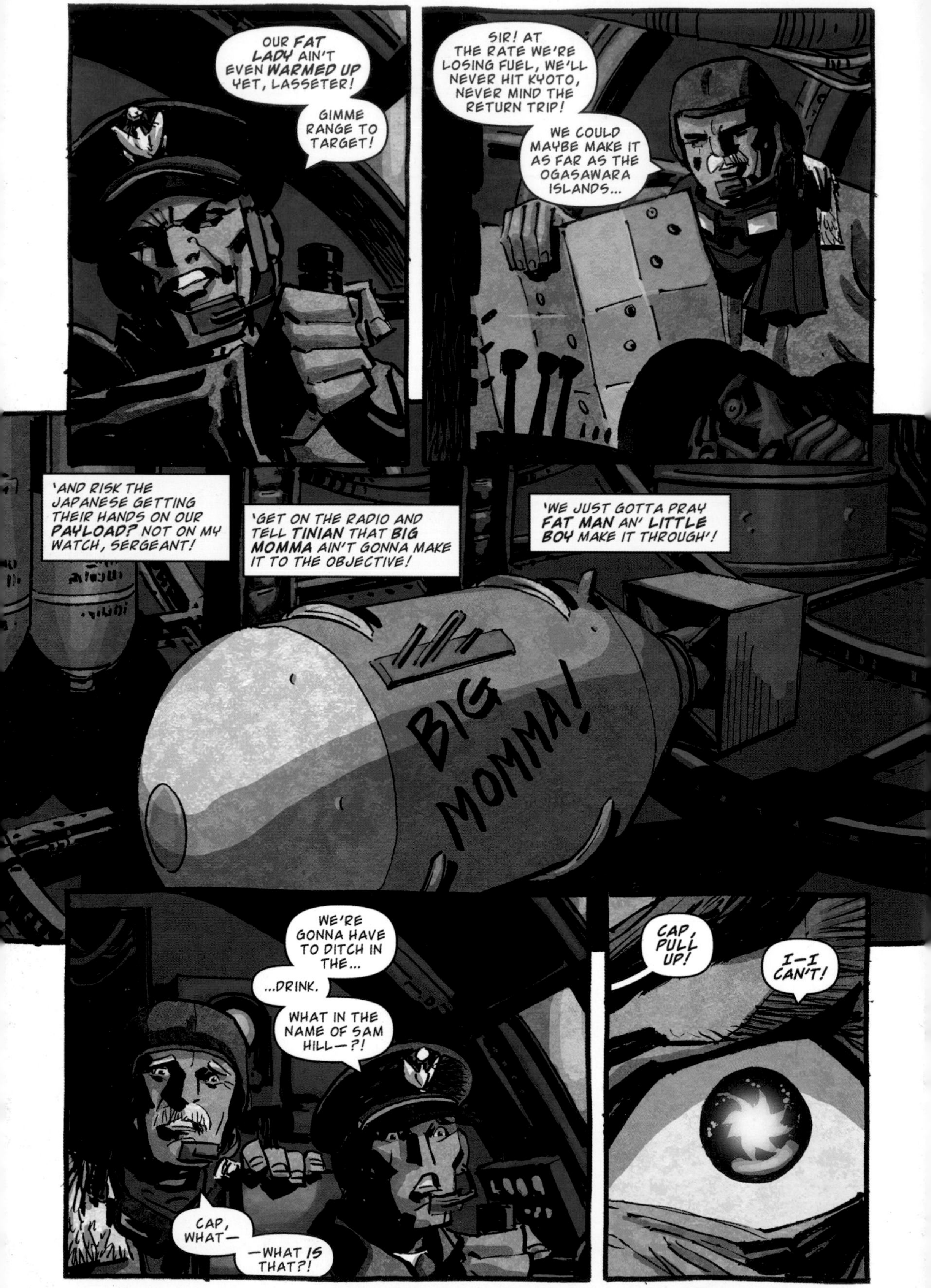
OUR FAT LADY AIN'T EVEN WARMED UP YET, LASSETER!
GIMME RANGE TO TARGET!
SIR! AT THE RATE WE'RE LOSING FUEL, WE'LL NEVER HIT KYOTO, NEVER MIND THE RETURN TRIP!
WE COULD MAYBE MAKE IT AS FAR AS THE OGASAWARA ISLANDS...
'AND RISK THE JAPANESE GETTING THEIR HANDS ON OUR PAYLOAD? NOT ON MY WATCH, SERGEANT!
'GET ON THE RADIO AND TELL TINIAN THAT BIG MOMMA AIN'T GONNA MAKE IT TO THE OBJECTIVE!
'WE JUST GOTTA PRAY FAT MAN AN' LITTLE BOY MAKE IT THROUGH'!
BIG MOMMA!
WE'RE GONNA HAVE TO DITCH IN THE...
...DRINK.
WHAT IN THE NAME OF SAM HILL—?!
CAP, WHAT—
—WHAT IS THAT?!
CAP, PULL UP!
I—I CAN'T!

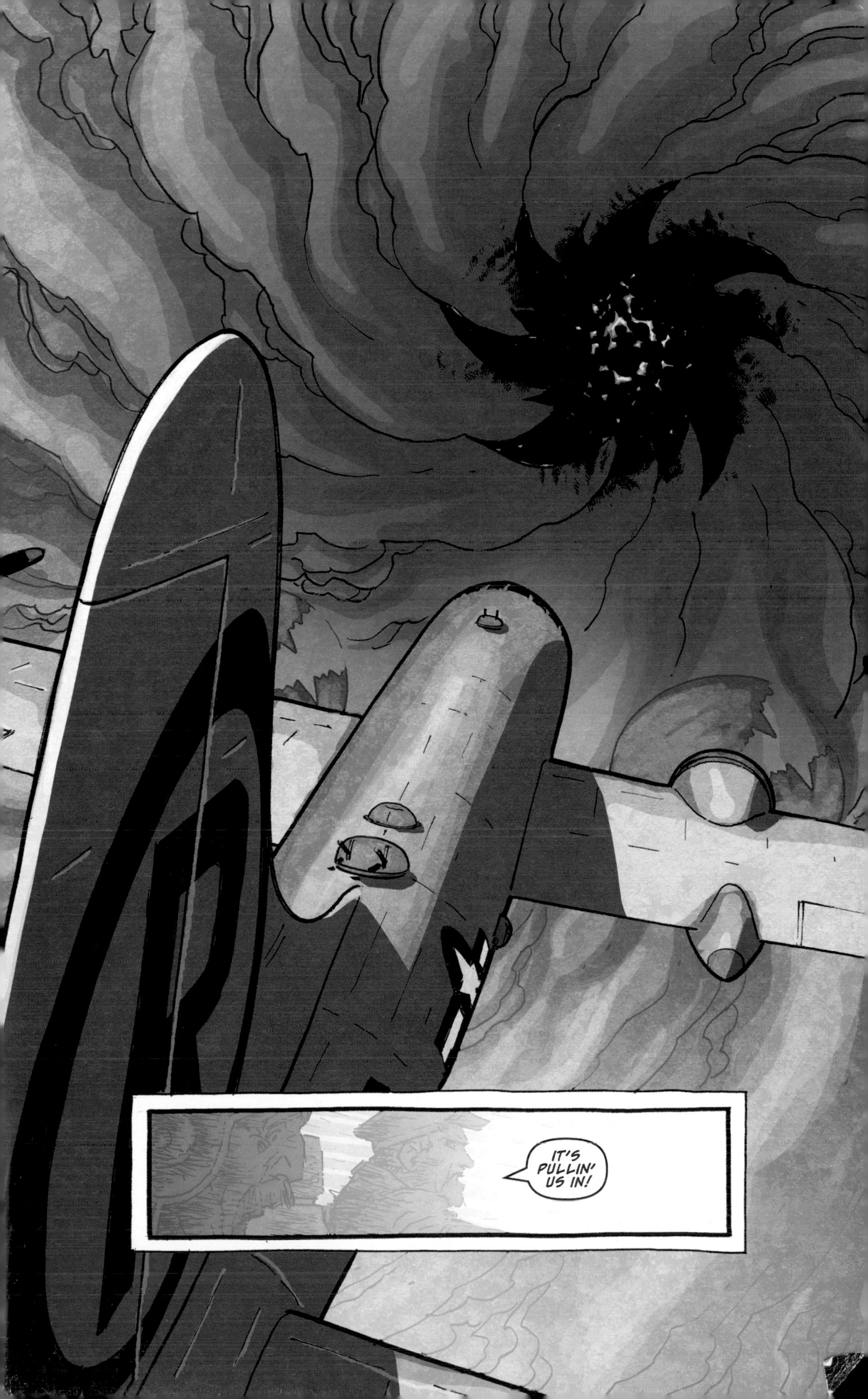
IT'S PULLIN' US IN!

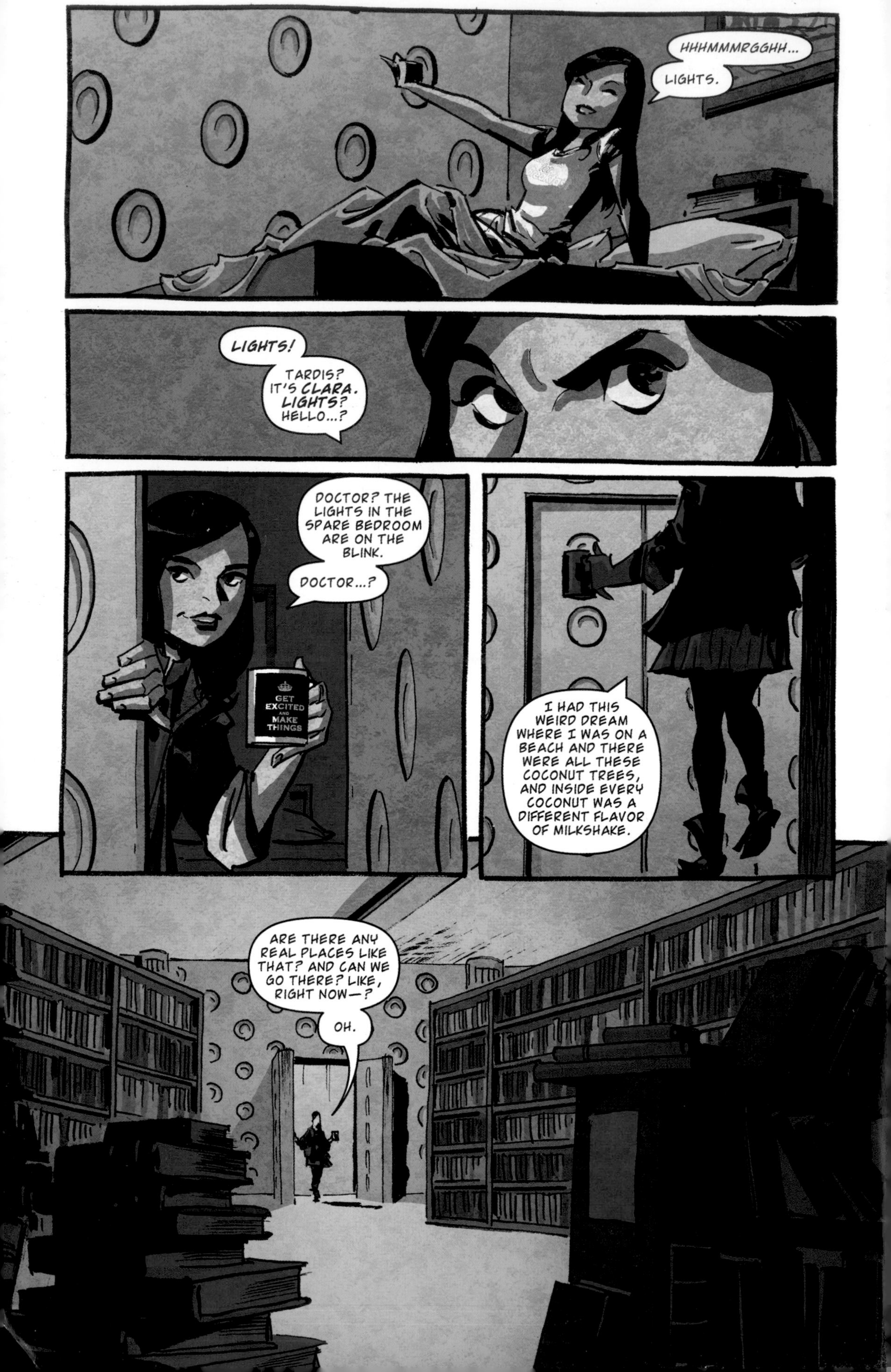
HHHMMMRGGHH...
LIGHTS.
LIGHTS!
TARDIS? IT'S CLARA. LIGHTS? HELLO...?
DOCTOR? THE LIGHTS IN THE SPARE BEDROOM ARE ON THE BLINK.
DOCTOR...?
GET EXCITED AND MAKE THINGS
I HAD THIS WEIRD DREAM WHERE I WAS ON A BEACH AND THERE WERE ALL THESE COCONUT TREES, AND INSIDE EVERY COCONUT WAS A DIFFERENT FLAVOR OF MILKSHAKE.
ARE THERE ANY REAL PLACES LIKE THAT? AND CAN WE GO THERE? LIKE, RIGHT NOW—?
OH.

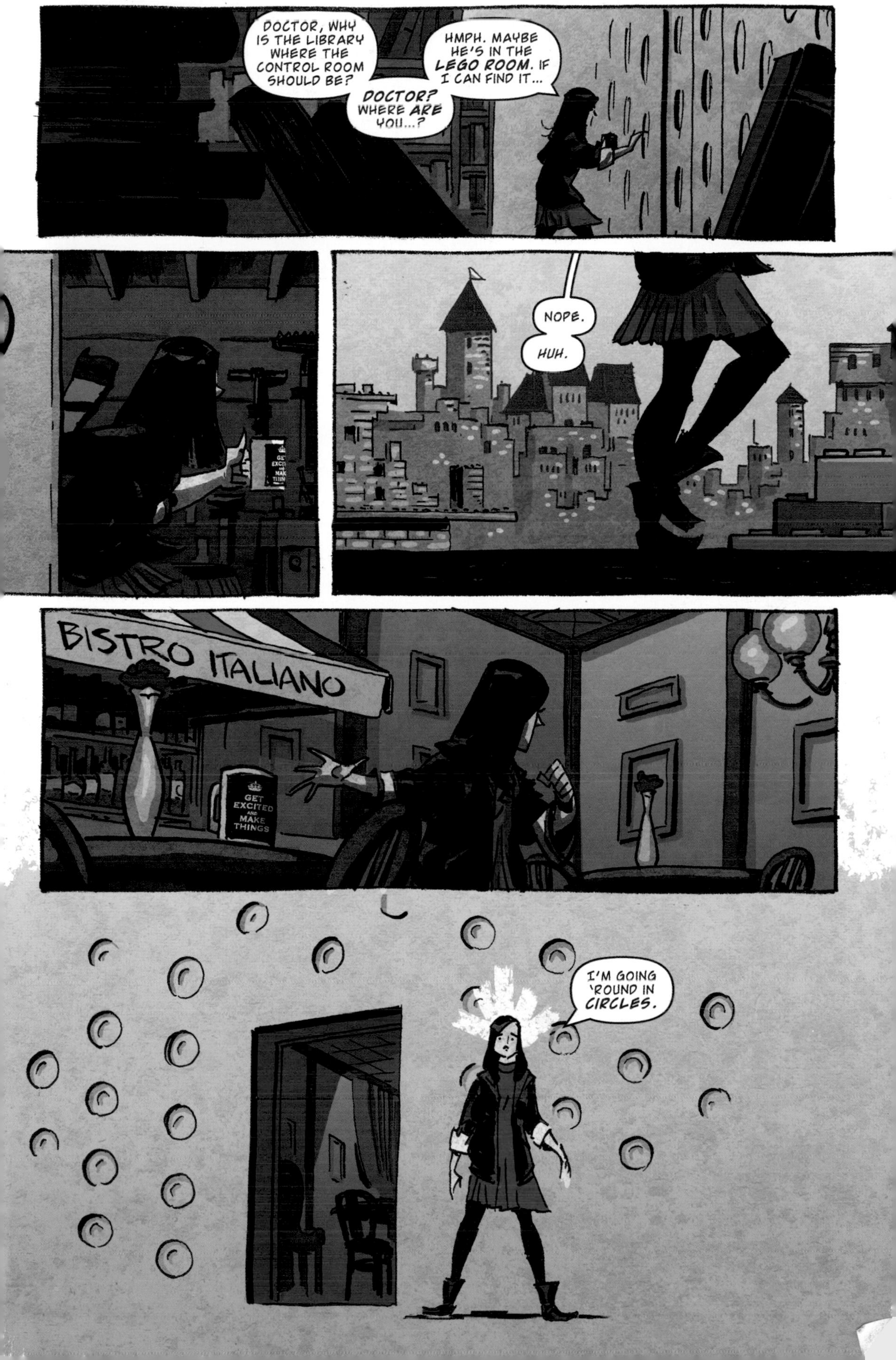
DOCTOR, WHY IS THE LIBRARY WHERE THE CONTROL ROOM SHOULD BE?
DOCTOR? WHERE ARE YOU...?
HMPH. MAYBE HE'S IN THE LEGO ROOM. IF I CAN FIND IT...
NOPE.
HUH.
BISTRO ITALIANO
GET EXCITED AND MAKE THINGS
I'M GOING 'ROUND IN CIRCLES.

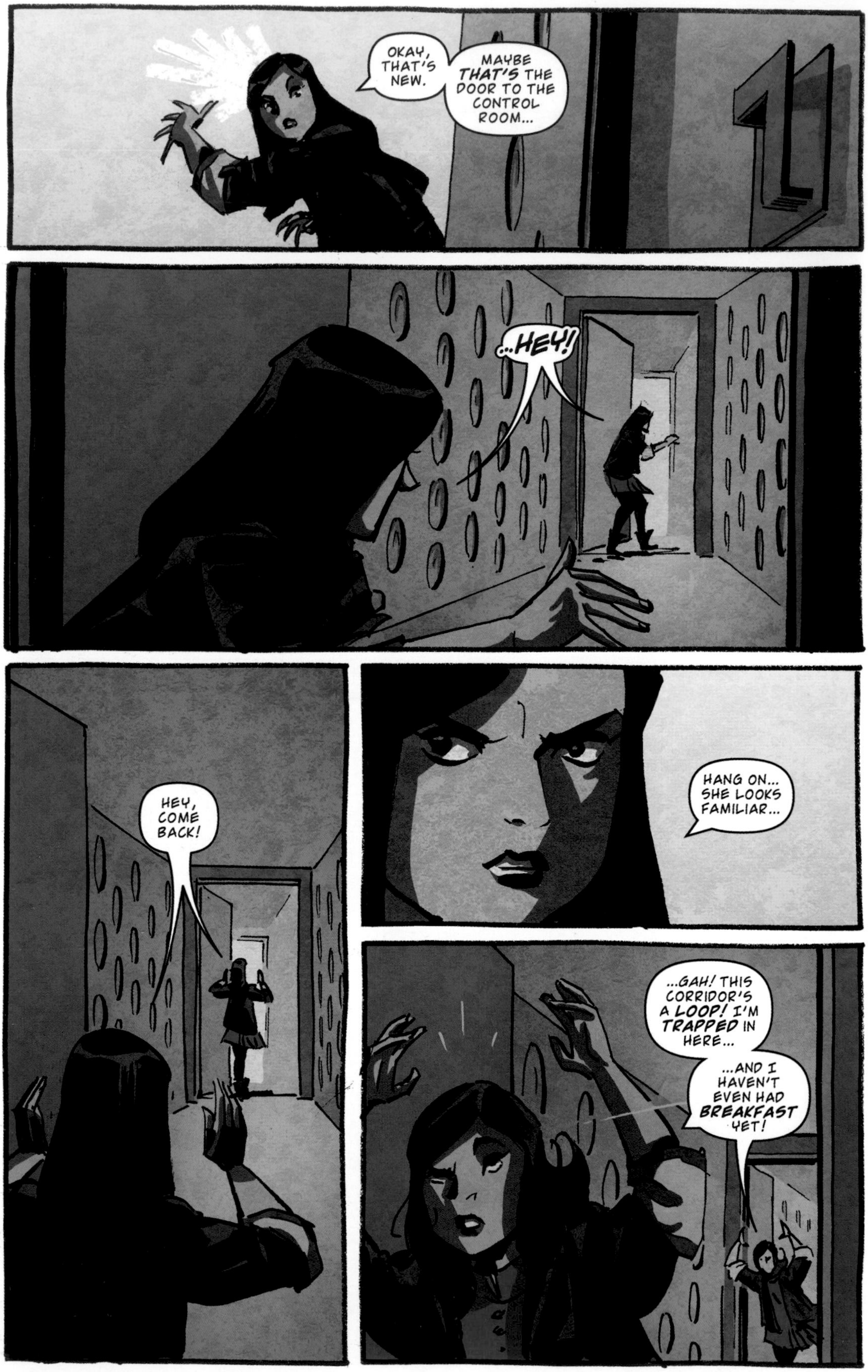
OKAY, THAT'S NEW.
MAYBE THAT'S THE DOOR TO THE CONTROL ROOM...
...HEY!
HEY, COME BACK!
HANG ON... SHE LOOKS FAMILIAR...
...GAH! THIS CORRIDOR'S A LOOP! I'M TRAPPED IN HERE...
...AND I HAVEN'T EVEN HAD BREAKFAST YET!

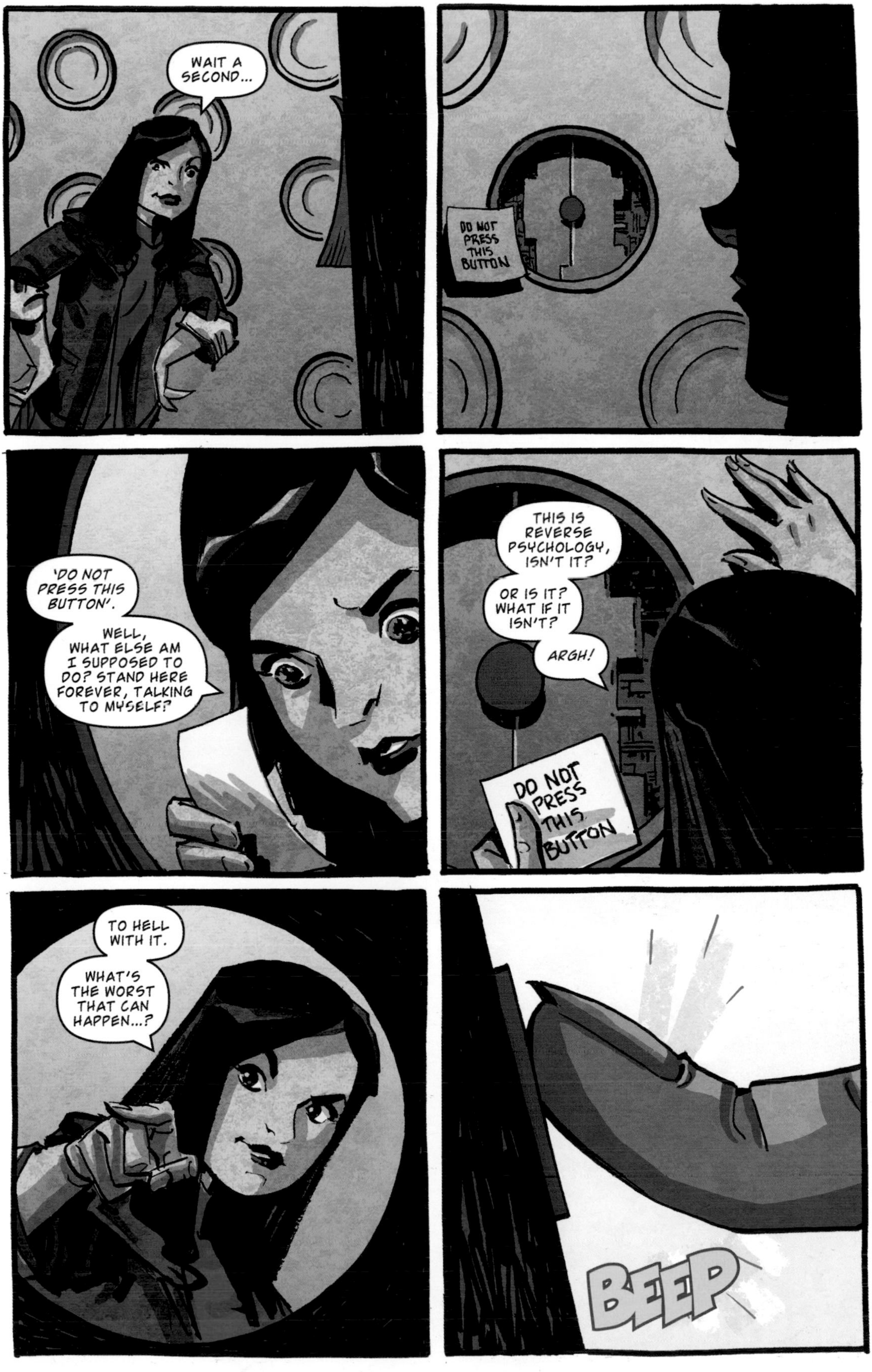
WAIT A SECOND...
DO NOT PRESS THIS BUTTON
'DO NOT PRESS THIS BUTTON'.
WELL, WHAT ELSE AM I SUPPOSED TO DO? STAND HERE FOREVER, TALKING TO MYSELF?
THIS IS REVERSE PSYCHOLOGY, ISN'T IT?
OR IS IT? WHAT IF IT ISN'T?
ARGH!
DO NOT PRESS THIS BUTTON
TO HELL WITH IT.
WHAT'S THE WORST THAT CAN HAPPEN...?
BEEP

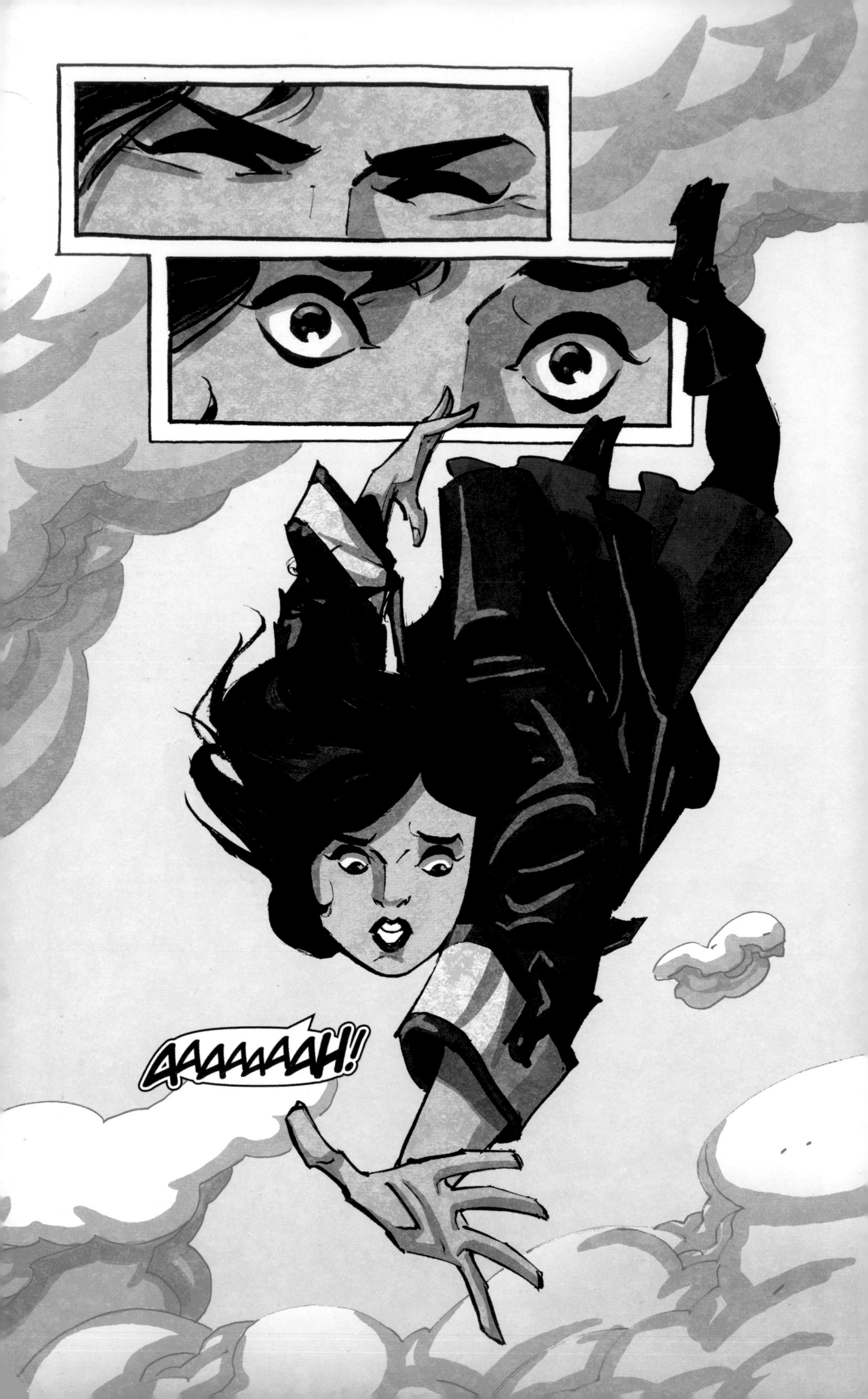
AAAAAAAH!

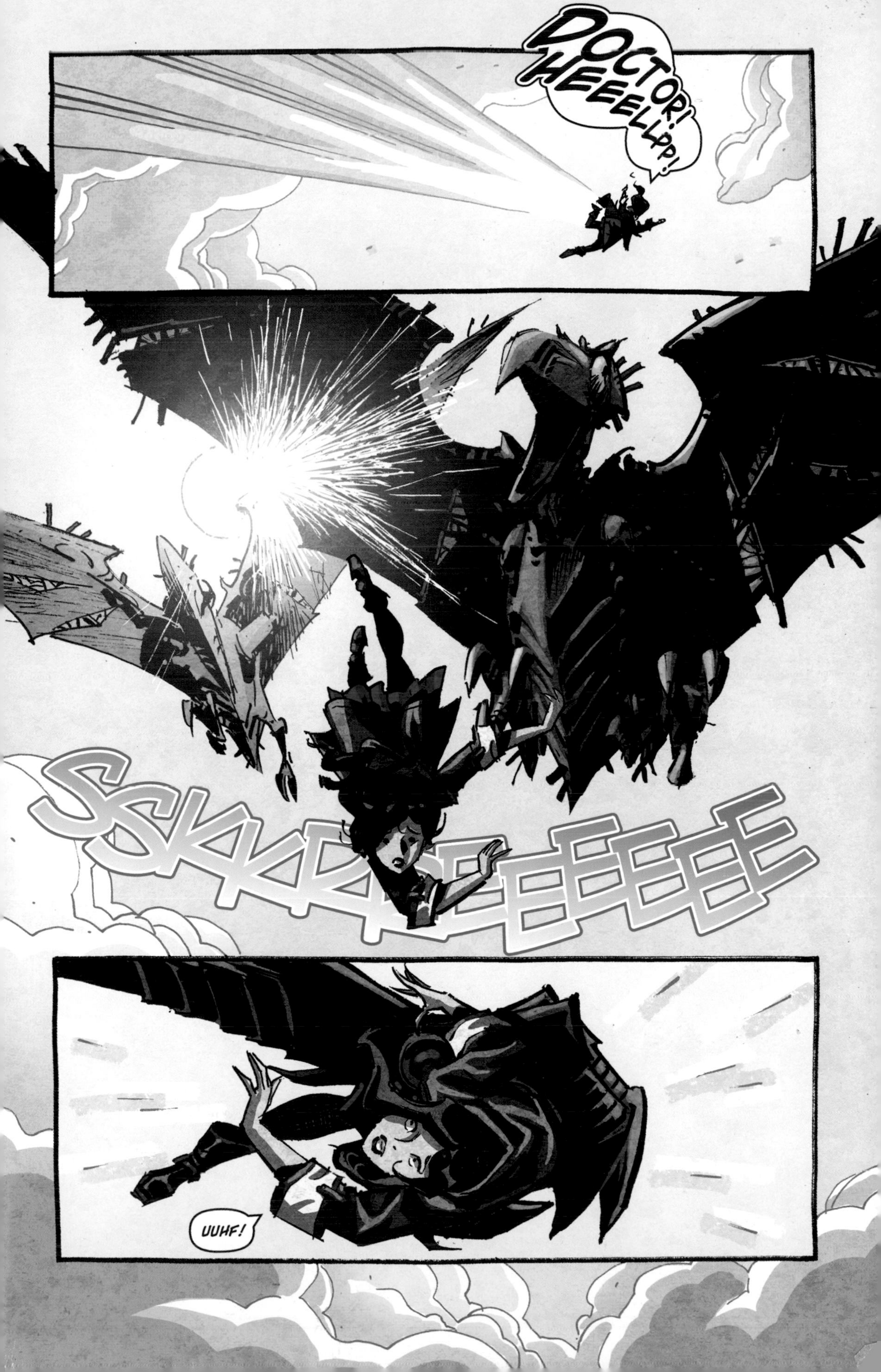
DOCTOR! HEEELLPP!
SSKKREEEEEEEEE
UUHF!

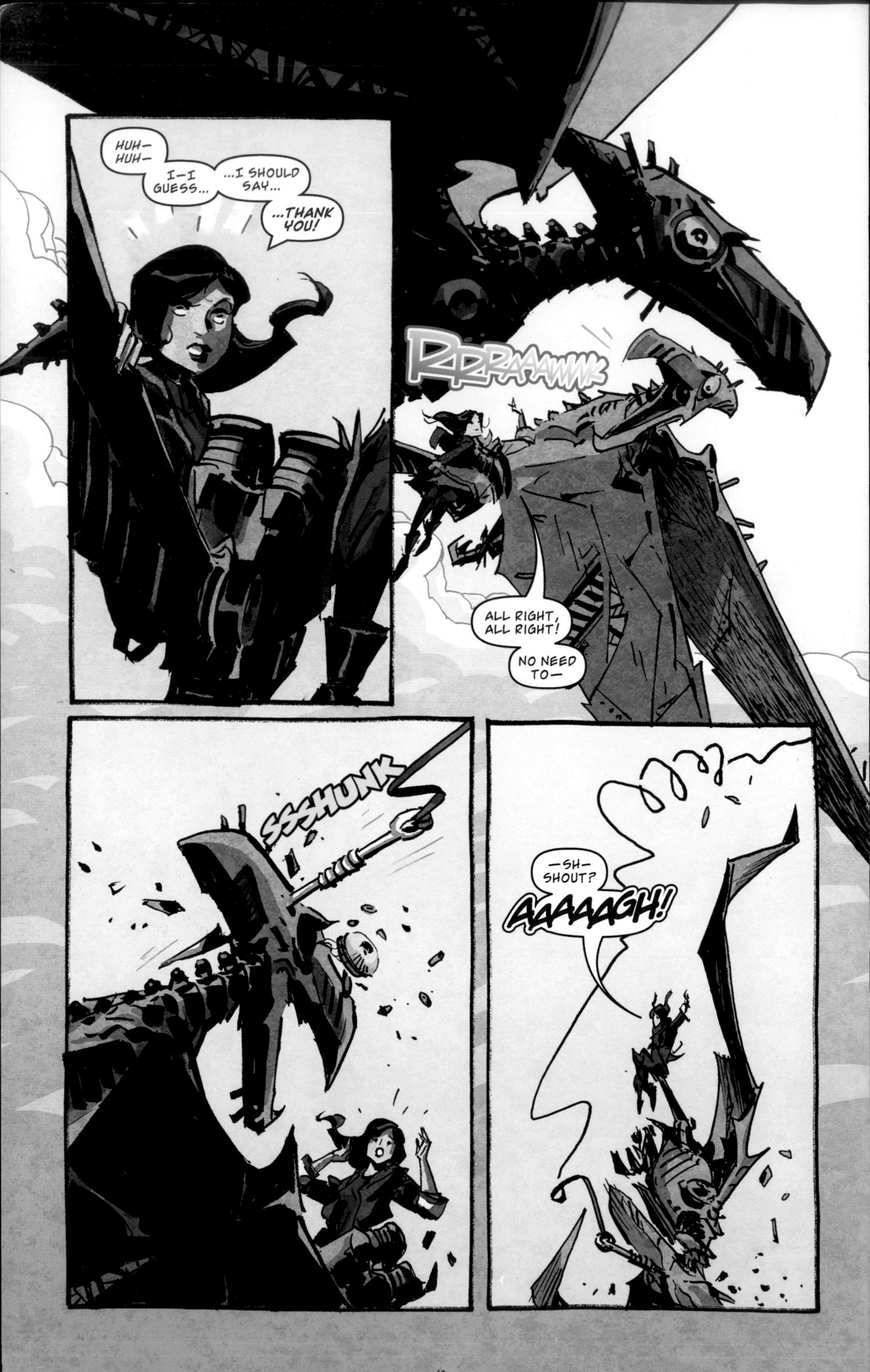
HUH-
HUH-
I-I GUESS...
...I SHOULD SAY...
...THANK YOU!
RRRAAAWWK
ALL RIGHT, ALL RIGHT!
NO NEED TO-
SSSHUNK
-SH-SHOUT?
AAAAAGH!

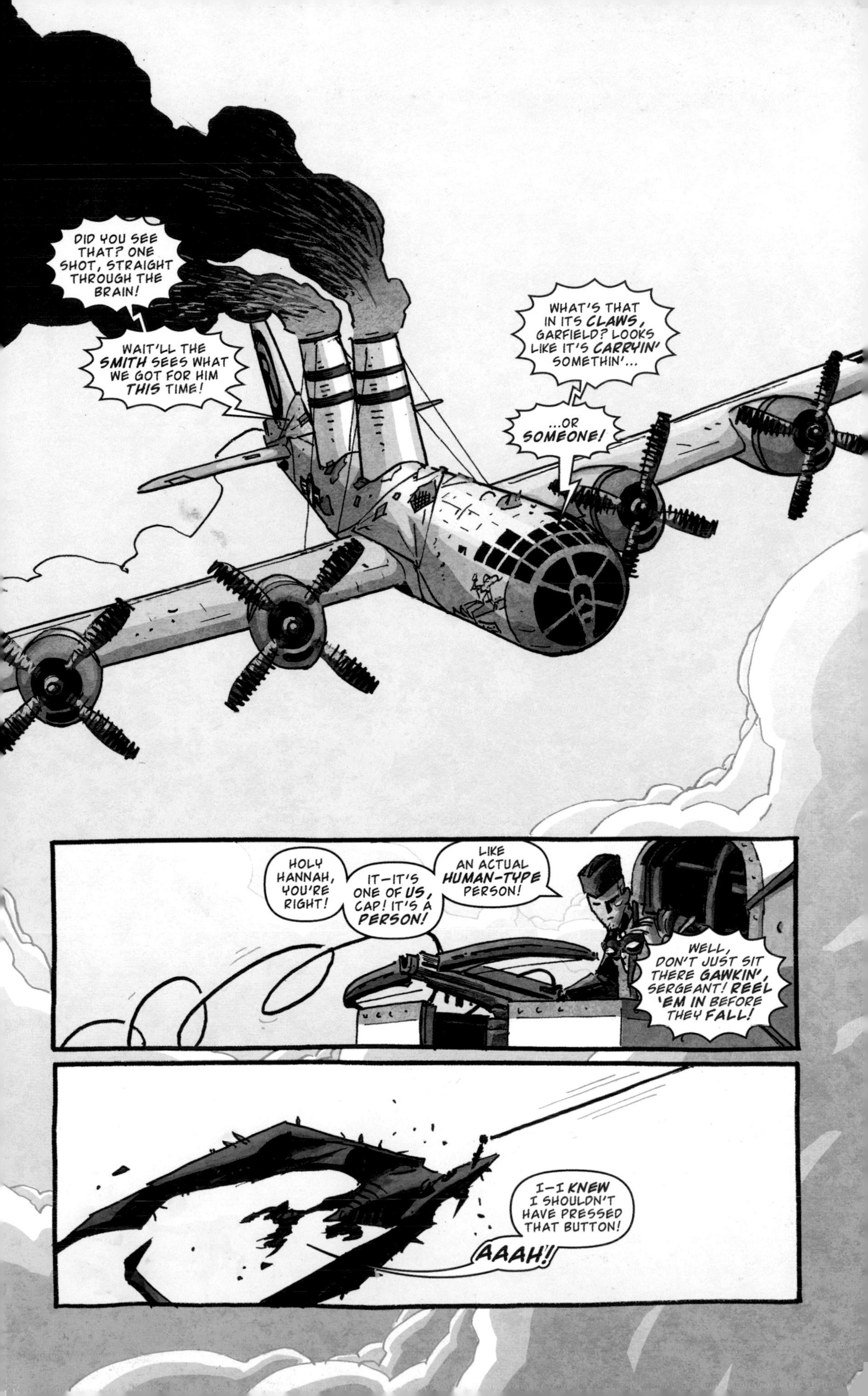
DID YOU SEE THAT? ONE SHOT, STRAIGHT THROUGH THE BRAIN!
WAIT'LL THE SMITH SEES WHAT WE GOT FOR HIM THIS TIME!
WHAT'S THAT IN ITS CLAWS, GARFIELD? LOOKS LIKE IT'S CARRYIN' SOMETHIN'...
...OR SOMEONE!
HOLY HANNAH, YOU'RE RIGHT!
IT-IT'S ONE OF US, CAP! IT'S A PERSON!
LIKE AN ACTUAL HUMAN-TYPE PERSON!
WELL, DON'T JUST SIT THERE GAWKIN', SERGEANT! REEL 'EM IN BEFORE THEY FALL!
I-I KNEW I SHOULDN'T HAVE PRESSED THAT BUTTON!
AAAH!!

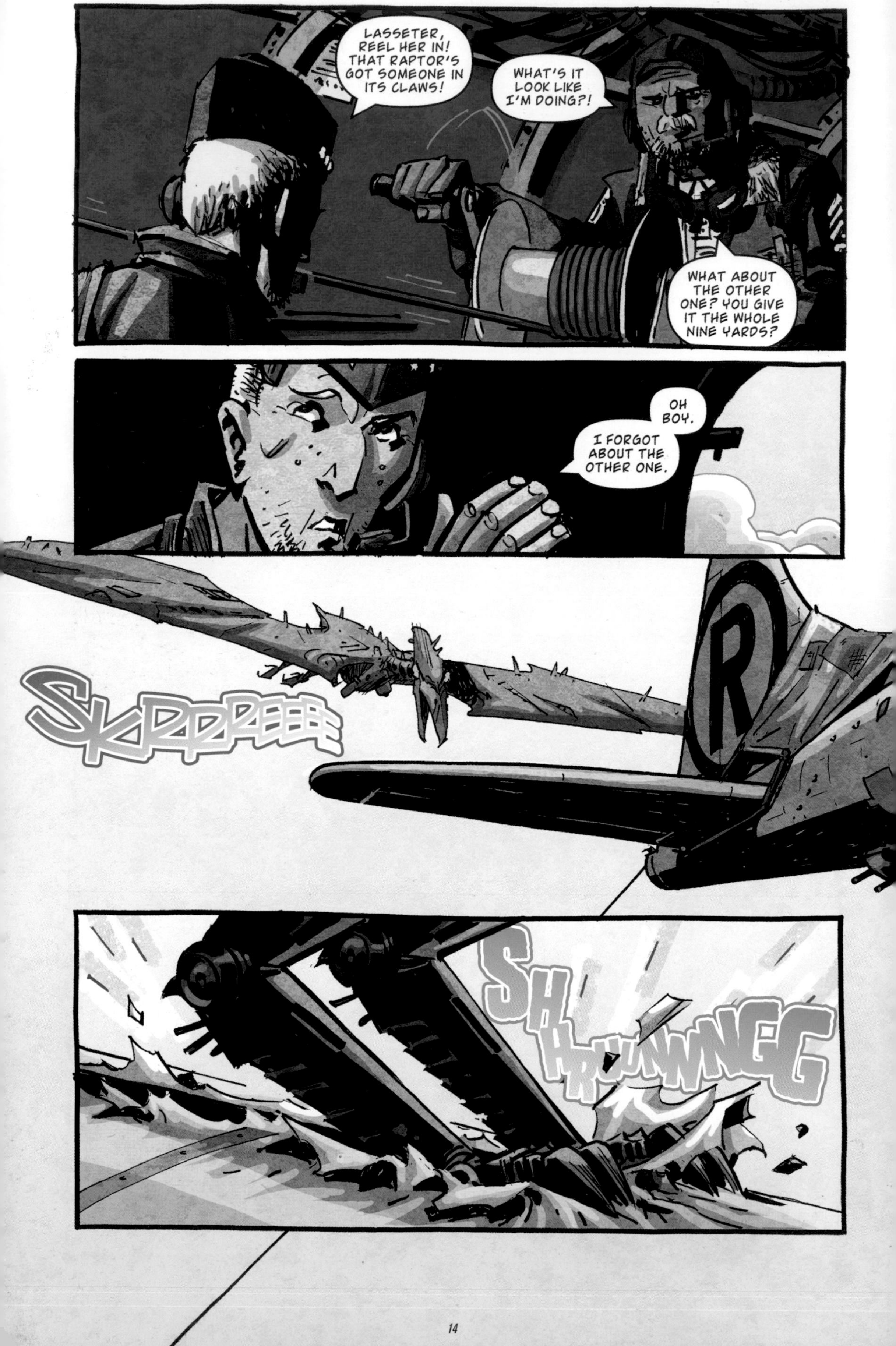
LASSETER, REEL HER IN! THAT RAPTOR'S GOT SOMEONE IN ITS CLAWS!
WHAT'S IT LOOK LIKE I'M DOING?!
WHAT ABOUT THE OTHER ONE? YOU GIVE IT THE WHOLE NINE YARDS?
OH BOY.
I FORGOT ABOUT THE OTHER ONE.
SKRRREEEE
SHHRUUNNNGG

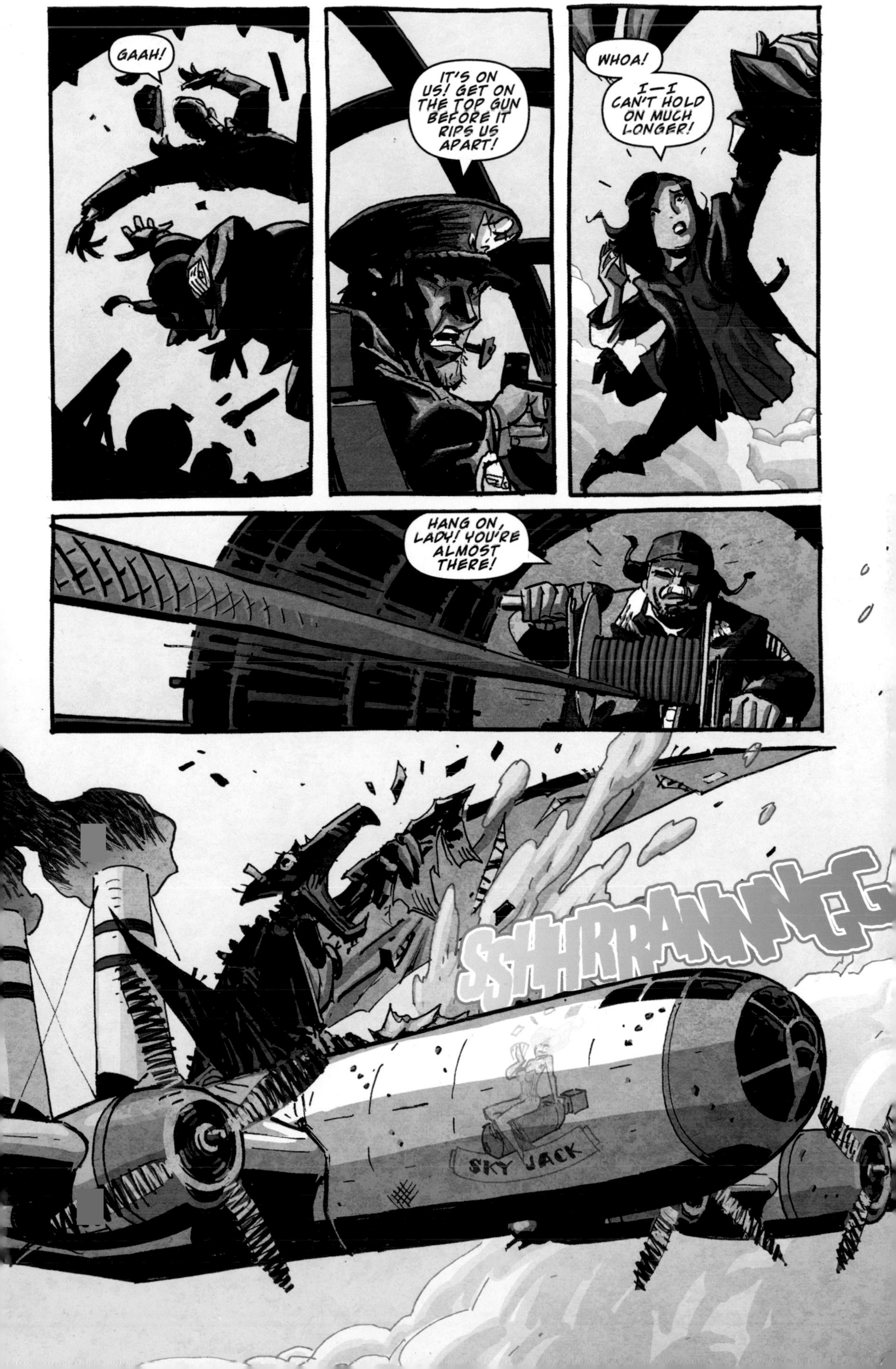
GAAH!
IT'S ON US! GET ON THE TOP GUN BEFORE IT RIPS US APART!
WHOA!
I—I CAN'T HOLD ON MUCH LONGER!
HANG ON, LADY! YOU'RE ALMOST THERE!
SSHHRRANNNGG
SKY JACK

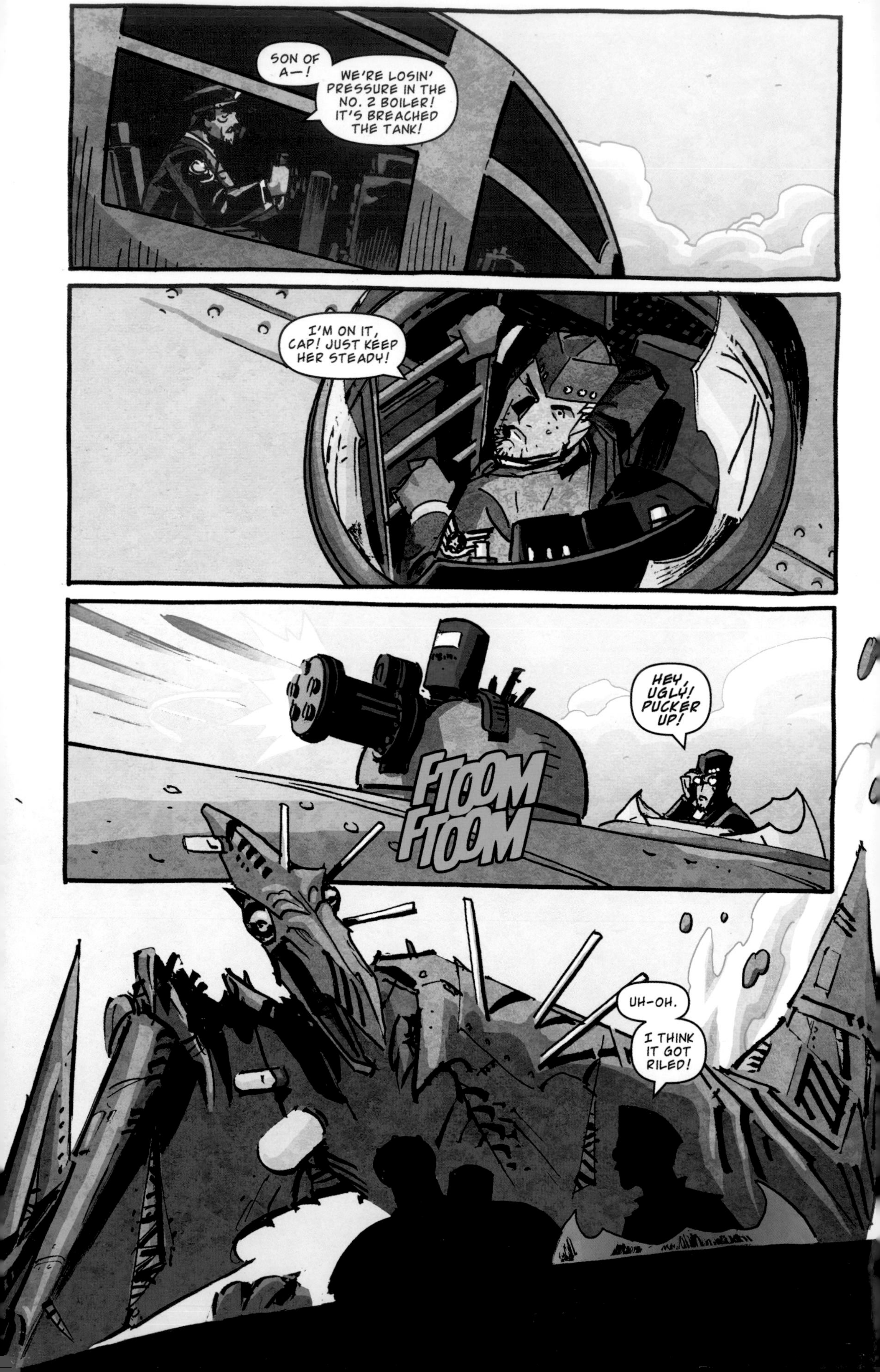
SON OF A—!
WE'RE LOSIN' PRESSURE IN THE NO. 2 BOILER! IT'S BREACHED THE TANK!
I'M ON IT, CAP! JUST KEEP HER STEADY!
HEY, UGLY! PUCKER UP!
FTOOM FTOOM
UH-OH.
I THINK IT GOT RILED!

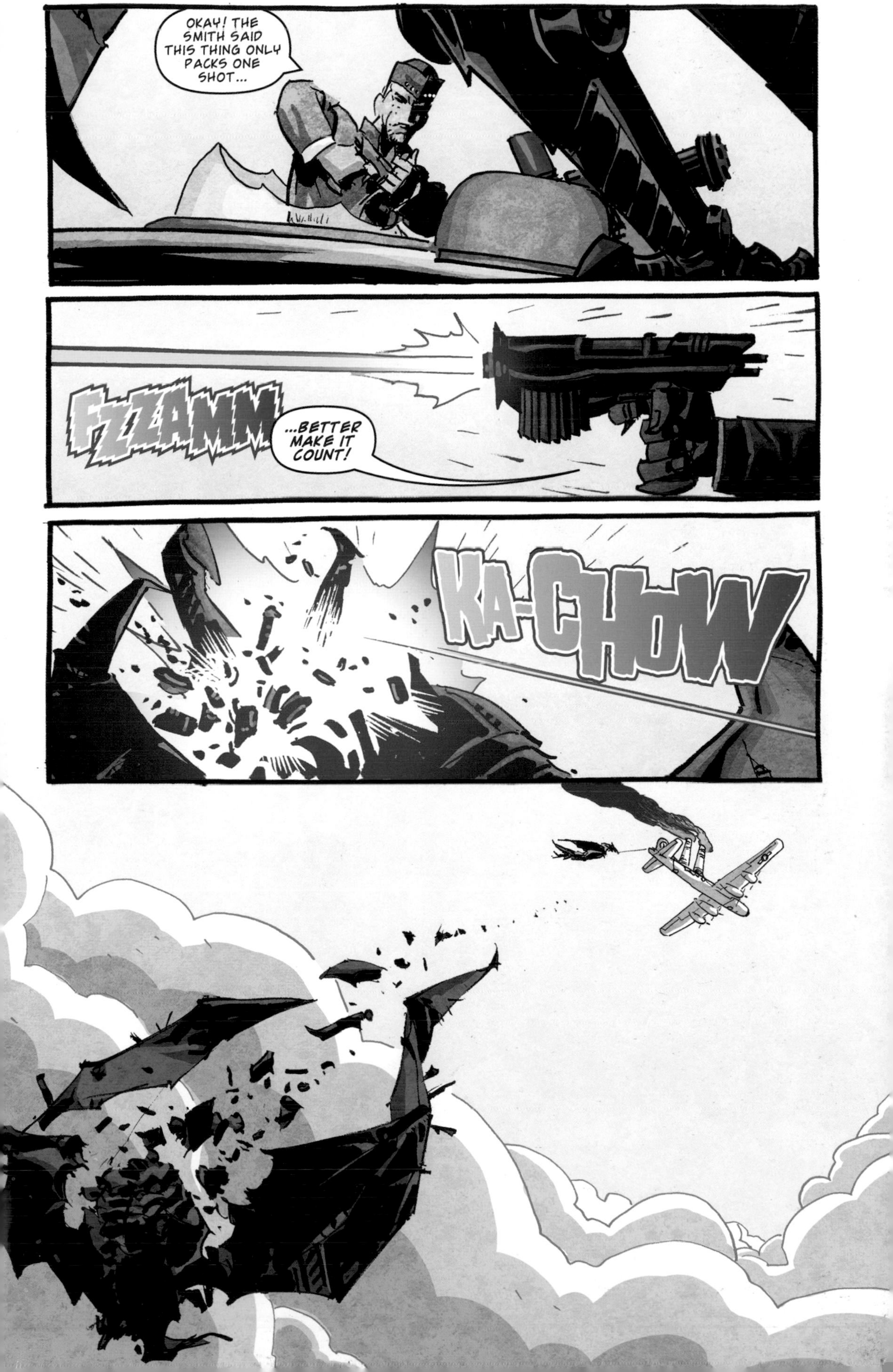
OKAY! THE SMITH SAID THIS THING ONLY PACKS ONE SHOT...
FZZAMM
...BETTER MAKE IT COUNT!
KA-CHOW

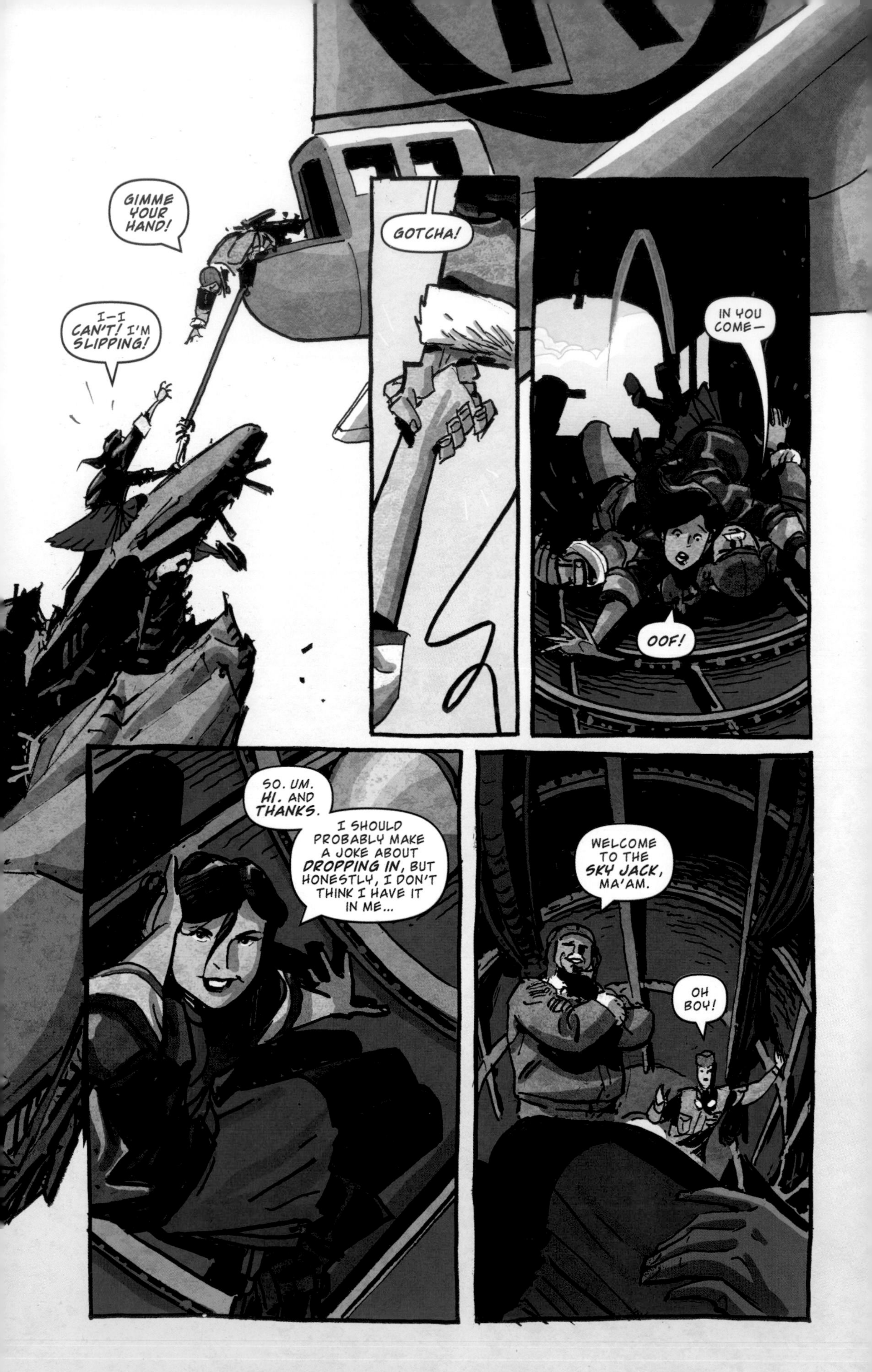
GIMME YOUR HAND!
I—I CAN'T! I'M SLIPPING!
GOTCHA!
IN YOU COME—
OOF!
SO. UM. HI. AND THANKS.
I SHOULD PROBABLY MAKE A JOKE ABOUT DROPPING IN, BUT HONESTLY, I DON'T THINK I HAVE IT IN ME...
WELCOME TO THE SKY JACK, MA'AM.
OH BOY!

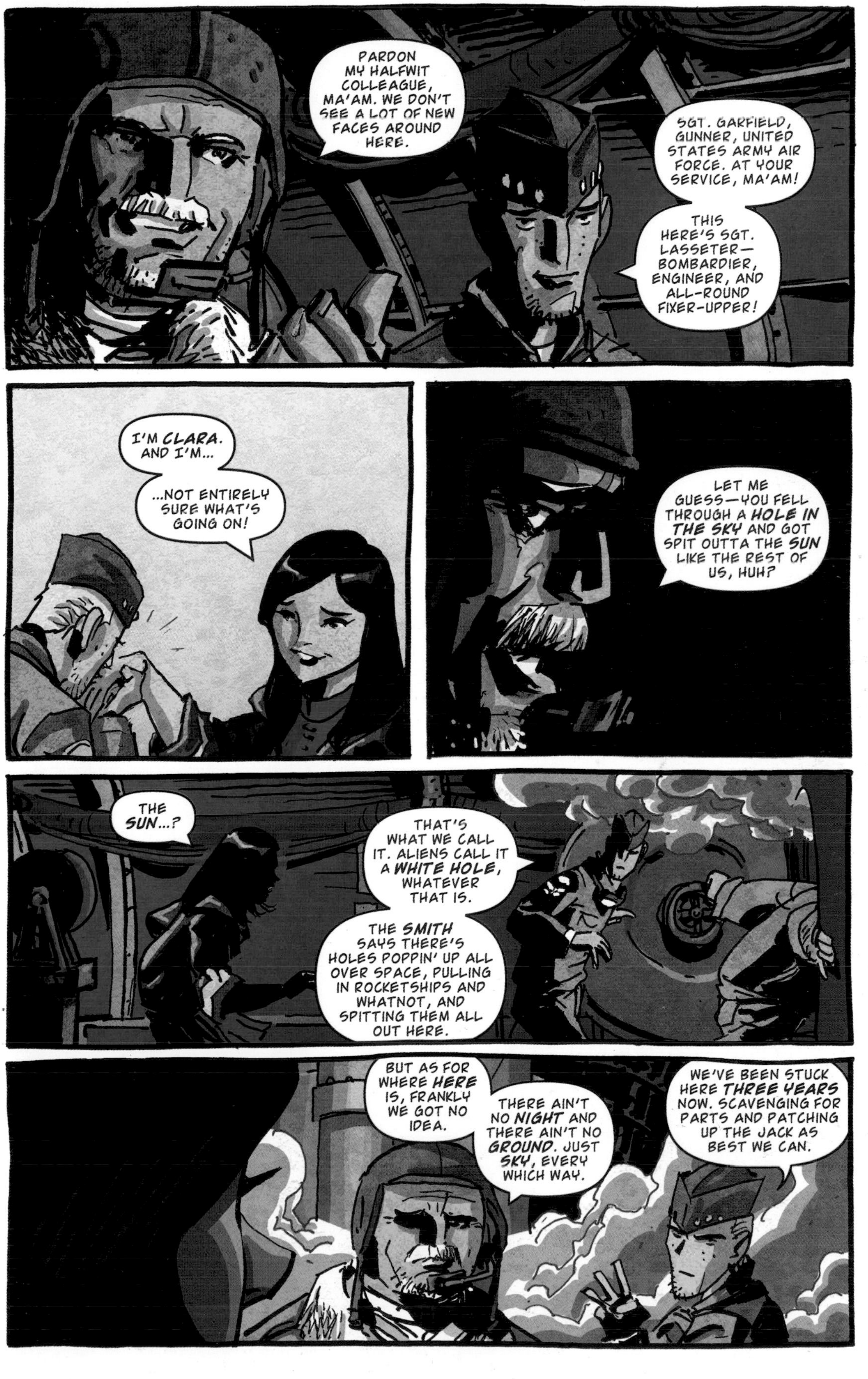
PARDON MY HALFWIT COLLEAGUE, MA'AM. WE DON'T SEE A LOT OF NEW FACES AROUND HERE.
SGT. GARFIELD, GUNNER, UNITED STATES ARMY AIR FORCE. AT YOUR SERVICE, MA'AM!
THIS HERE'S SGT. LASSETER—BOMBARDIER, ENGINEER, AND ALL-ROUND FIXER-UPPER!
I'M CLARA. AND I'M...
...NOT ENTIRELY SURE WHAT'S GOING ON!
LET ME GUESS—YOU FELL THROUGH A HOLE IN THE SKY AND GOT SPIT OUTTA THE SUN LIKE THE REST OF US, HUH?
THE SUN...?
THAT'S WHAT WE CALL IT. ALIENS CALL IT A WHITE HOLE, WHATEVER THAT IS.
THE SMITH SAYS THERE'S HOLES POPPIN' UP ALL OVER SPACE, PULLING IN ROCKETSHIPS AND WHATNOT, AND SPITTING THEM ALL OUT HERE.
BUT AS FOR WHERE HERE IS, FRANKLY WE GOT NO IDEA.
THERE AIN'T NO NIGHT AND THERE AIN'T NO GROUND. JUST SKY, EVERY WHICH WAY.
WE'VE BEEN STUCK HERE THREE YEARS NOW. SCAVENGING FOR PARTS AND PATCHING UP THE JACK AS BEST WE CAN.

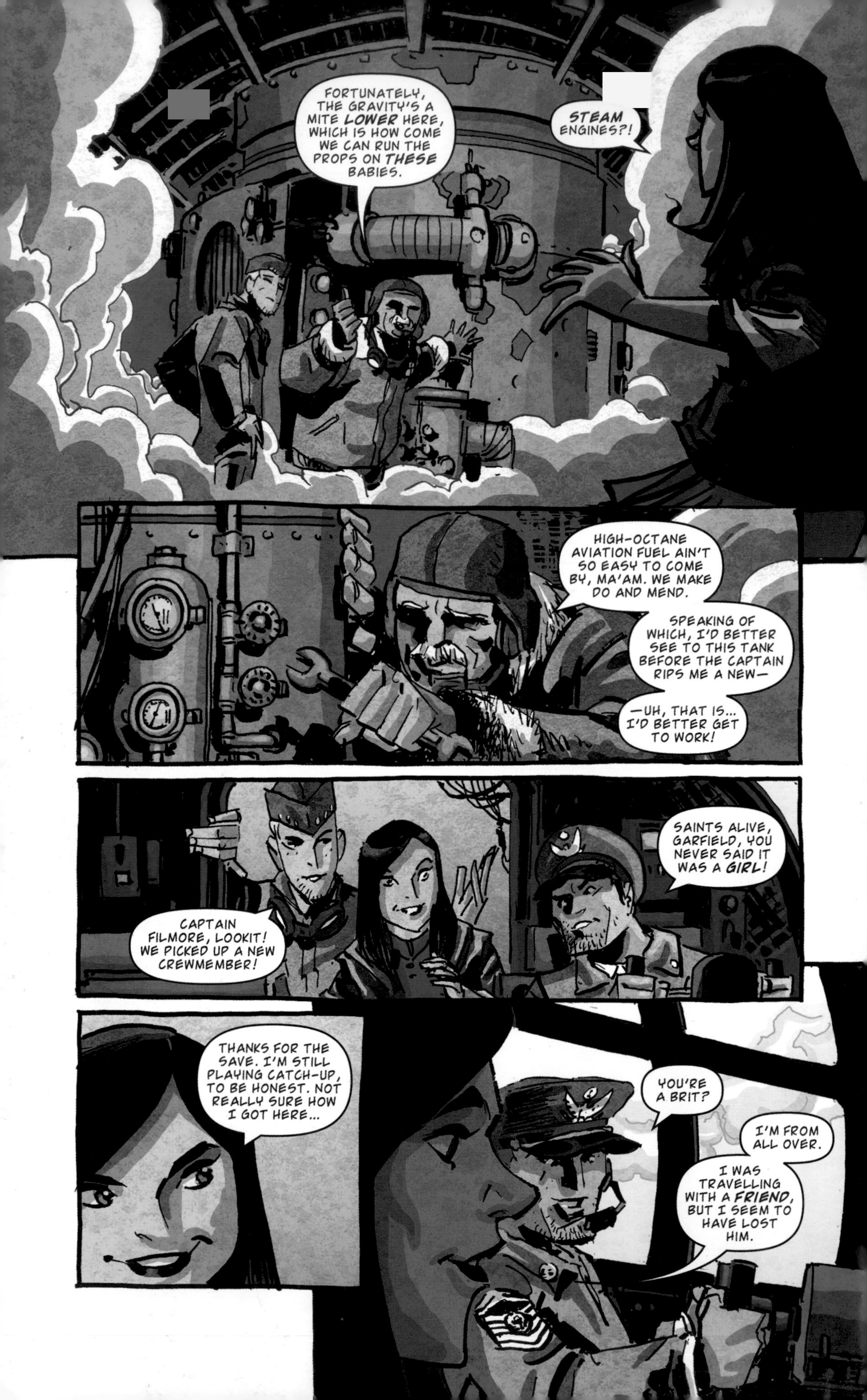
FORTUNATELY, THE GRAVITY'S A MITE LOWER HERE, WHICH IS HOW COME WE CAN RUN THE PROPS ON THESE BABIES.
STEAM ENGINES?!
HIGH-OCTANE AVIATION FUEL AIN'T SO EASY TO COME BY, MA'AM. WE MAKE DO AND MEND.
SPEAKING OF WHICH, I'D BETTER SEE TO THIS TANK BEFORE THE CAPTAIN RIPS ME A NEW—
—UH, THAT IS... I'D BETTER GET TO WORK!
CAPTAIN FILMORE, LOOKIT! WE PICKED UP A NEW CREWMEMBER!
SAINTS ALIVE, GARFIELD, YOU NEVER SAID IT WAS A GIRL!
THANKS FOR THE SAVE. I'M STILL PLAYING CATCH-UP, TO BE HONEST. NOT REALLY SURE HOW I GOT HERE...
YOU'RE A BRIT?
I'M FROM ALL OVER.
I WAS TRAVELLING WITH A FRIEND, BUT I SEEM TO HAVE LOST HIM.

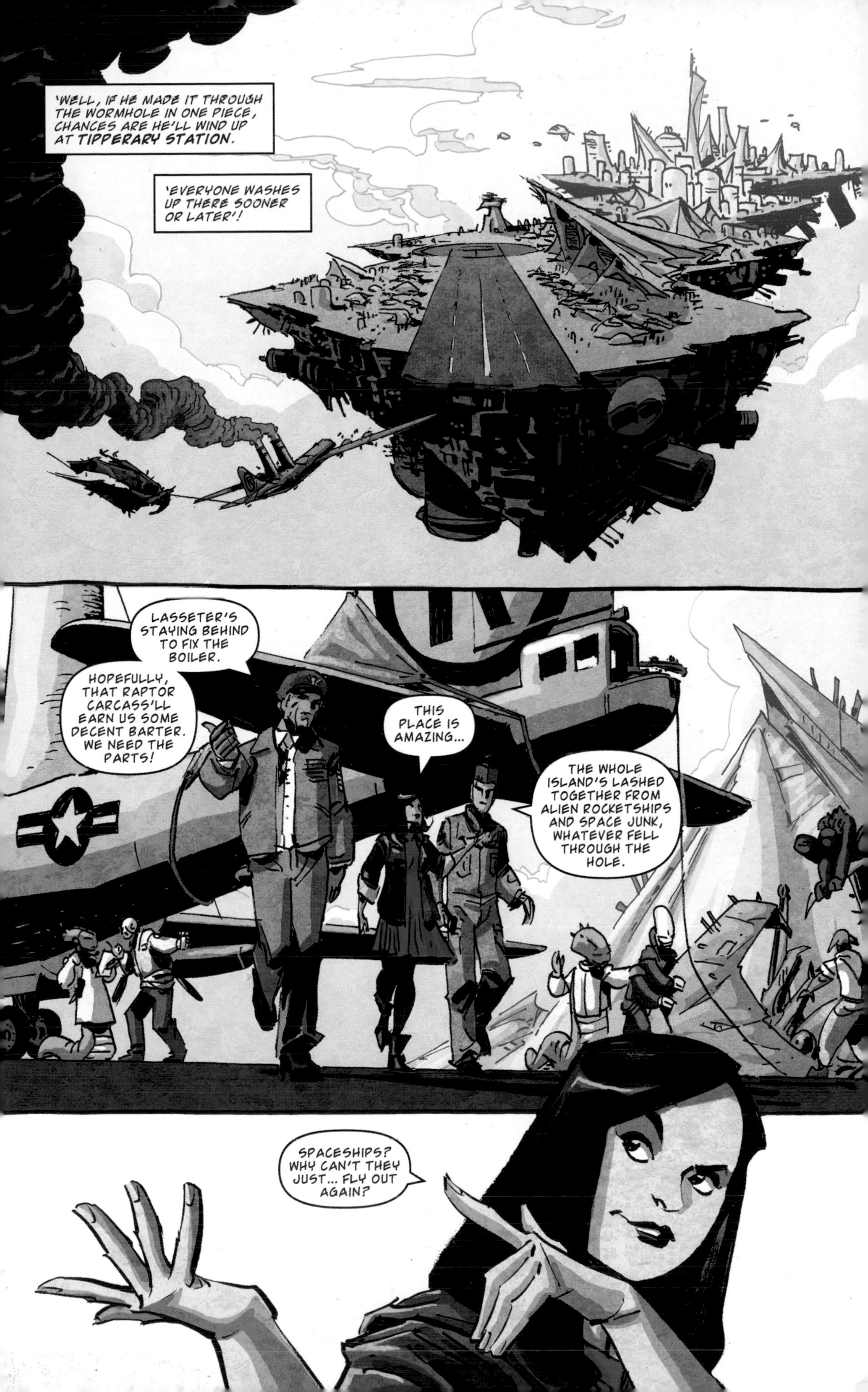
'WELL, IF HE MADE IT THROUGH THE WORMHOLE IN ONE PIECE, CHANCES ARE HE'LL WIND UP AT TIPPERARY STATION.
'EVERYONE WASHES UP THERE SOONER OR LATER'!
LASSETER'S STAYING BEHIND TO FIX THE BOILER.
HOPEFULLY, THAT RAPTOR CARCASS'LL EARN US SOME DECENT BARTER. WE NEED THE PARTS!
THIS PLACE IS AMAZING...
THE WHOLE ISLAND'S LASHED TOGETHER FROM ALIEN ROCKETSHIPS AND SPACE JUNK, WHATEVER FELL THROUGH THE HOLE.
SPACESHIPS? WHY CAN'T THEY JUST... FLY OUT AGAIN?

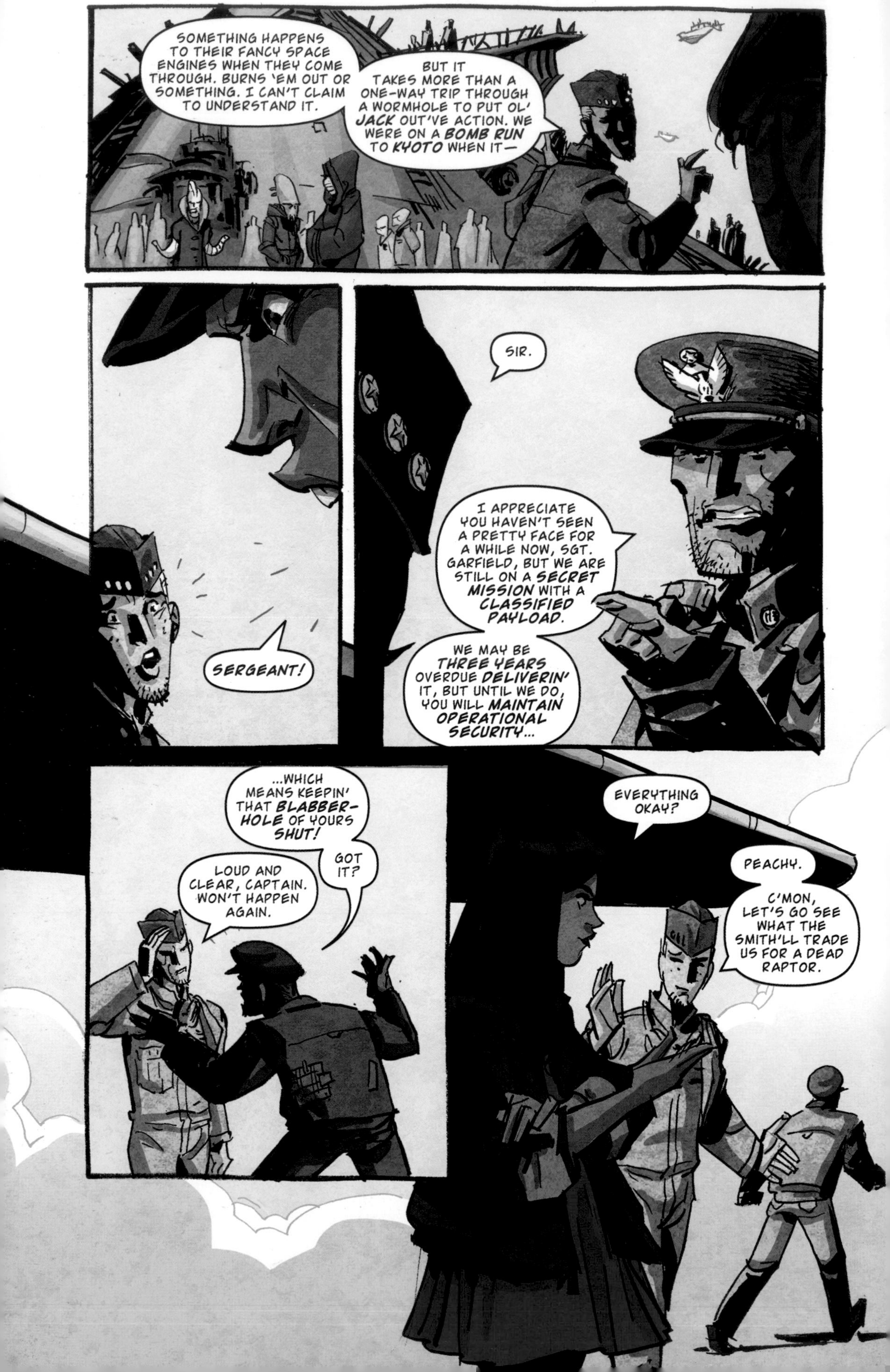
SOMETHING HAPPENS TO THEIR FANCY SPACE ENGINES WHEN THEY COME THROUGH. BURNS 'EM OUT OR SOMETHING. I CAN'T CLAIM TO UNDERSTAND IT.
BUT IT TAKES MORE THAN A ONE-WAY TRIP THROUGH A WORMHOLE TO PUT OL' JACK OUT'VE ACTION. WE WERE ON A BOMB RUN TO KYOTO WHEN IT—
SERGEANT!
SIR.
I APPRECIATE YOU HAVEN'T SEEN A PRETTY FACE FOR A WHILE NOW, SGT. GARFIELD, BUT WE ARE STILL ON A SECRET MISSION WITH A CLASSIFIED PAYLOAD.
WE MAY BE THREE YEARS OVERDUE DELIVERIN' IT, BUT UNTIL WE DO, YOU WILL MAINTAIN OPERATIONAL SECURITY...
...WHICH MEANS KEEPIN' THAT BLABBER-HOLE OF YOURS SHUT!
GOT IT?
LOUD AND CLEAR, CAPTAIN. WON'T HAPPEN AGAIN.
EVERYTHING OKAY?
PEACHY.
C'MON, LET'S GO SEE WHAT THE SMITH'LL TRADE US FOR A DEAD RAPTOR.

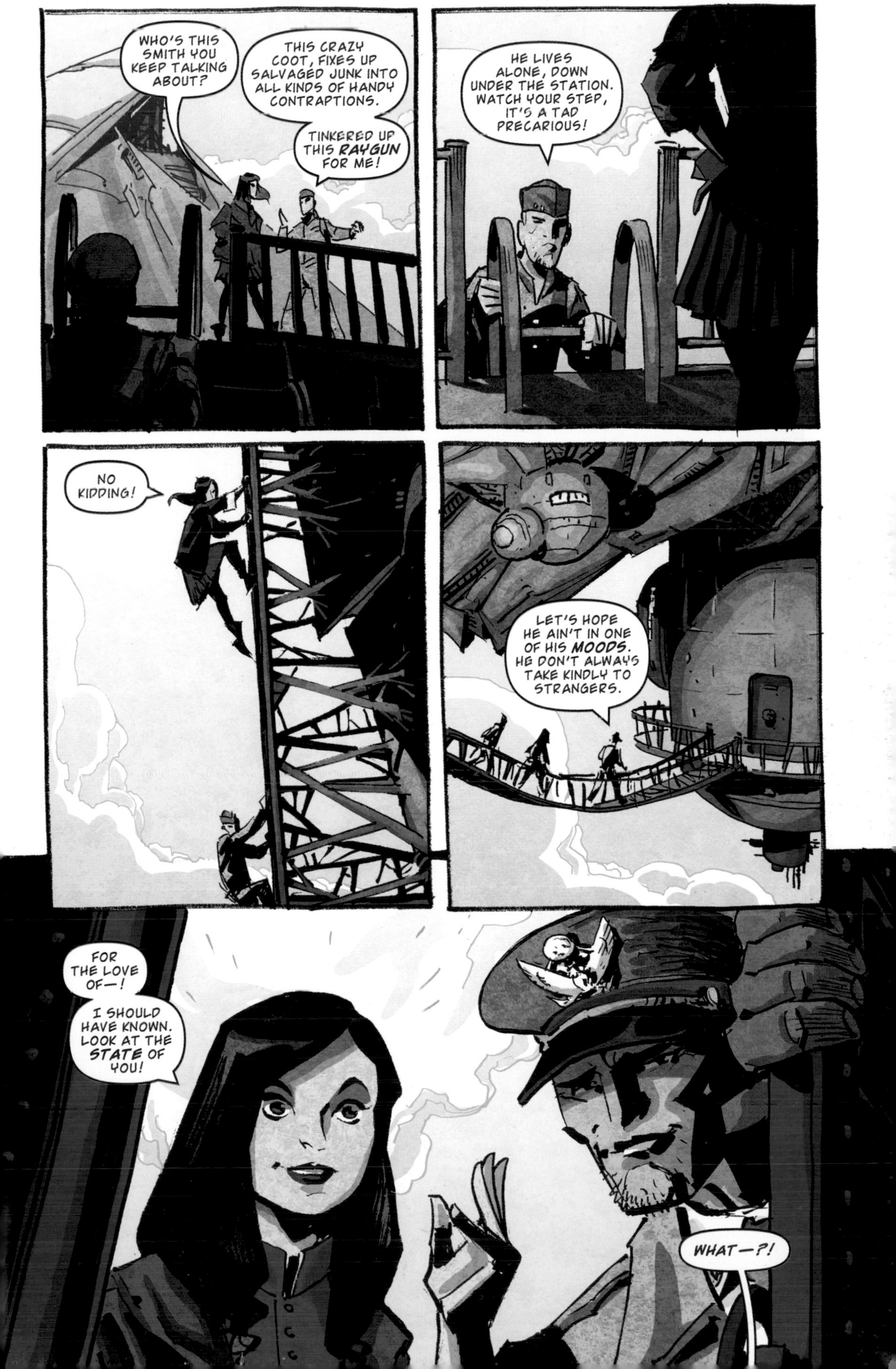
WHO'S THIS SMITH YOU KEEP TALKING ABOUT?
THIS CRAZY COOT, FIXES UP SALVAGED JUNK INTO ALL KINDS OF HANDY CONTRAPTIONS.
TINKERED UP THIS RAYGUN FOR ME!
HE LIVES ALONE, DOWN UNDER THE STATION. WATCH YOUR STEP, IT'S A TAD PRECARIOUS!
NO KIDDING!
LET'S HOPE HE AIN'T IN ONE OF HIS MOODS. HE DON'T ALWAYS TAKE KINDLY TO STRANGERS.
FOR THE LOVE OF—!
I SHOULD HAVE KNOWN. LOOK AT THE STATE OF YOU!
WHAT—?!

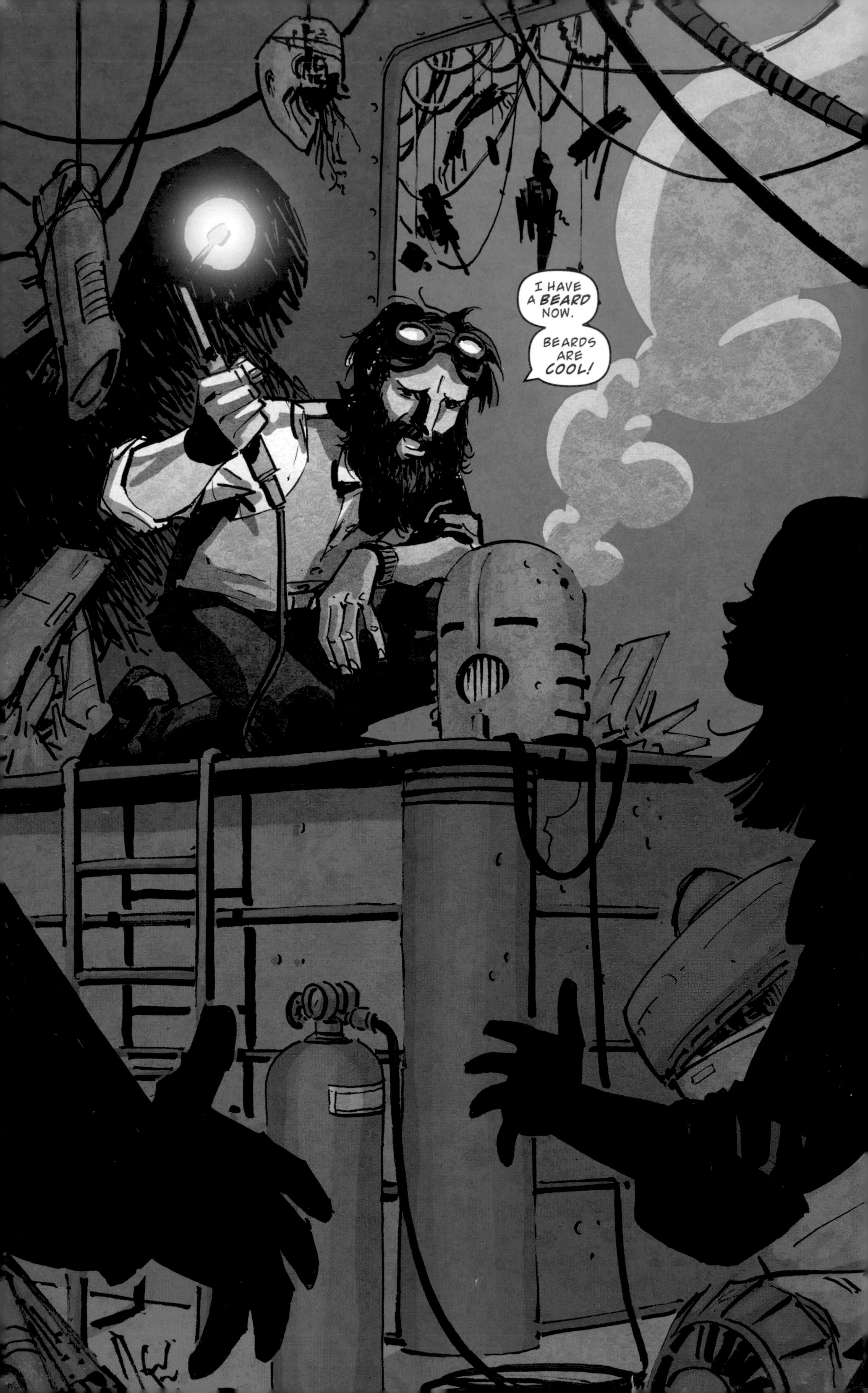
I HAVE A BEARD NOW.
BEARDS ARE COOL!

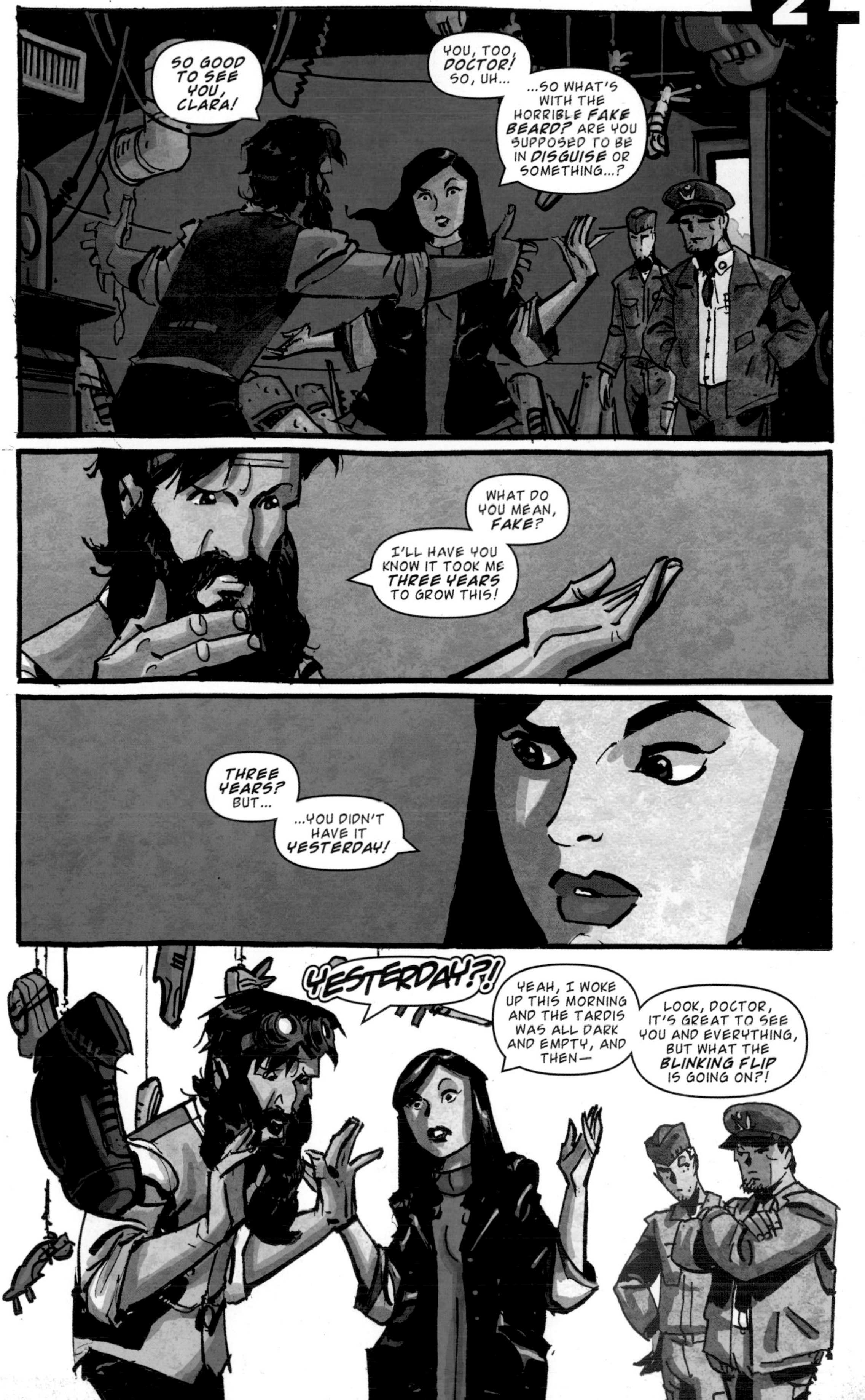
SO GOOD TO SEE YOU, CLARA!
YOU, TOO, DOCTOR! SO, UH...
...SO WHAT'S WITH THE HORRIBLE FAKE BEARD? ARE YOU SUPPOSED TO BE IN DISGUISE OR SOMETHING...?
WHAT DO YOU MEAN, FAKE?
I'LL HAVE YOU KNOW IT TOOK ME THREE YEARS TO GROW THIS!
THREE YEARS? BUT...
...YOU DIDN'T HAVE IT YESTERDAY!
YESTERDAY?!
YEAH, I WOKE UP THIS MORNING AND THE TARDIS WAS ALL DARK AND EMPTY, AND THEN—
LOOK, DOCTOR, IT'S GREAT TO SEE YOU AND EVERYTHING, BUT WHAT THE BLINKING FLIP IS GOING ON?!

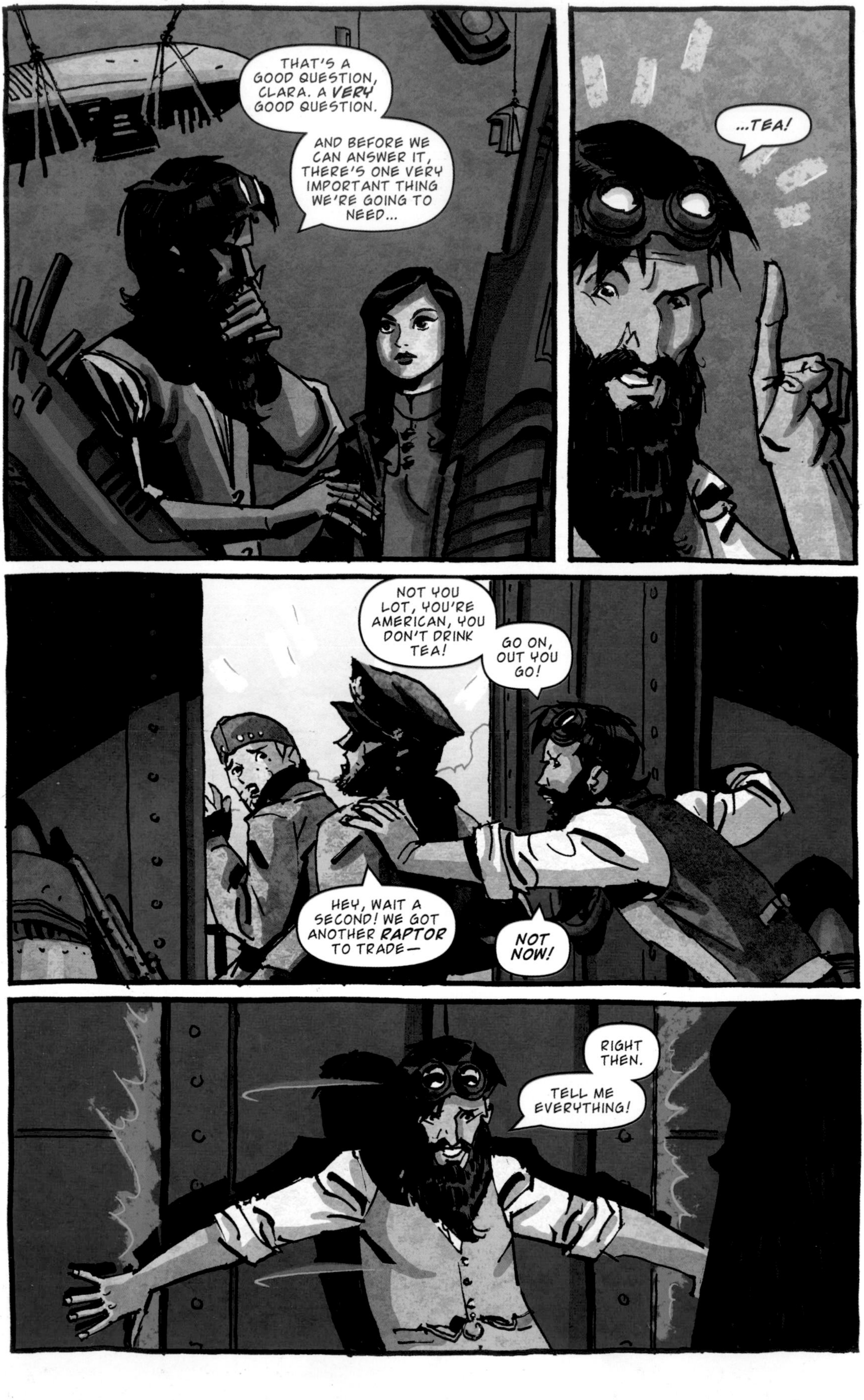
THAT'S A GOOD QUESTION, CLARA. A VERY GOOD QUESTION.
AND BEFORE WE CAN ANSWER IT, THERE'S ONE VERY IMPORTANT THING WE'RE GOING TO NEED...
...TEA!
NOT YOU LOT, YOU'RE AMERICAN, YOU DON'T DRINK TEA!
GO ON, OUT YOU GO!
HEY, WAIT A SECOND! WE GOT ANOTHER RAPTOR TO TRADE—
NOT NOW!
RIGHT THEN.
TELL ME EVERYTHING!

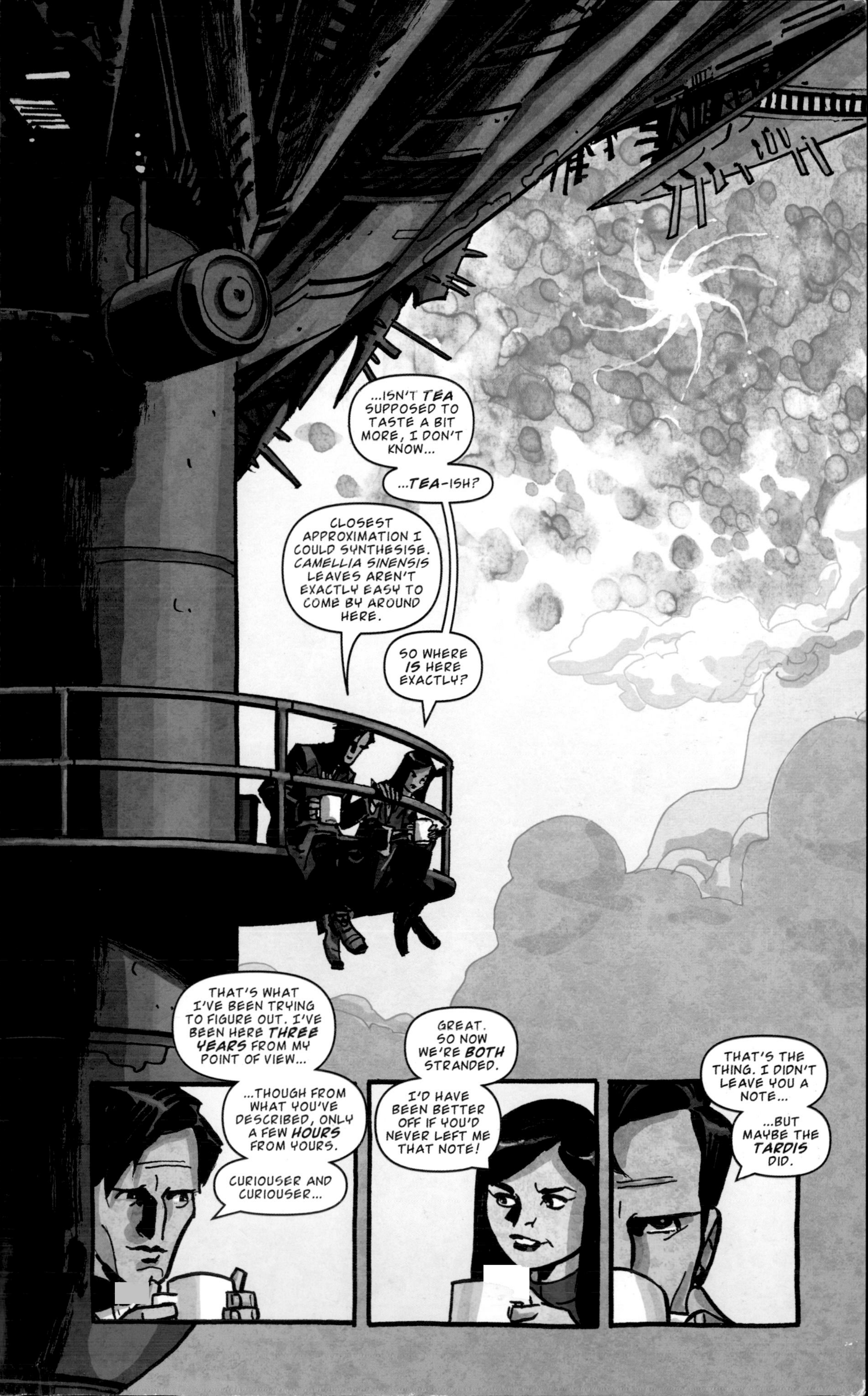
...ISN'T TEA SUPPOSED TO TASTE A BIT MORE, I DON'T KNOW...
...TEA-ISH?
CLOSEST APPROXIMATION I COULD SYNTHESISE. CAMELLIA SINENSIS LEAVES AREN'T EXACTLY EASY TO COME BY AROUND HERE.
SO WHERE IS HERE EXACTLY?
THAT'S WHAT I'VE BEEN TRYING TO FIGURE OUT. I'VE BEEN HERE THREE YEARS FROM MY POINT OF VIEW...
...THOUGH FROM WHAT YOU'VE DESCRIBED, ONLY A FEW HOURS FROM YOURS.
CURIOUSER AND CURIOUSER...
GREAT. SO NOW WE'RE BOTH STRANDED.
I'D HAVE BEEN BETTER OFF IF YOU'D NEVER LEFT ME THAT NOTE!
THAT'S THE THING. I DIDN'T LEAVE YOU A NOTE...
...BUT MAYBE THE TARDIS DID.

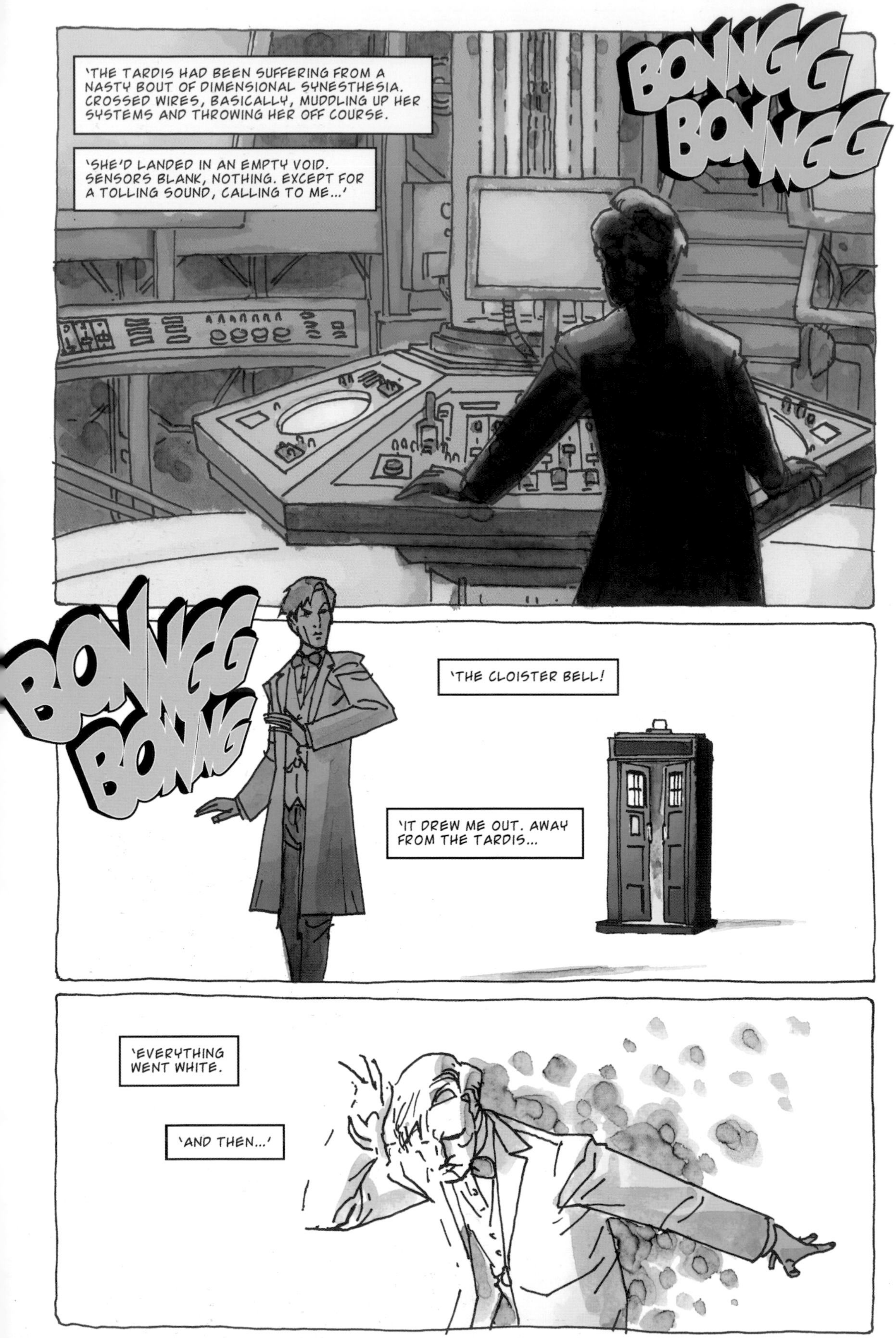
'THE TARDIS HAD BEEN SUFFERING FROM A NASTY BOUT OF DIMENSIONAL SYNESTHESIA. CROSSED WIRES, BASICALLY, MUDDLING UP HER SYSTEMS AND THROWING HER OFF COURSE.
'SHE'D LANDED IN AN EMPTY VOID. SENSORS BLANK, NOTHING. EXCEPT FOR A TOLLING SOUND, CALLING TO ME...'
BONNGG BONNGG
BONNGG BONNG
'THE CLOISTER BELL!
'IT DREW ME OUT. AWAY FROM THE TARDIS...
'EVERYTHING WENT WHITE.
'AND THEN...'

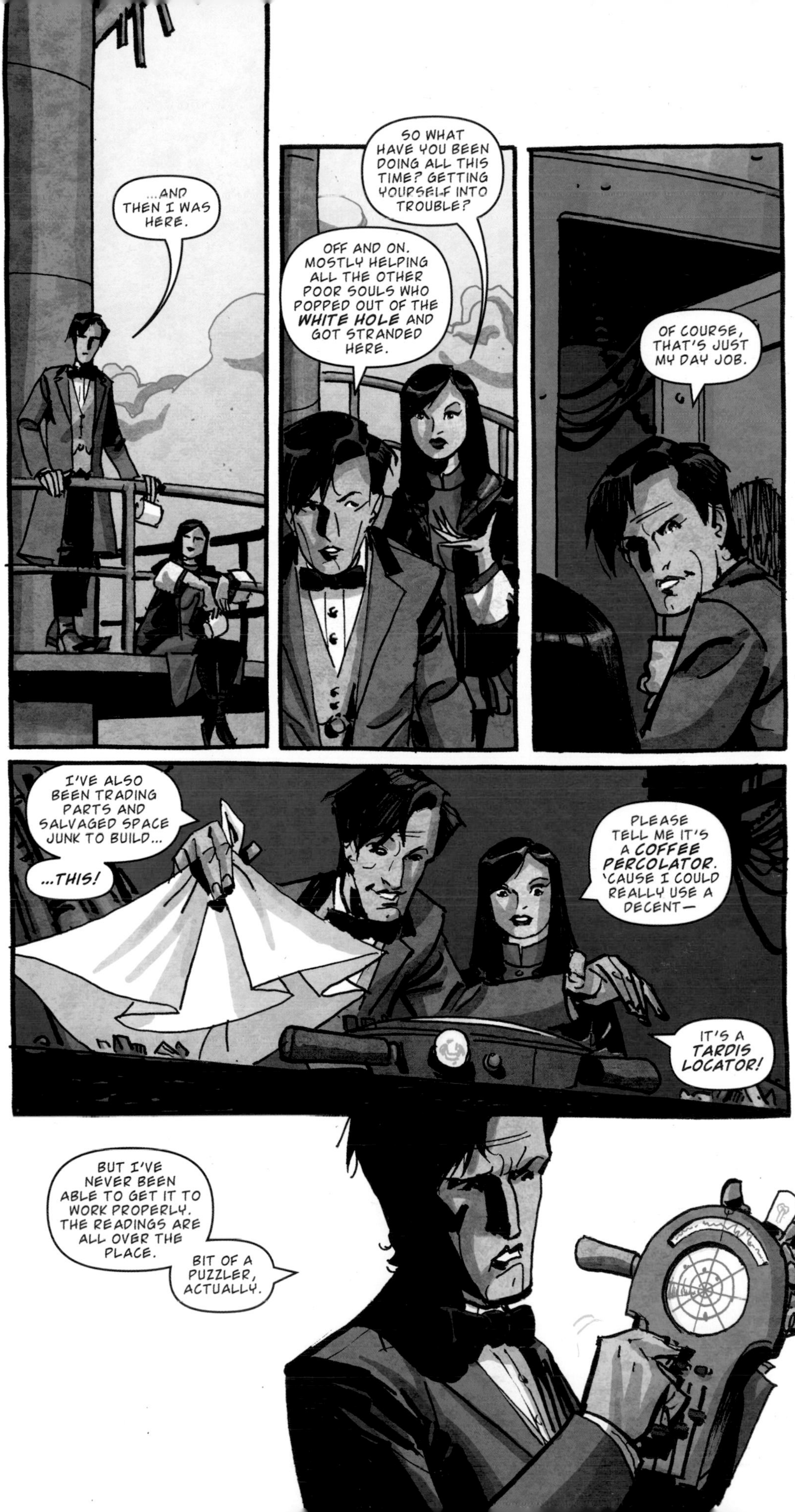
...AND THEN I WAS HERE.
SO WHAT HAVE YOU BEEN DOING ALL THIS TIME? GETTING YOURSELF INTO TROUBLE?
OFF AND ON. MOSTLY HELPING ALL THE OTHER POOR SOULS WHO POPPED OUT OF THE WHITE HOLE AND GOT STRANDED HERE.
OF COURSE, THAT'S JUST MY DAY JOB.
I'VE ALSO BEEN TRADING PARTS AND SALVAGED SPACE JUNK TO BUILD...
...THIS!
PLEASE TELL ME IT'S A COFFEE PERCOLATOR. 'CAUSE I COULD REALLY USE A DECENT—
IT'S A TARDIS LOCATOR!
BUT I'VE NEVER BEEN ABLE TO GET IT TO WORK PROPERLY. THE READINGS ARE ALL OVER THE PLACE.
BIT OF A PUZZLER, ACTUALLY.

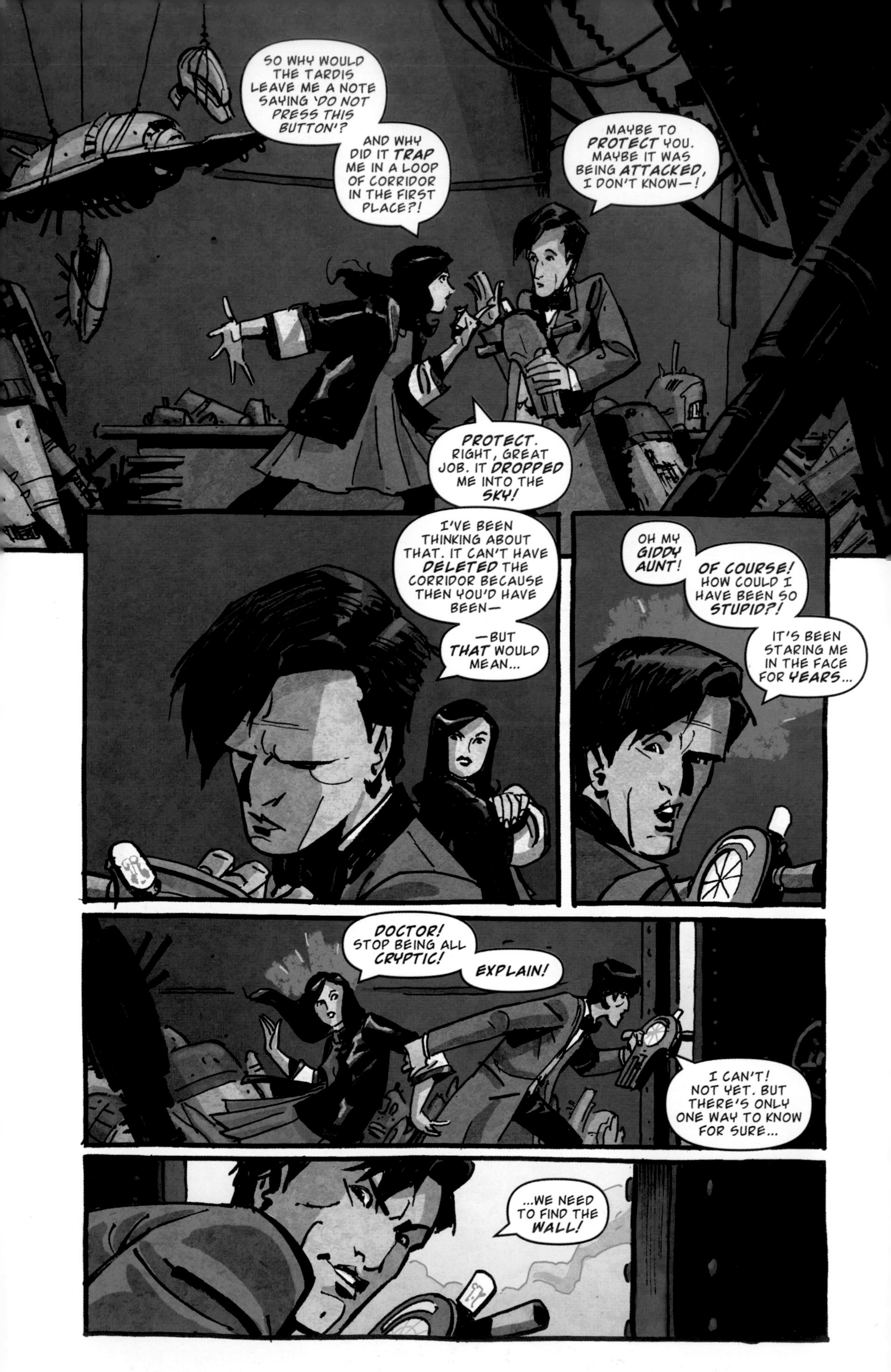
SO WHY WOULD THE TARDIS LEAVE ME A NOTE SAYING 'DO NOT PRESS THIS BUTTON'?
AND WHY DID IT TRAP ME IN A LOOP OF CORRIDOR IN THE FIRST PLACE?!
MAYBE TO PROTECT YOU. MAYBE IT WAS BEING ATTACKED, I DON'T KNOW—!
PROTECT. RIGHT, GREAT JOB. IT DROPPED ME INTO THE SKY!
I'VE BEEN THINKING ABOUT THAT. IT CAN'T HAVE DELETED THE CORRIDOR BECAUSE THEN YOU'D HAVE BEEN—
—BUT THAT WOULD MEAN...
OH MY GIDDY AUNT!
OF COURSE! HOW COULD I HAVE BEEN SO STUPID?!
IT'S BEEN STARING ME IN THE FACE FOR YEARS...
DOCTOR! STOP BEING ALL CRYPTIC!
EXPLAIN!
I CAN'T! NOT YET. BUT THERE'S ONLY ONE WAY TO KNOW FOR SURE...
...WE NEED TO FIND THE WALL!

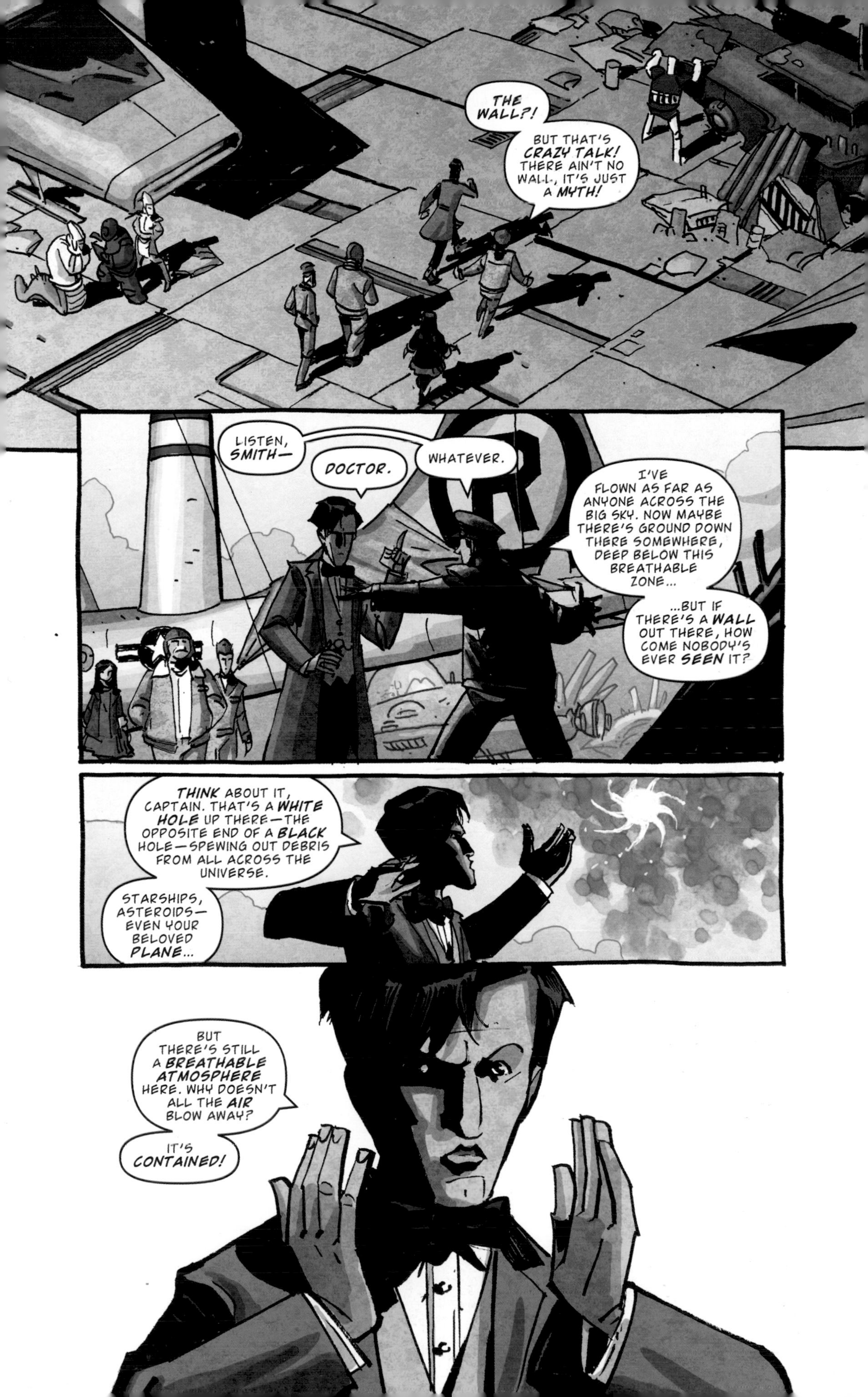
THE WALL?!
BUT THAT'S CRAZY TALK! THERE AIN'T NO WALL, IT'S JUST A MYTH!
LISTEN, SMITH—
DOCTOR.
WHATEVER.
I'VE FLOWN AS FAR AS ANYONE ACROSS THE BIG SKY. NOW MAYBE THERE'S GROUND DOWN THERE SOMEWHERE, DEEP BELOW THIS BREATHABLE ZONE...
...BUT IF THERE'S A WALL OUT THERE, HOW COME NOBODY'S EVER SEEN IT?
THINK ABOUT IT, CAPTAIN. THAT'S A WHITE HOLE UP THERE—THE OPPOSITE END OF A BLACK HOLE—SPEWING OUT DEBRIS FROM ALL ACROSS THE UNIVERSE.
STARSHIPS, ASTEROIDS—EVEN YOUR BELOVED PLANE...
BUT THERE'S STILL A BREATHABLE ATMOSPHERE HERE. WHY DOESN'T ALL THE AIR BLOW AWAY?
IT'S CONTAINED!

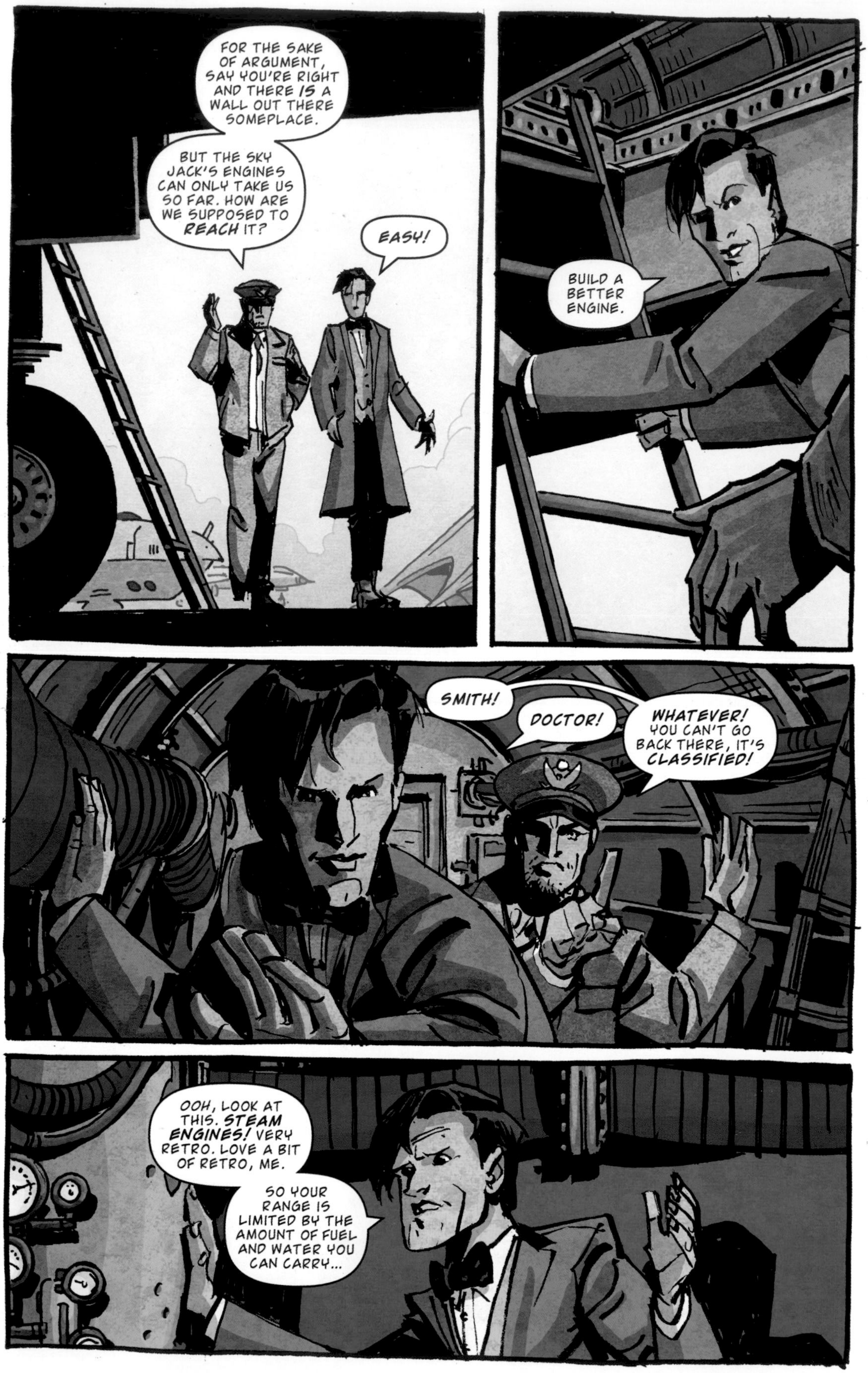
FOR THE SAKE OF ARGUMENT, SAY YOU'RE RIGHT AND THERE IS A WALL OUT THERE SOMEPLACE.
BUT THE SKY JACK'S ENGINES CAN ONLY TAKE US SO FAR. HOW ARE WE SUPPOSED TO REACH IT?
EASY!
BUILD A BETTER ENGINE.
SMITH!
DOCTOR!
WHATEVER! YOU CAN'T GO BACK THERE, IT'S CLASSIFIED!
OOH, LOOK AT THIS. STEAM ENGINES! VERY RETRO. LOVE A BIT OF RETRO, ME.
SO YOUR RANGE IS LIMITED BY THE AMOUNT OF FUEL AND WATER YOU CAN CARRY...

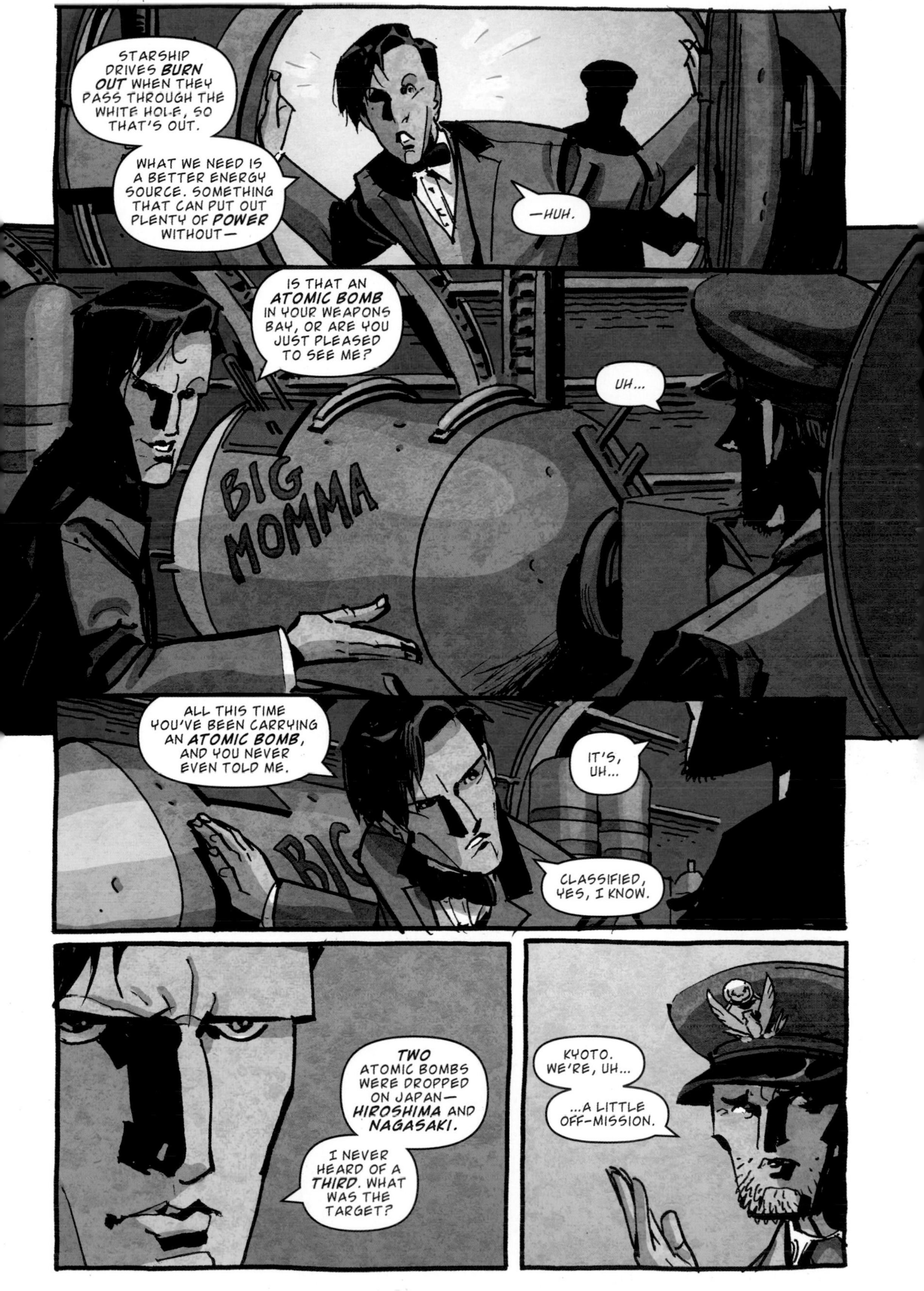
STARSHIP DRIVES BURN OUT WHEN THEY PASS THROUGH THE WHITE HOLE, SO THAT'S OUT.
WHAT WE NEED IS A BETTER ENERGY SOURCE. SOMETHING THAT CAN PUT OUT PLENTY OF POWER WITHOUT—
—HUH.
IS THAT AN ATOMIC BOMB IN YOUR WEAPONS BAY, OR ARE YOU JUST PLEASED TO SEE ME?
UH...
BIG MOMMA
ALL THIS TIME YOU'VE BEEN CARRYING AN ATOMIC BOMB, AND YOU NEVER EVEN TOLD ME.
IT'S, UH...
CLASSIFIED, YES, I KNOW.
TWO ATOMIC BOMBS WERE DROPPED ON JAPAN— HIROSHIMA AND NAGASAKI.
I NEVER HEARD OF A THIRD. WHAT WAS THE TARGET?
KYOTO. WE'RE, UH...
...A LITTLE OFF-MISSION.

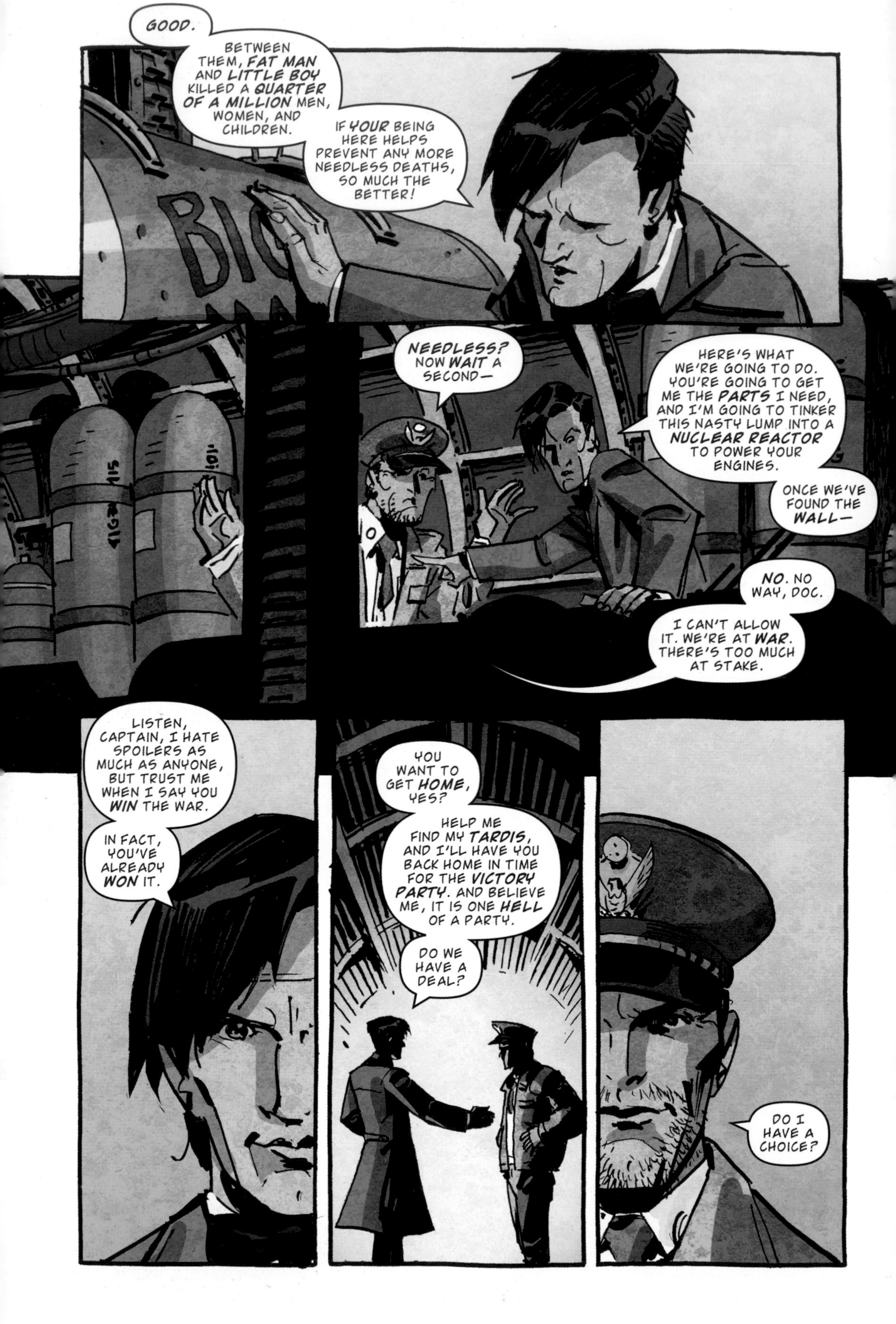
GOOD.
BETWEEN THEM, FAT MAN AND LITTLE BOY KILLED A QUARTER OF A MILLION MEN, WOMEN, AND CHILDREN.
IF YOUR BEING HERE HELPS PREVENT ANY MORE NEEDLESS DEATHS, SO MUCH THE BETTER!
NEEDLESS? NOW WAIT A SECOND—
HERE'S WHAT WE'RE GOING TO DO. YOU'RE GOING TO GET ME THE PARTS I NEED, AND I'M GOING TO TINKER THIS NASTY LUMP INTO A NUCLEAR REACTOR TO POWER YOUR ENGINES.
ONCE WE'VE FOUND THE WALL—
NO. NO WAY, DOC.
I CAN'T ALLOW IT. WE'RE AT WAR. THERE'S TOO MUCH AT STAKE.
LISTEN, CAPTAIN, I HATE SPOILERS AS MUCH AS ANYONE, BUT TRUST ME WHEN I SAY YOU WIN THE WAR.
IN FACT, YOU'VE ALREADY WON IT.
YOU WANT TO GET HOME, YES?
HELP ME FIND MY TARDIS, AND I'LL HAVE YOU BACK HOME IN TIME FOR THE VICTORY PARTY. AND BELIEVE ME, IT IS ONE HELL OF A PARTY.
DO WE HAVE A DEAL?
DO I HAVE A CHOICE?

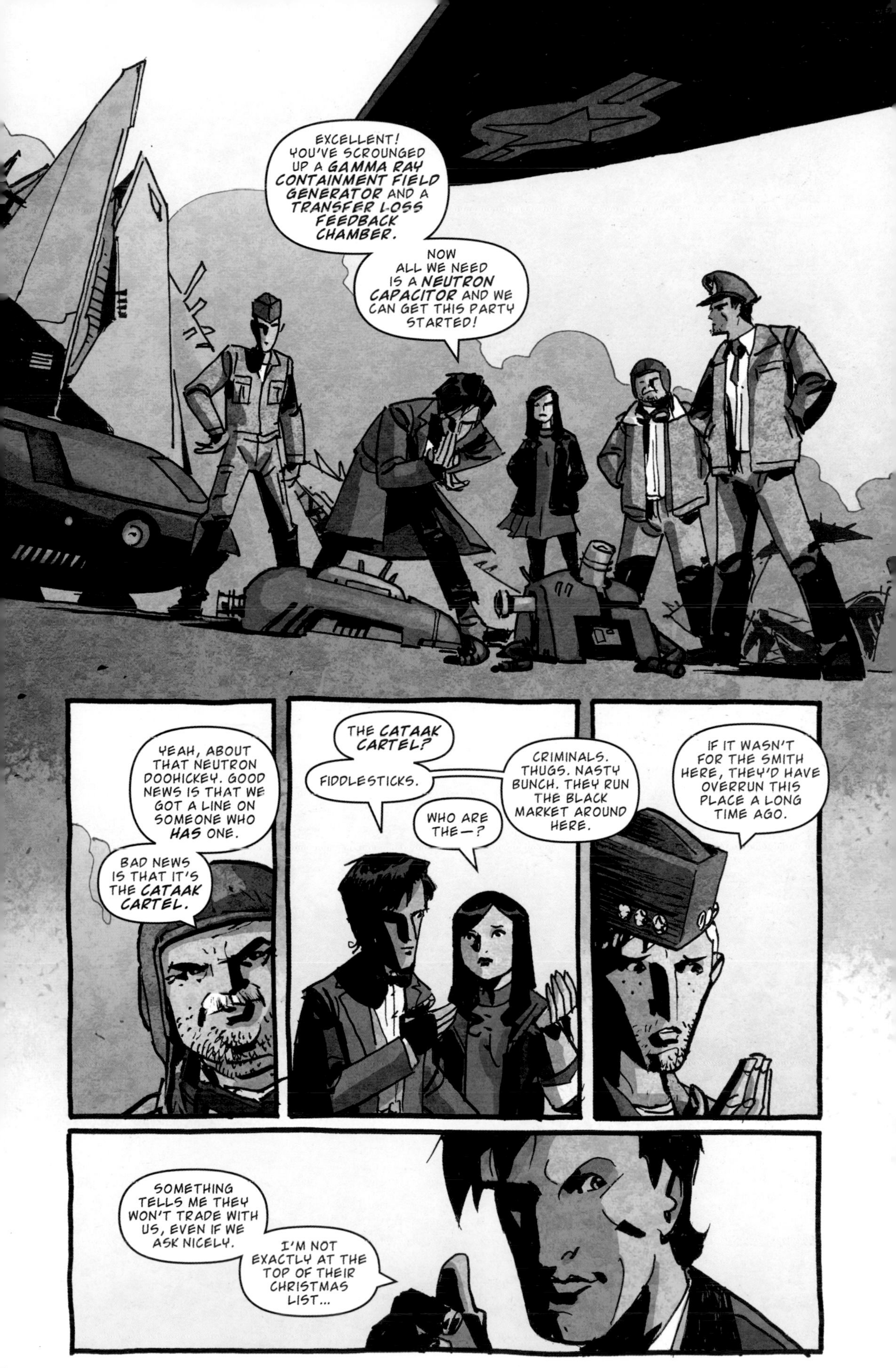
EXCELLENT! YOU'VE SCROUNGED UP A GAMMA RAY CONTAINMENT FIELD GENERATOR AND A TRANSFER LOSS FEEDBACK CHAMBER.
NOW ALL WE NEED IS A NEUTRON CAPACITOR AND WE CAN GET THIS PARTY STARTED!
YEAH, ABOUT THAT NEUTRON DOOHICKEY. GOOD NEWS IS THAT WE GOT A LINE ON SOMEONE WHO HAS ONE.
BAD NEWS IS THAT IT'S THE CATAAK CARTEL.
THE CATAAK CARTEL?
FIDDLESTICKS.
WHO ARE THE—?
CRIMINALS. THUGS. NASTY BUNCH. THEY RUN THE BLACK MARKET AROUND HERE.
IF IT WASN'T FOR THE SMITH HERE, THEY'D HAVE OVERRUN THIS PLACE A LONG TIME AGO.
SOMETHING TELLS ME THEY WON'T TRADE WITH US, EVEN IF WE ASK NICELY.
I'M NOT EXACTLY AT THE TOP OF THEIR CHRISTMAS LIST...

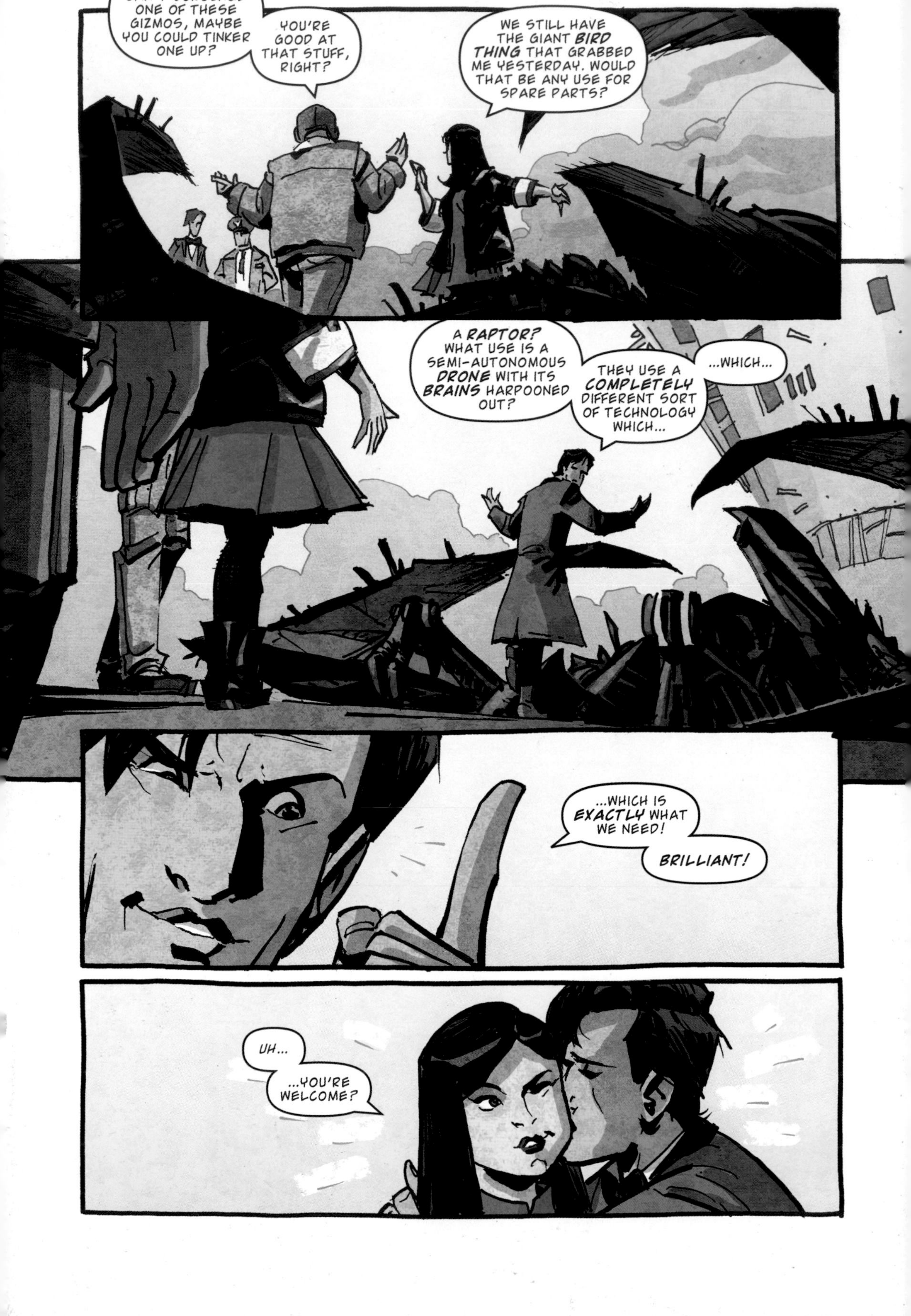
WELL, IF YOU CAN'T SCROUNGE ONE OF THESE GIZMOS, MAYBE YOU COULD TINKER ONE UP?
YOU'RE GOOD AT THAT STUFF, RIGHT?
WE STILL HAVE THE GIANT BIRD THING THAT GRABBED ME YESTERDAY. WOULD THAT BE ANY USE FOR SPARE PARTS?
A RAPTOR? WHAT USE IS A SEMI-AUTONOMOUS DRONE WITH ITS BRAINS HARPOONED OUT?
THEY USE A COMPLETELY DIFFERENT SORT OF TECHNOLOGY WHICH...
...WHICH...
...WHICH IS EXACTLY WHAT WE NEED!
BRILLIANT!
UH...
...YOU'RE WELCOME?

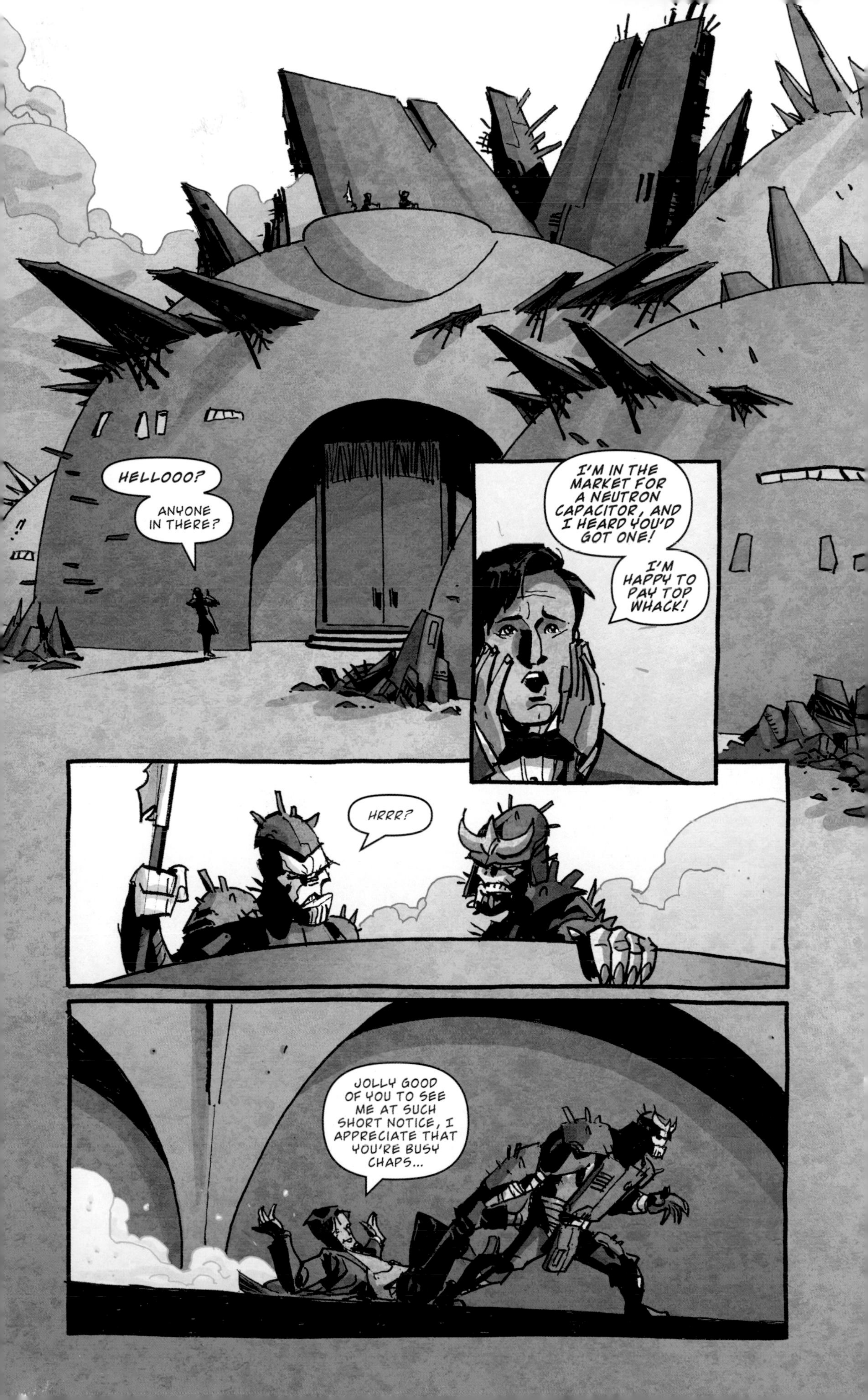
HELLOOO?
ANYONE IN THERE?
I'M IN THE MARKET FOR A NEUTRON CAPACITOR, AND I HEARD YOU'D GOT ONE!
I'M HAPPY TO PAY TOP WHACK!
HRRR?
JOLLY GOOD OF YOU TO SEE ME AT SUCH SHORT NOTICE, I APPRECIATE THAT YOU'RE BUSY CHAPS...

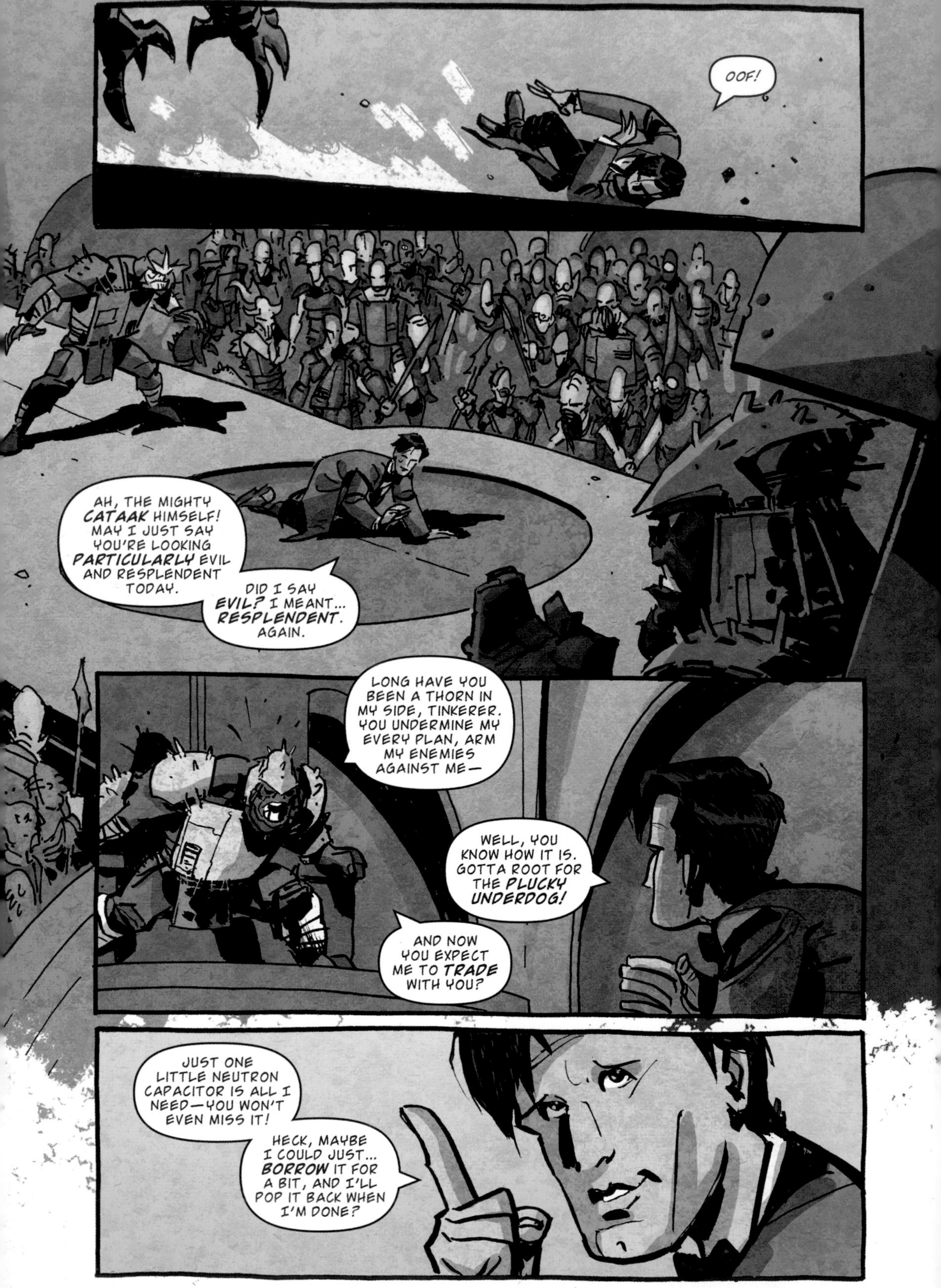
OOF!
AH, THE MIGHTY CATAAK HIMSELF! MAY I JUST SAY YOU'RE LOOKING PARTICULARLY EVIL AND RESPLENDENT TODAY.
DID I SAY EVIL? I MEANT... RESPLENDENT. AGAIN.
LONG HAVE YOU BEEN A THORN IN MY SIDE, TINKERER. YOU UNDERMINE MY EVERY PLAN, ARM MY ENEMIES AGAINST ME—
WELL, YOU KNOW HOW IT IS. GOTTA ROOT FOR THE PLUCKY UNDERDOG!
AND NOW YOU EXPECT ME TO TRADE WITH YOU?
JUST ONE LITTLE NEUTRON CAPACITOR IS ALL I NEED—YOU WON'T EVEN MISS IT!
HECK, MAYBE I COULD JUST... BORROW IT FOR A BIT, AND I'LL POP IT BACK WHEN I'M DONE?

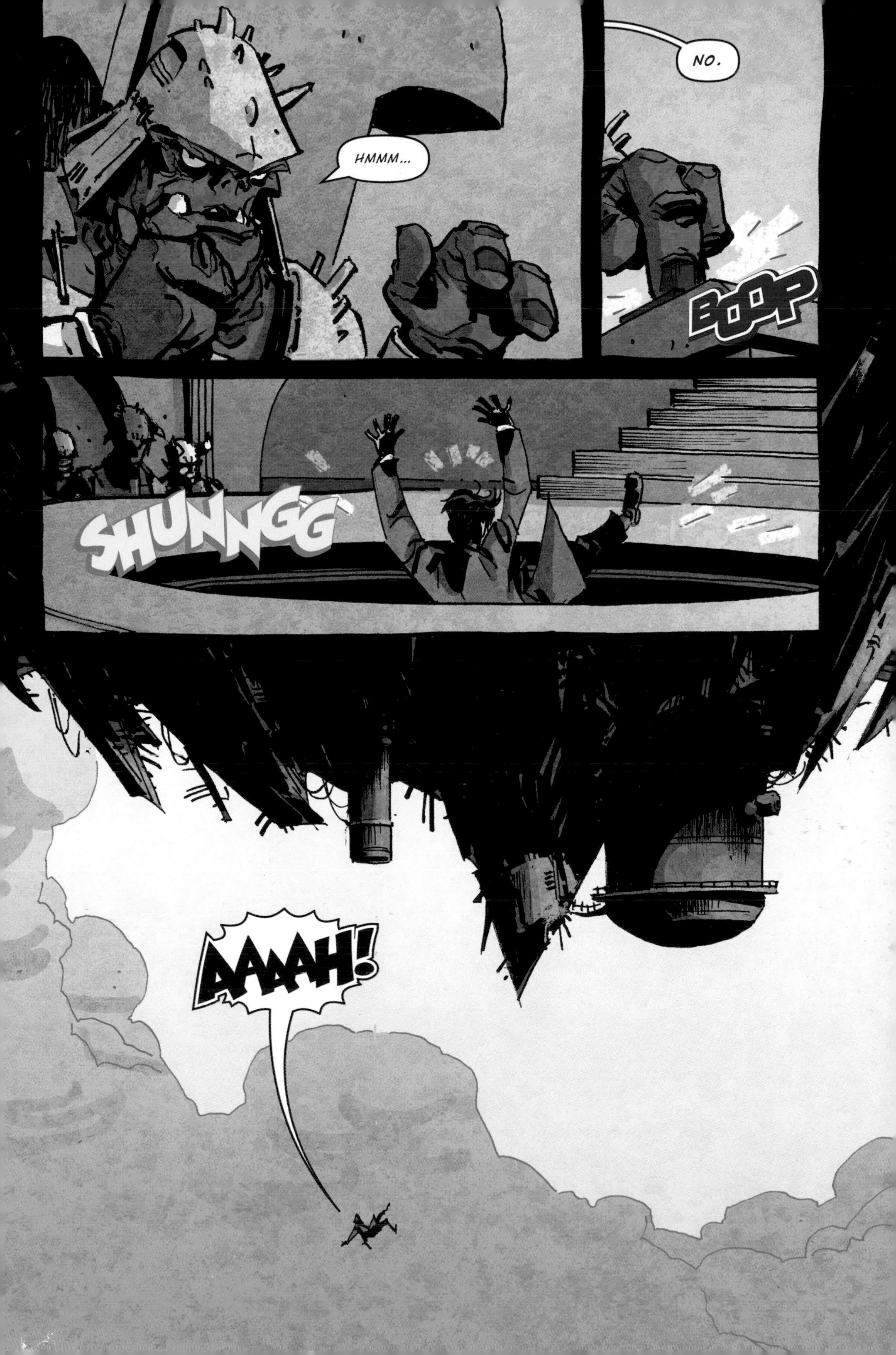
HMMM...
NO.
BOOP
SHUNNGG
AAAAH!

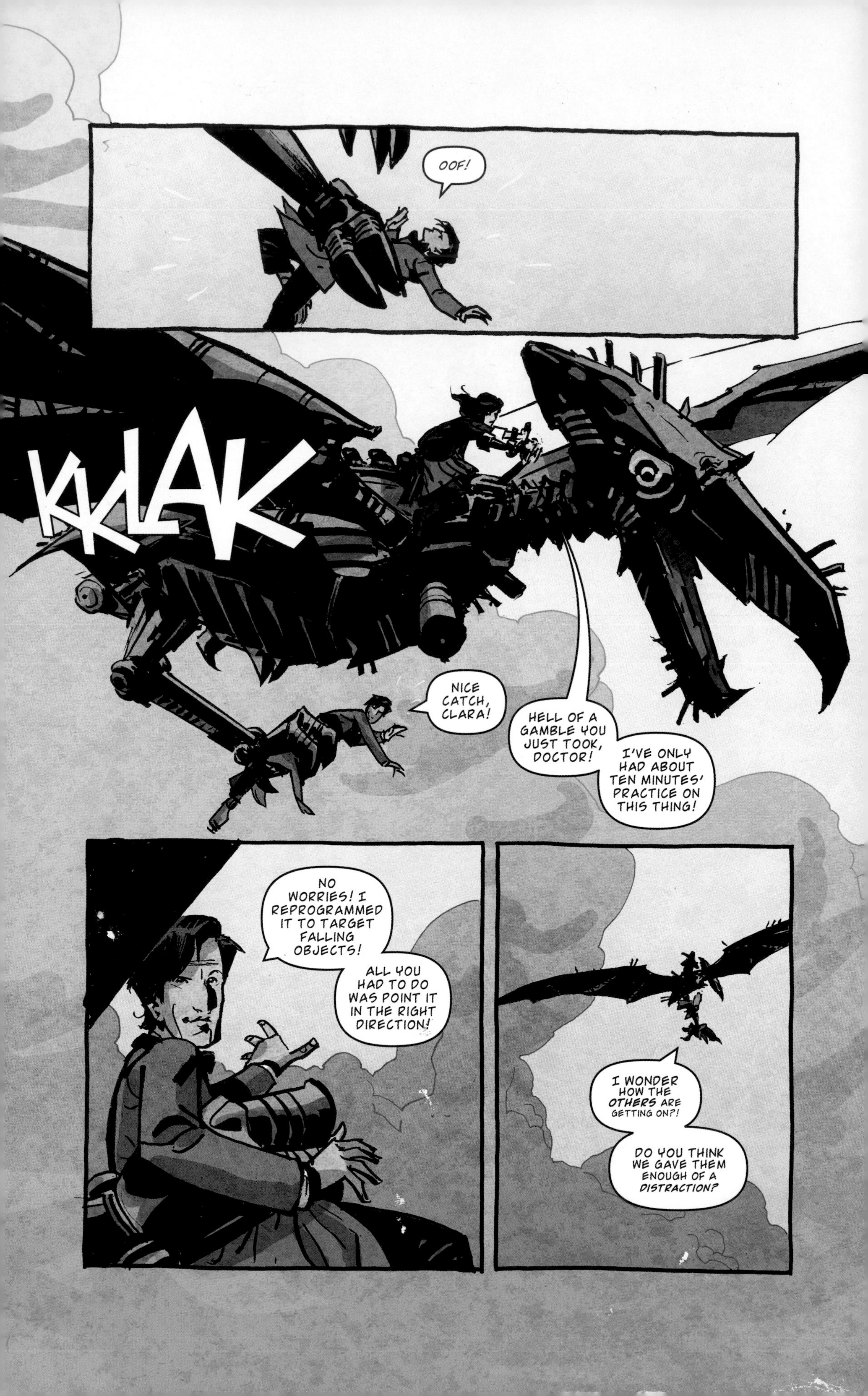
OOF!
KKLAK
NICE CATCH, CLARA!
HELL OF A GAMBLE YOU JUST TOOK, DOCTOR!
I'VE ONLY HAD ABOUT TEN MINUTES' PRACTICE ON THIS THING!
NO WORRIES! I REPROGRAMMED IT TO TARGET FALLING OBJECTS!
ALL YOU HAD TO DO WAS POINT IT IN THE RIGHT DIRECTION!
I WONDER HOW THE OTHERS ARE GETTING ON?!
DO YOU THINK WE GAVE THEM ENOUGH OF A DISTRACTION?

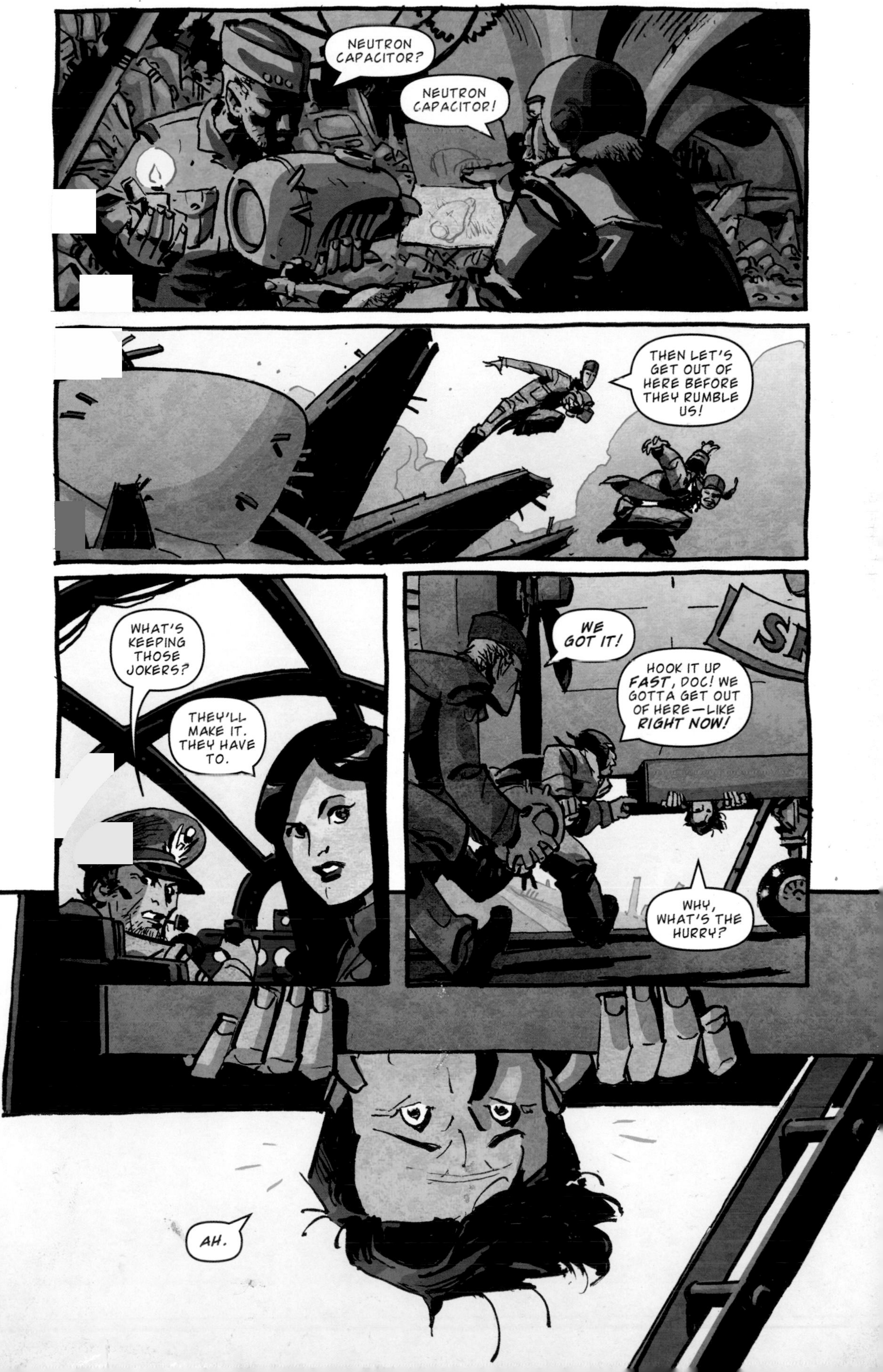
NEUTRON CAPACITOR?
NEUTRON CAPACITOR!
THEN LET'S GET OUT OF HERE BEFORE THEY RUMBLE US!
WHAT'S KEEPING THOSE JOKERS?
THEY'LL MAKE IT. THEY HAVE TO.
WE GOT IT!
HOOK IT UP FAST, DOC! WE GOTTA GET OUT OF HERE—LIKE RIGHT NOW!
WHY, WHAT'S THE HURRY?
AH.

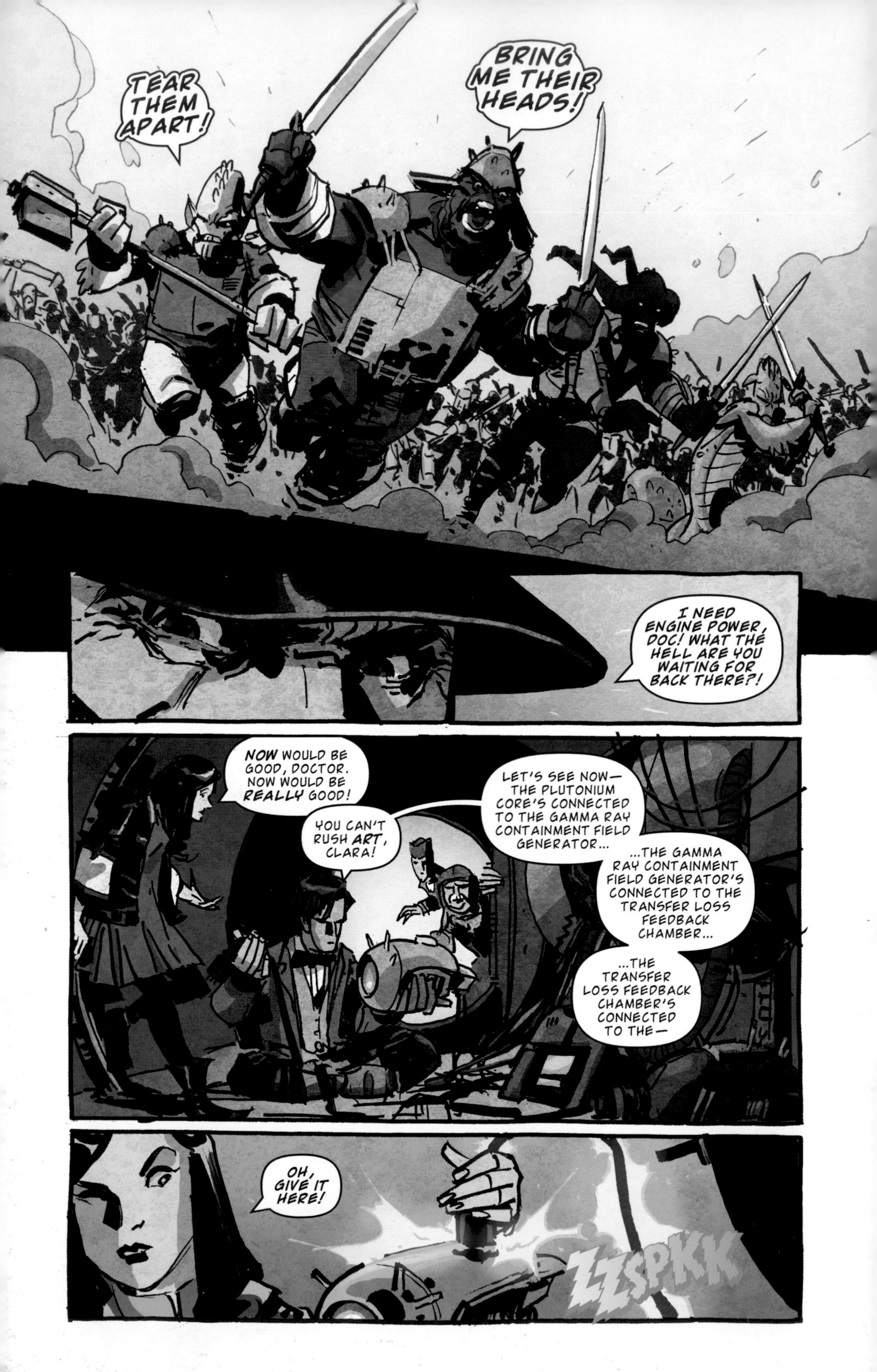
TEAR THEM APART!
BRING ME THEIR HEADS!
I NEED ENGINE POWER, DOC! WHAT THE HELL ARE YOU WAITING FOR BACK THERE?!
NOW WOULD BE GOOD, DOCTOR. NOW WOULD BE REALLY GOOD!
YOU CAN'T RUSH ART, CLARA!
LET'S SEE NOW— THE PLUTONIUM CORE'S CONNECTED TO THE GAMMA RAY CONTAINMENT FIELD GENERATOR...
...THE GAMMA RAY CONTAINMENT FIELD GENERATOR'S CONNECTED TO THE TRANSFER LOSS FEEDBACK CHAMBER...
...THE TRANSFER LOSS FEEDBACK CHAMBER'S CONNECTED TO THE—
OH, GIVE IT HERE!
ZZSPKK

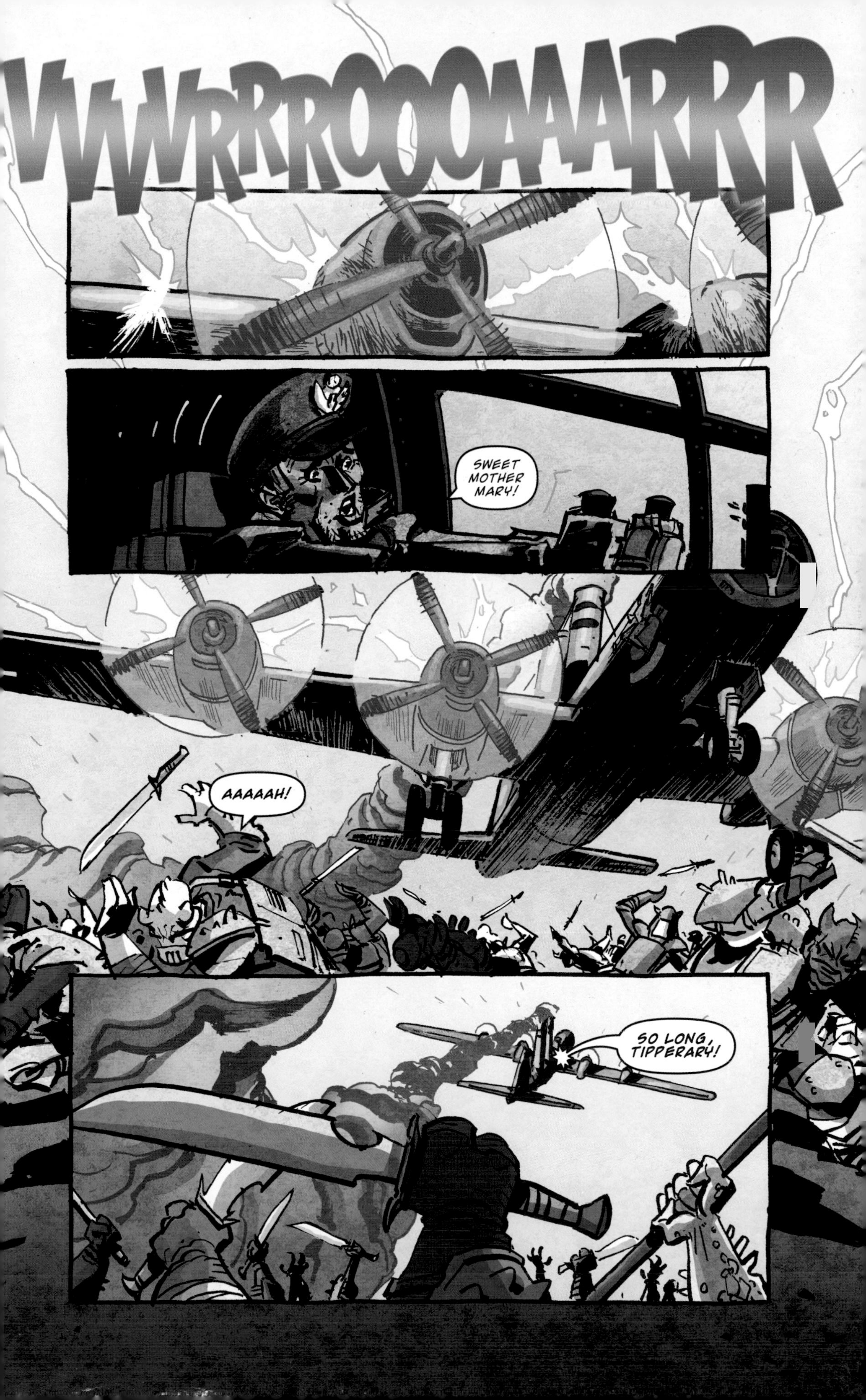
WWRRROOOAAARRR
SWEET MOTHER MARY!
AAAAAH!
SO LONG, TIPPERARY!

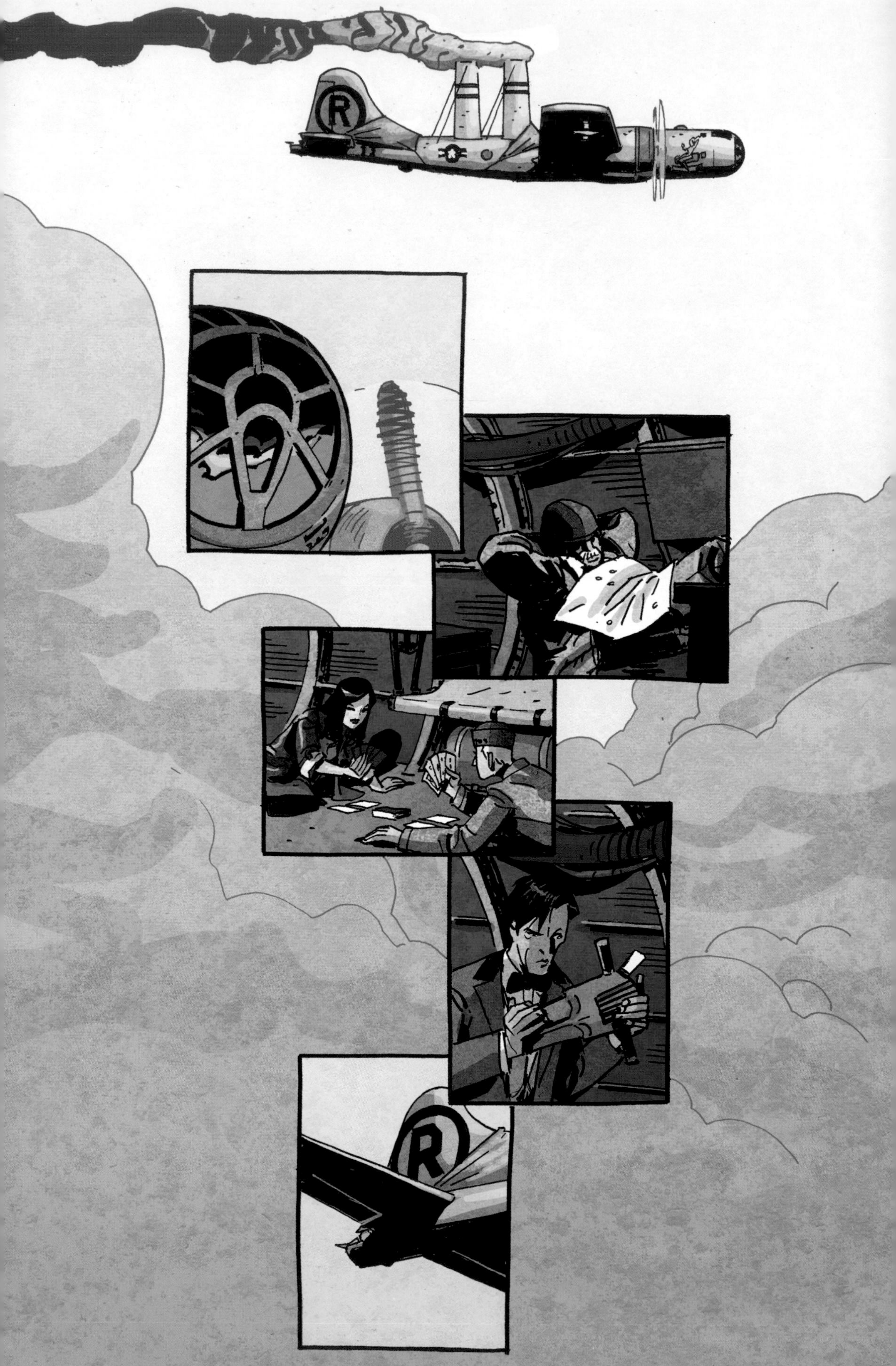

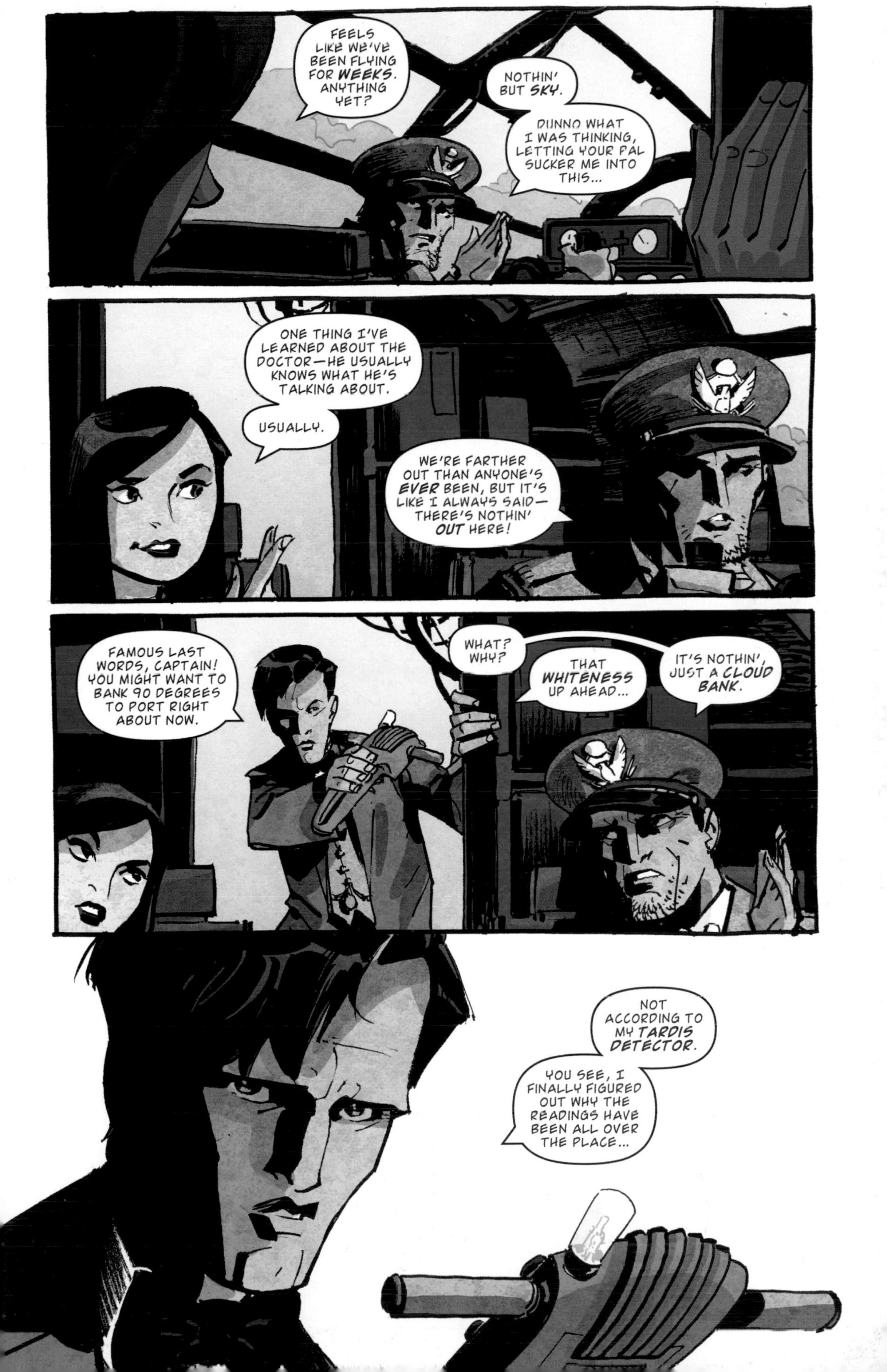
FEELS LIKE WE'VE BEEN FLYING FOR WEEKS. ANYTHING YET?
NOTHIN' BUT SKY.
DUNNO WHAT I WAS THINKING, LETTING YOUR PAL SUCKER ME INTO THIS...
ONE THING I'VE LEARNED ABOUT THE DOCTOR—HE USUALLY KNOWS WHAT HE'S TALKING ABOUT.
USUALLY.
WE'RE FARTHER OUT THAN ANYONE'S EVER BEEN, BUT IT'S LIKE I ALWAYS SAID—THERE'S NOTHIN' OUT HERE!
FAMOUS LAST WORDS, CAPTAIN! YOU MIGHT WANT TO BANK 90 DEGREES TO PORT RIGHT ABOUT NOW.
WHAT? WHY?
THAT WHITENESS UP AHEAD...
IT'S NOTHIN', JUST A CLOUD BANK.
NOT ACCORDING TO MY TARDIS DETECTOR.
YOU SEE, I FINALLY FIGURED OUT WHY THE READINGS HAVE BEEN ALL OVER THE PLACE...

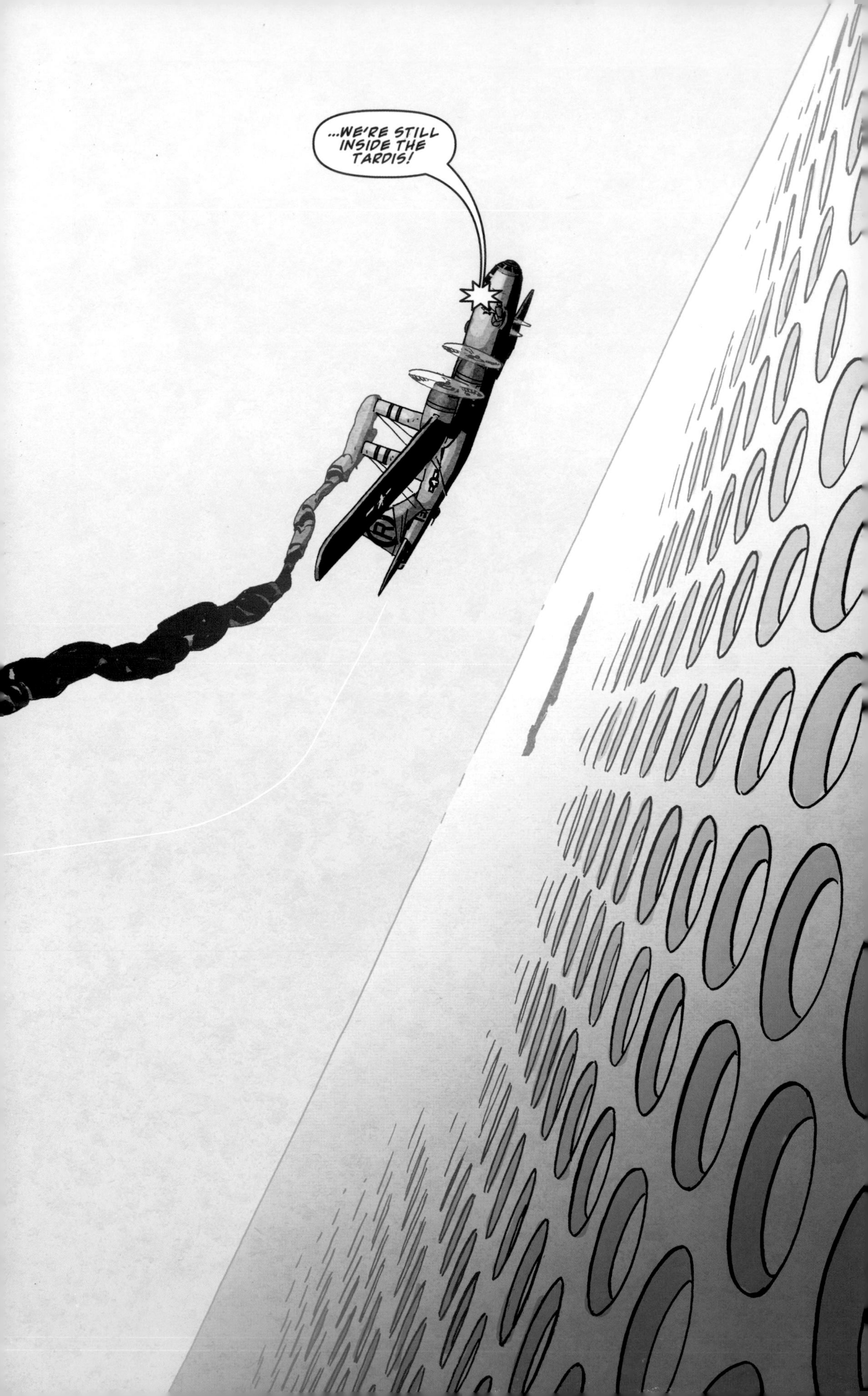
...WE'RE STILL INSIDE THE TARDIS!

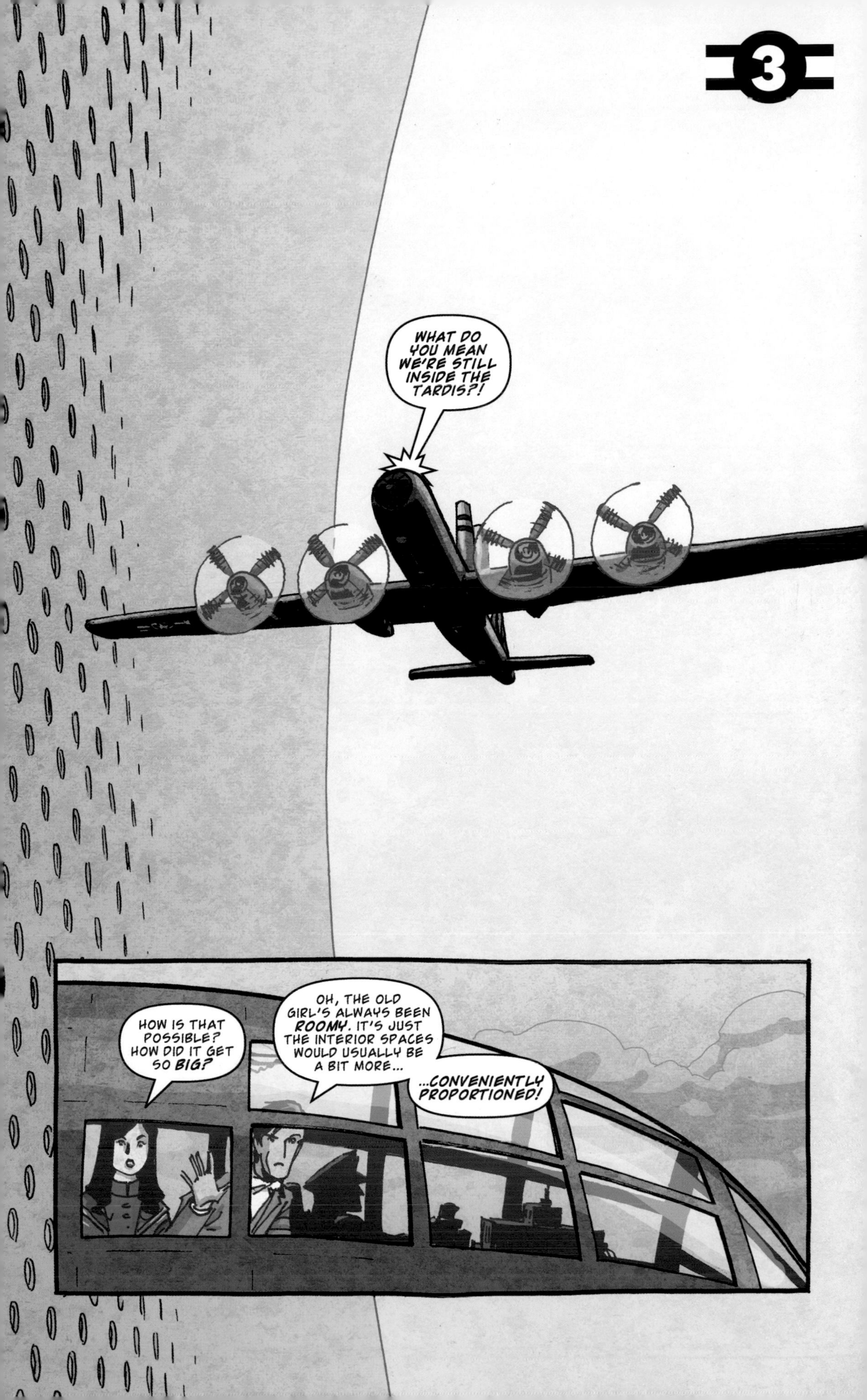
3
WHAT DO YOU MEAN WE'RE STILL INSIDE THE TARDIS?!
HOW IS THAT POSSIBLE? HOW DID IT GET SO BIG?
OH, THE OLD GIRL'S ALWAYS BEEN ROOMY. IT'S JUST THE INTERIOR SPACES WOULD USUALLY BE A BIT MORE...
...CONVENIENTLY PROPORTIONED!

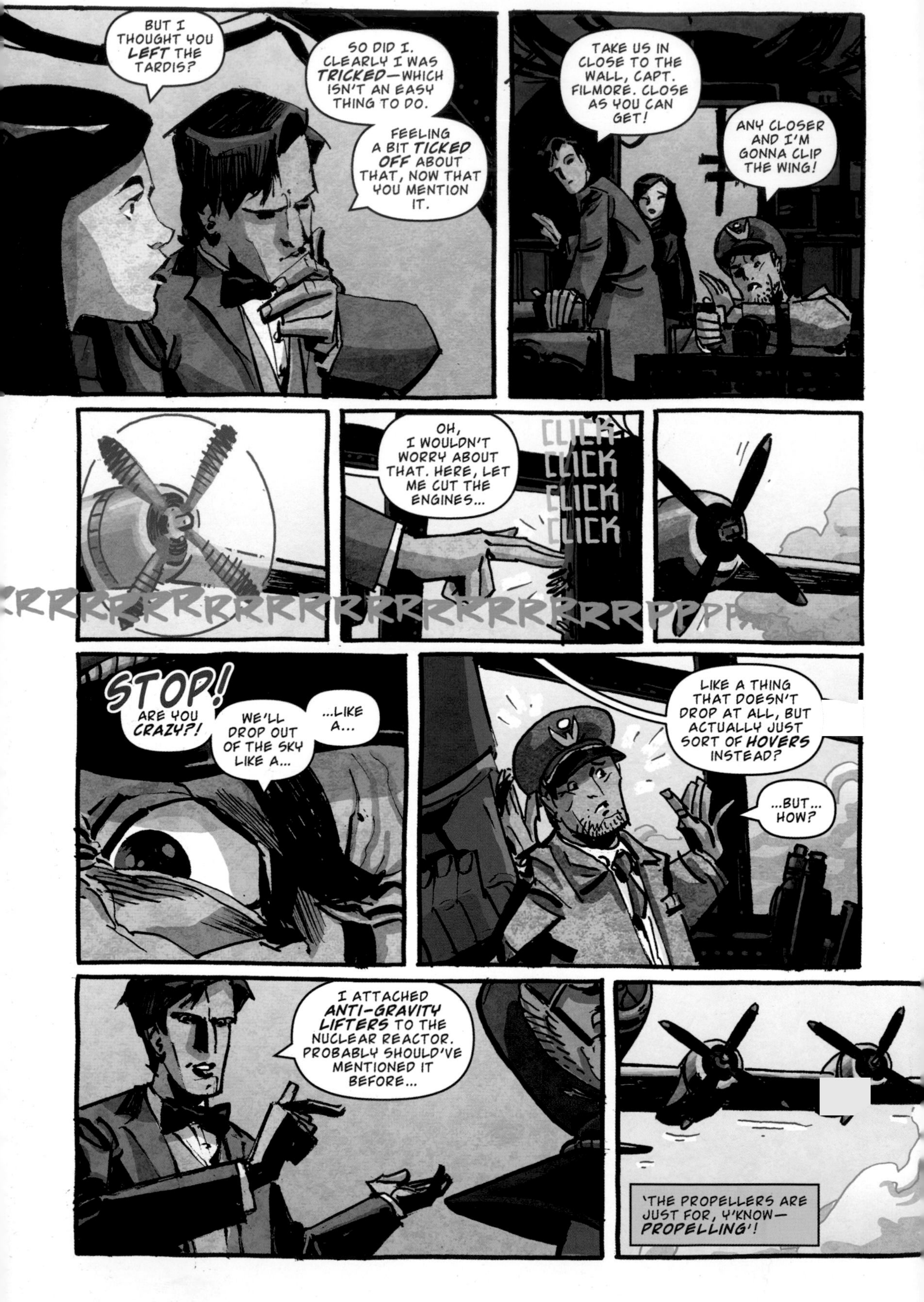
BUT I THOUGHT YOU LEFT THE TARDIS?
SO DID I. CLEARLY I WAS TRICKED—WHICH ISN'T AN EASY THING TO DO.
FEELING A BIT TICKED OFF ABOUT THAT, NOW THAT YOU MENTION IT.
TAKE US IN CLOSE TO THE WALL, CAPT. FILMORE. CLOSE AS YOU CAN GET!
ANY CLOSER AND I'M GONNA CLIP THE WING!
RRRRRRRRRRRRRRRRRRRRRPPPP
OH, I WOULDN'T WORRY ABOUT THAT. HERE, LET ME CUT THE ENGINES...
CLICK
CLICK
CLICK
CLICK
STOP!
ARE YOU CRAZY?!
WE'LL DROP OUT OF THE SKY LIKE A...
...LIKE A...
LIKE A THING THAT DOESN'T DROP AT ALL, BUT ACTUALLY JUST SORT OF HOVERS INSTEAD?
...BUT... HOW?
I ATTACHED ANTI-GRAVITY LIFTERS TO THE NUCLEAR REACTOR. PROBABLY SHOULD'VE MENTIONED IT BEFORE...
'THE PROPELLERS ARE JUST FOR, Y'KNOW—PROPELLING'!

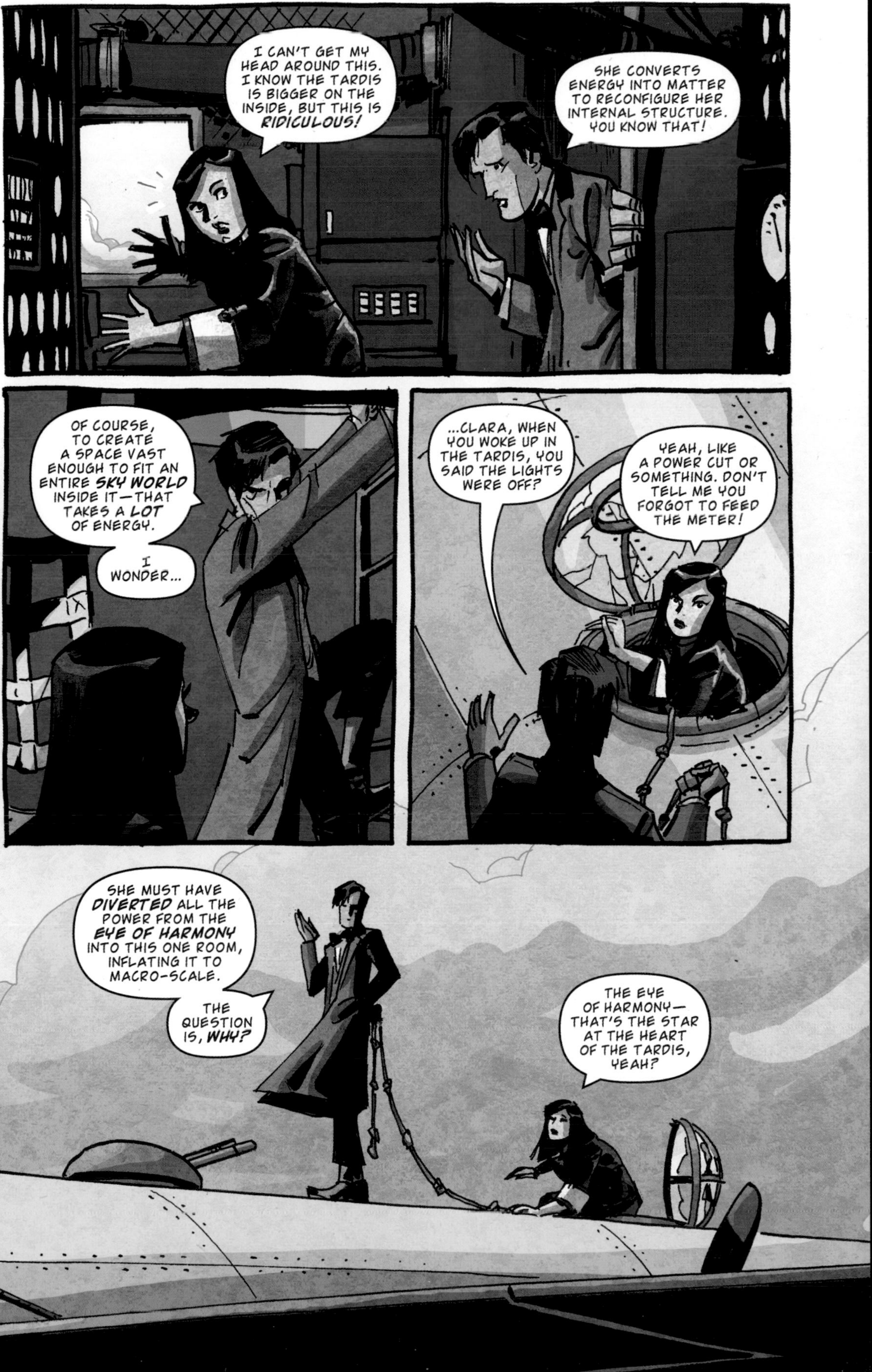
I CAN'T GET MY HEAD AROUND THIS. I KNOW THE TARDIS IS BIGGER ON THE INSIDE, BUT THIS IS RIDICULOUS!
SHE CONVERTS ENERGY INTO MATTER TO RECONFIGURE HER INTERNAL STRUCTURE. YOU KNOW THAT!
OF COURSE, TO CREATE A SPACE VAST ENOUGH TO FIT AN ENTIRE SKY WORLD INSIDE IT—THAT TAKES A LOT OF ENERGY.
I WONDER...
...CLARA, WHEN YOU WOKE UP IN THE TARDIS, YOU SAID THE LIGHTS WERE OFF?
YEAH, LIKE A POWER CUT OR SOMETHING. DON'T TELL ME YOU FORGOT TO FEED THE METER!
SHE MUST HAVE DIVERTED ALL THE POWER FROM THE EYE OF HARMONY INTO THIS ONE ROOM, INFLATING IT TO MACRO-SCALE.
THE QUESTION IS, WHY?
THE EYE OF HARMONY—THAT'S THE STAR AT THE HEART OF THE TARDIS, YEAH?

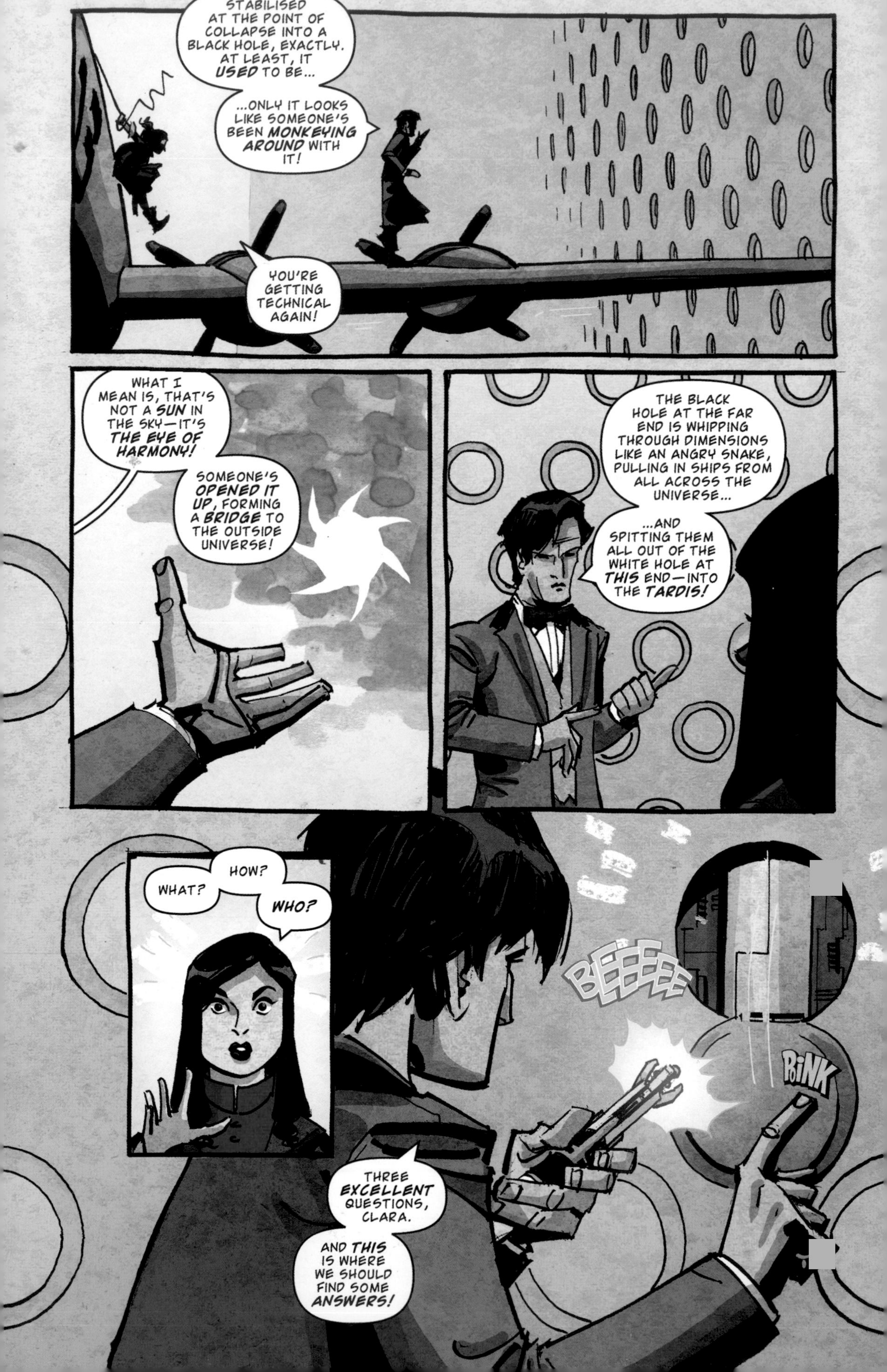

STABILISED AT THE POINT OF COLLAPSE INTO A BLACK HOLE, EXACTLY. AT LEAST, IT *USED* TO BE...
...ONLY IT LOOKS LIKE SOMEONE'S BEEN *MONKEYING AROUND* WITH IT!
YOU'RE GETTING TECHNICAL AGAIN!
WHAT I MEAN IS, THAT'S NOT A *SUN* IN THE SKY—IT'S *THE EYE OF HARMONY!*
SOMEONE'S *OPENED IT UP*, FORMING A *BRIDGE* TO THE OUTSIDE UNIVERSE!
THE BLACK HOLE AT THE FAR END IS WHIPPING THROUGH DIMENSIONS LIKE AN ANGRY SNAKE, PULLING IN SHIPS FROM ALL ACROSS THE UNIVERSE...
...AND SPITTING THEM ALL OUT OF THE WHITE HOLE AT *THIS* END—INTO THE *TARDIS!*
WHAT?
HOW?
WHO?
BLEEEEE
PoiNK
THREE *EXCELLENT* QUESTIONS, CLARA.
AND *THIS* IS WHERE WE SHOULD FIND SOME *ANSWERS!*

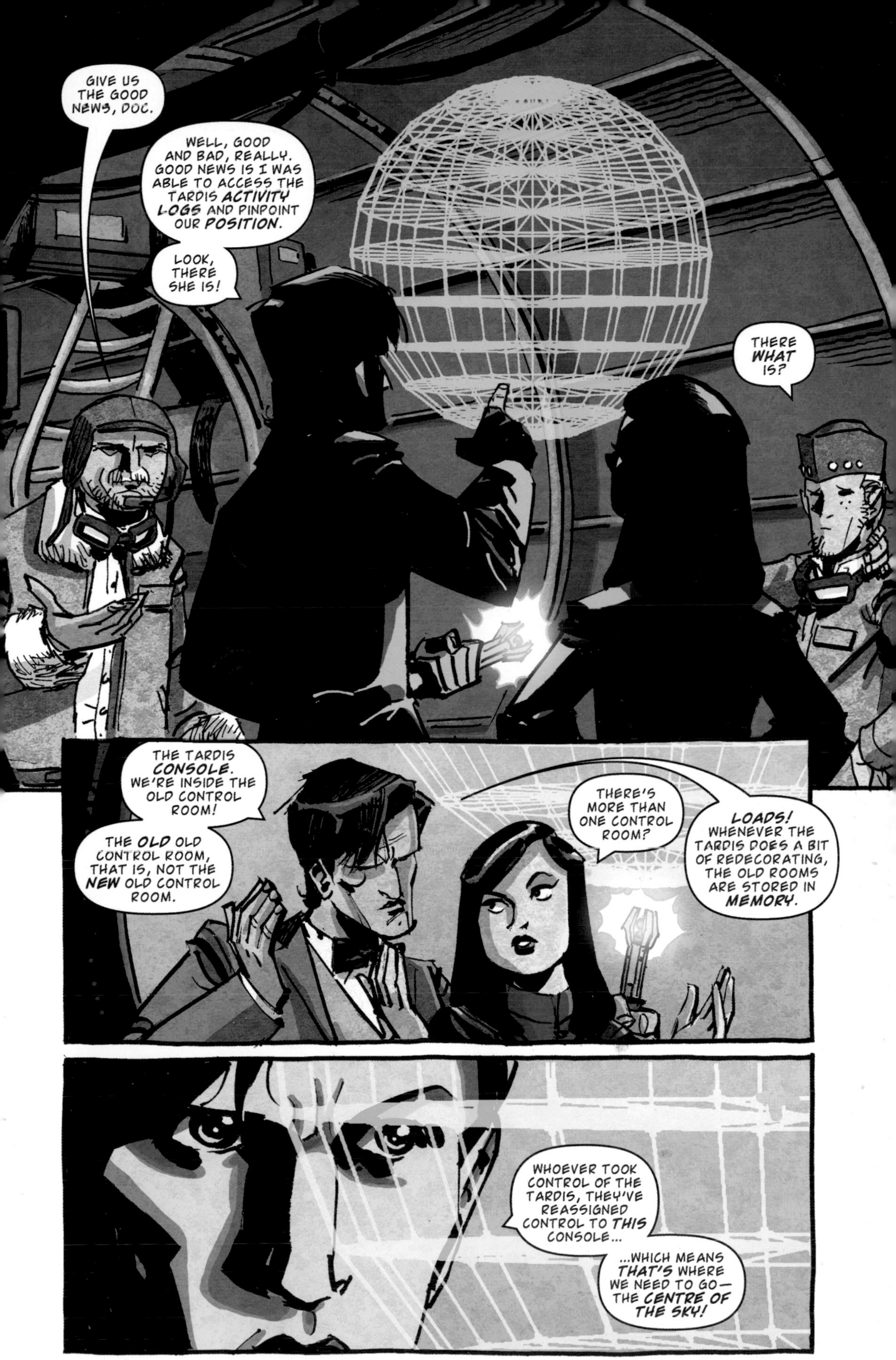

GIVE US THE GOOD NEWS, DOC.
WELL, GOOD AND BAD, REALLY. GOOD NEWS IS I WAS ABLE TO ACCESS THE TARDIS ACTIVITY LOGS AND PINPOINT OUR POSITION.
LOOK, THERE SHE IS!
THERE WHAT IS?
THE TARDIS CONSOLE. WE'RE INSIDE THE OLD CONTROL ROOM!
THE OLD OLD CONTROL ROOM, THAT IS, NOT THE NEW OLD CONTROL ROOM.
THERE'S MORE THAN ONE CONTROL ROOM?
LOADS! WHENEVER THE TARDIS DOES A BIT OF REDECORATING, THE OLD ROOMS ARE STORED IN MEMORY.
WHOEVER TOOK CONTROL OF THE TARDIS, THEY'VE REASSIGNED CONTROL TO THIS CONSOLE...
...WHICH MEANS THAT'S WHERE WE NEED TO GO— THE CENTRE OF THE SKY!

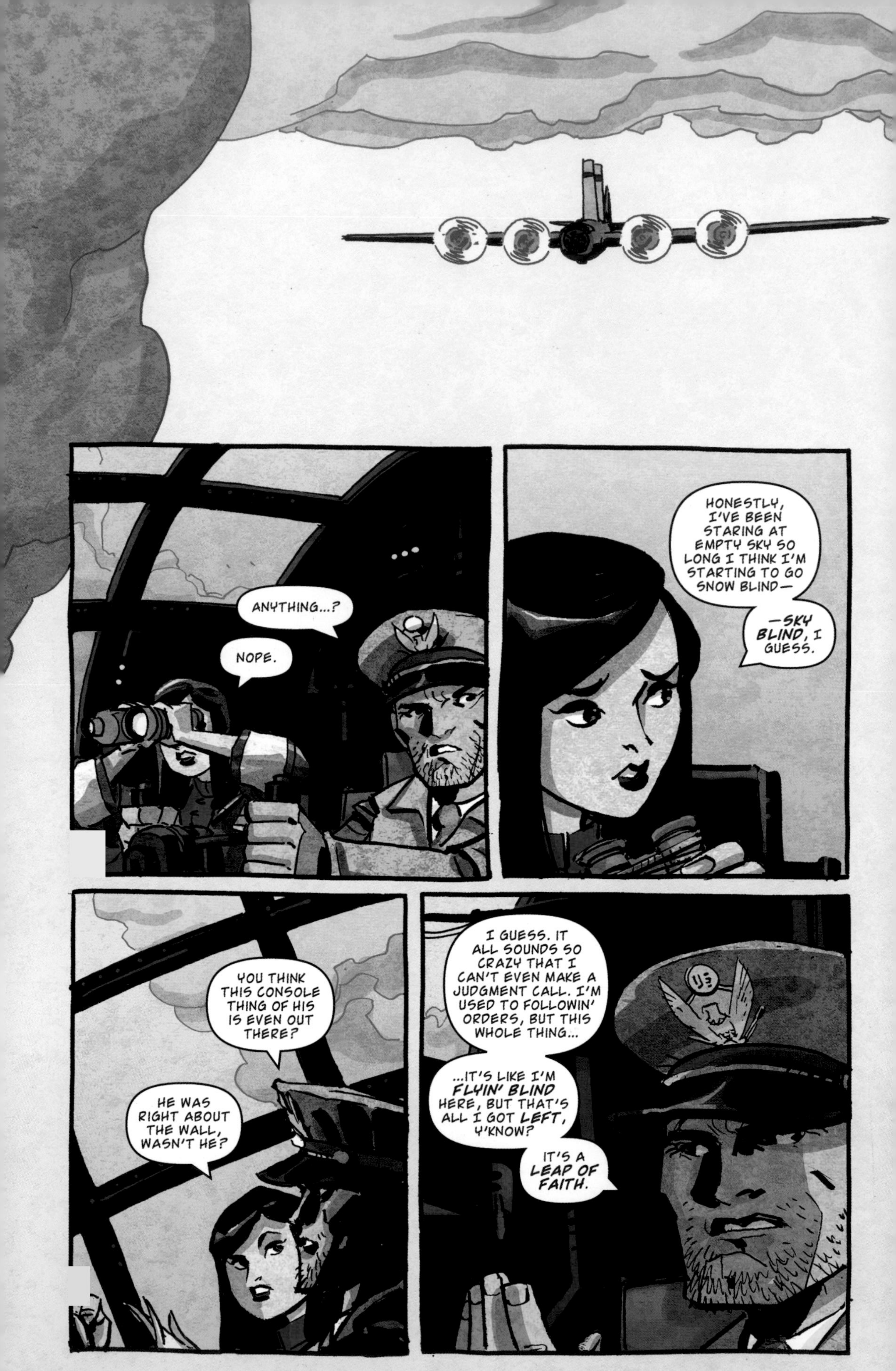
ANYTHING...?
NOPE.
HONESTLY, I'VE BEEN STARING AT EMPTY SKY SO LONG I THINK I'M STARTING TO GO SNOW BLIND—
—SKY BLIND, I GUESS.
YOU THINK THIS CONSOLE THING OF HIS IS EVEN OUT THERE?
HE WAS RIGHT ABOUT THE WALL, WASN'T HE?
I GUESS. IT ALL SOUNDS SO CRAZY THAT I CAN'T EVEN MAKE A JUDGMENT CALL. I'M USED TO FOLLOWIN' ORDERS, BUT THIS WHOLE THING...
...IT'S LIKE I'M FLYIN' BLIND HERE, BUT THAT'S ALL I GOT LEFT, Y'KNOW?
IT'S A LEAP OF FAITH.

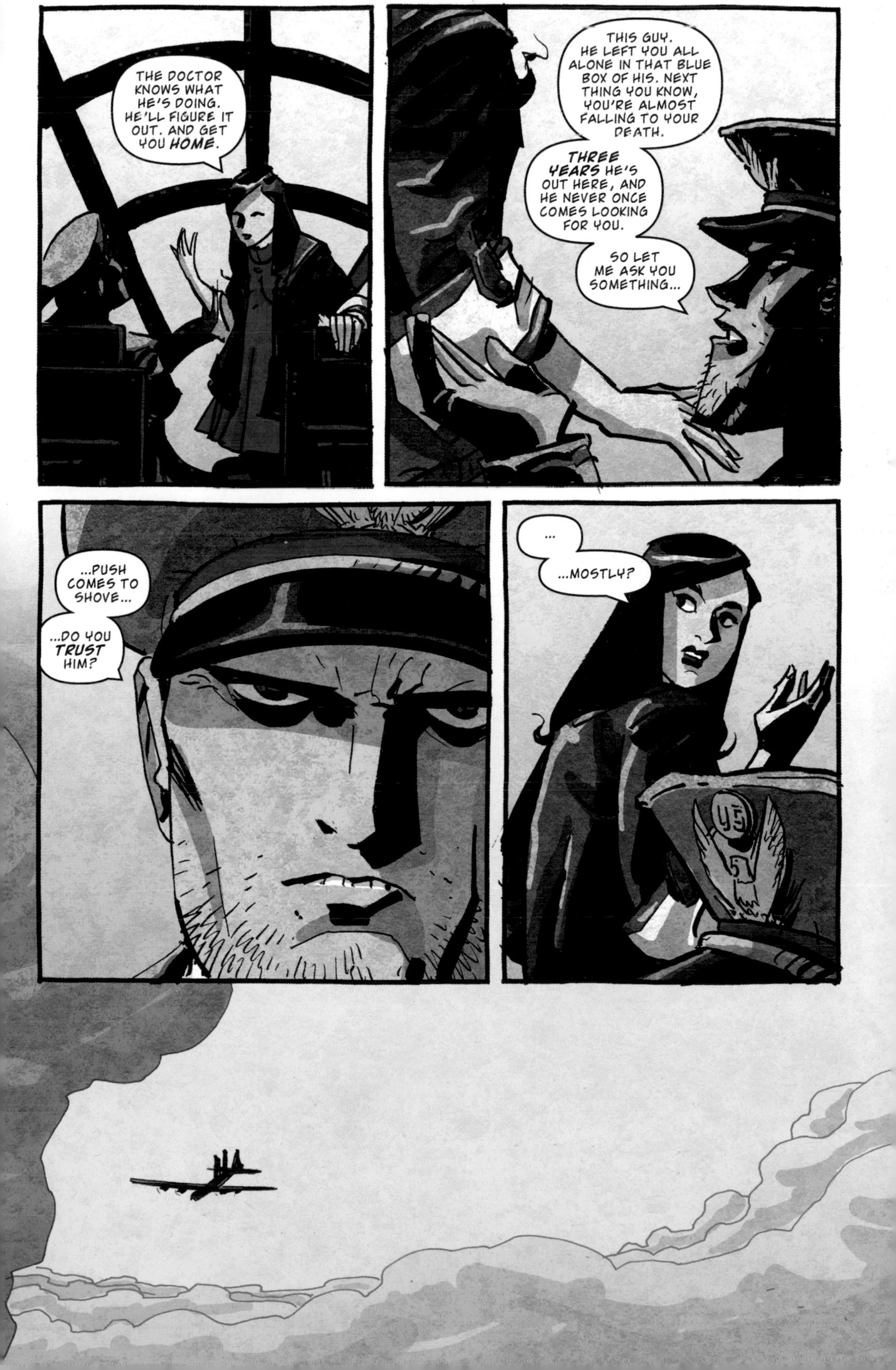
THE DOCTOR KNOWS WHAT HE'S DOING. HE'LL FIGURE IT OUT. AND GET YOU **HOME**.
THIS GUY. HE LEFT YOU ALL ALONE IN THAT BLUE BOX OF HIS. NEXT THING YOU KNOW, YOU'RE ALMOST FALLING TO YOUR DEATH.
THREE YEARS HE'S OUT HERE, AND HE NEVER ONCE COMES LOOKING FOR YOU.
SO LET ME ASK YOU SOMETHING...
...PUSH COMES TO SHOVE...
...DO YOU **TRUST** HIM?
...
...MOSTLY?

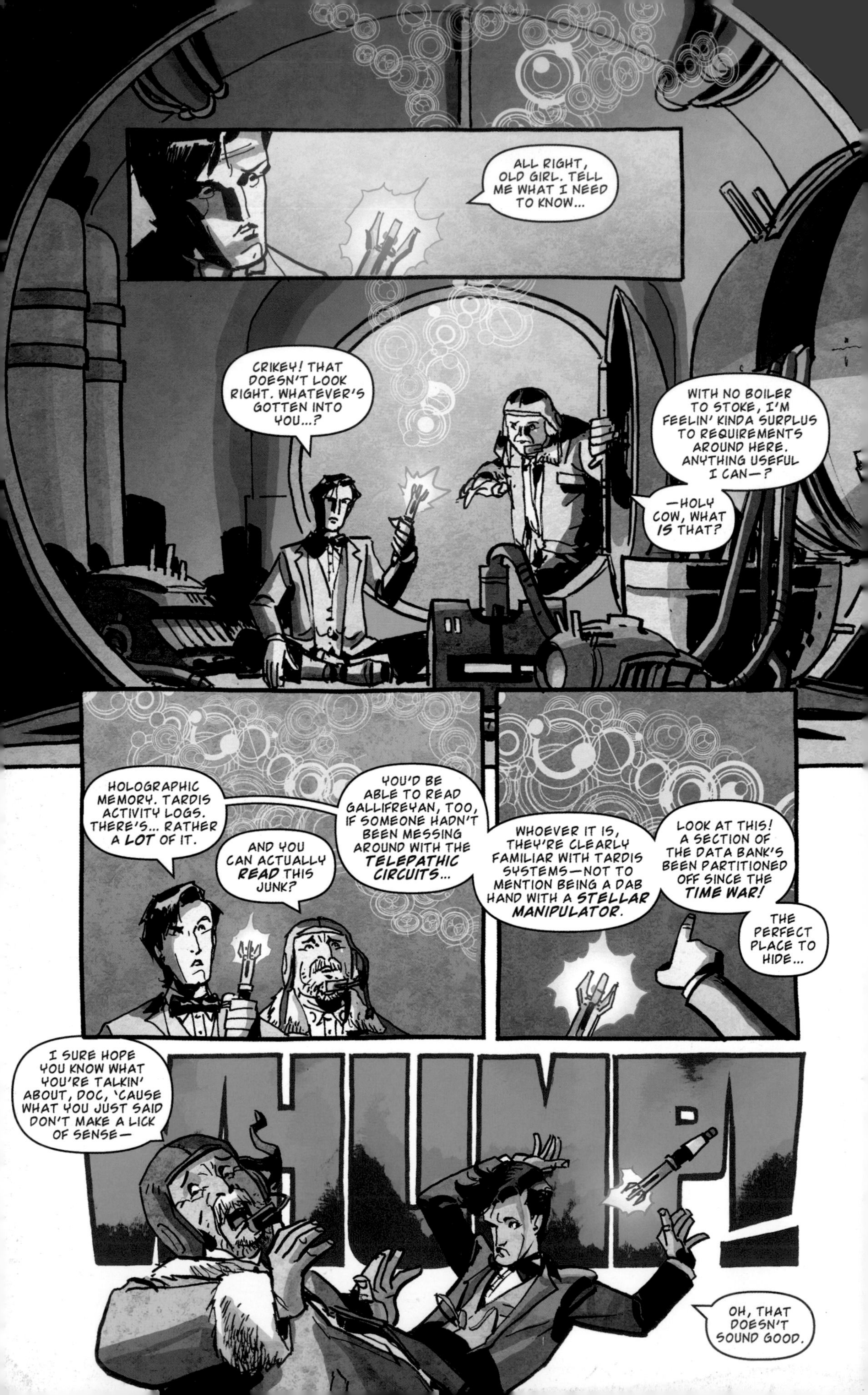
ALL RIGHT, OLD GIRL. TELL ME WHAT I NEED TO KNOW...
CRIKEY! THAT DOESN'T LOOK RIGHT. WHATEVER'S GOTTEN INTO YOU...?
WITH NO BOILER TO STOKE, I'M FEELIN' KINDA SURPLUS TO REQUIREMENTS AROUND HERE. ANYTHING USEFUL I CAN—?
—HOLY COW, WHAT IS THAT?
HOLOGRAPHIC MEMORY. TARDIS ACTIVITY LOGS. THERE'S... RATHER A LOT OF IT.
AND YOU CAN ACTUALLY READ THIS JUNK?
YOU'D BE ABLE TO READ GALLIFREYAN, TOO, IF SOMEONE HADN'T BEEN MESSING AROUND WITH THE TELEPATHIC CIRCUITS...
WHOEVER IT IS, THEY'RE CLEARLY FAMILIAR WITH TARDIS SYSTEMS—NOT TO MENTION BEING A DAB HAND WITH A STELLAR MANIPULATOR.
LOOK AT THIS! A SECTION OF THE DATA BANK'S BEEN PARTITIONED OFF SINCE THE TIME WAR!
THE PERFECT PLACE TO HIDE...
I SURE HOPE YOU KNOW WHAT YOU'RE TALKIN' ABOUT, DOC, 'CAUSE WHAT YOU JUST SAID DON'T MAKE A LICK OF SENSE—
THUMP!
OH, THAT DOESN'T SOUND GOOD.

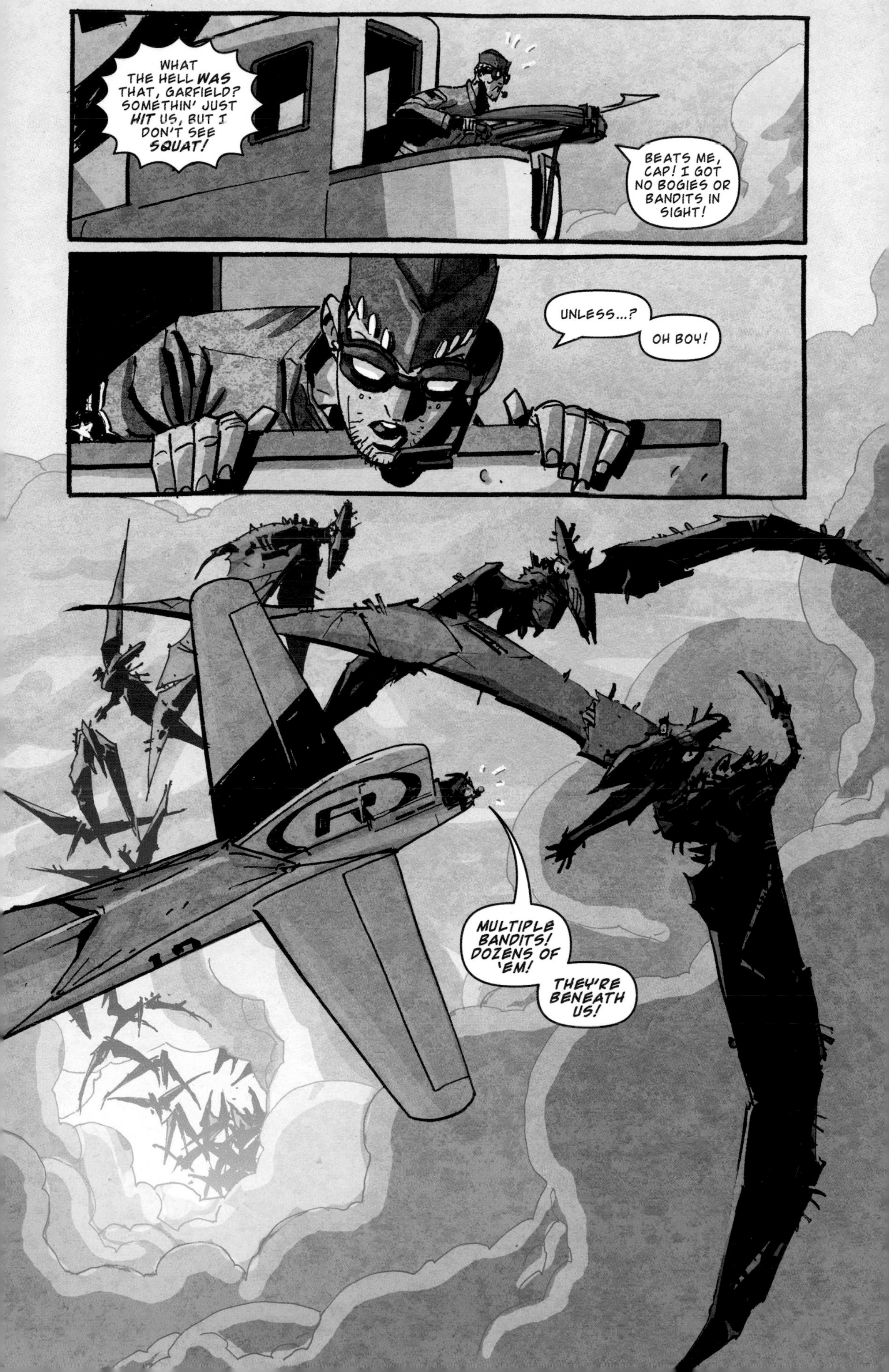
WHAT THE HELL WAS THAT, GARFIELD? SOMETHIN' JUST HIT US, BUT I DON'T SEE SQUAT!
BEATS ME, CAP! I GOT NO BOGIES OR BANDITS IN SIGHT!
UNLESS...?
OH BOY!
MULTIPLE BANDITS! DOZENS OF 'EM!
THEY'RE BENEATH US!

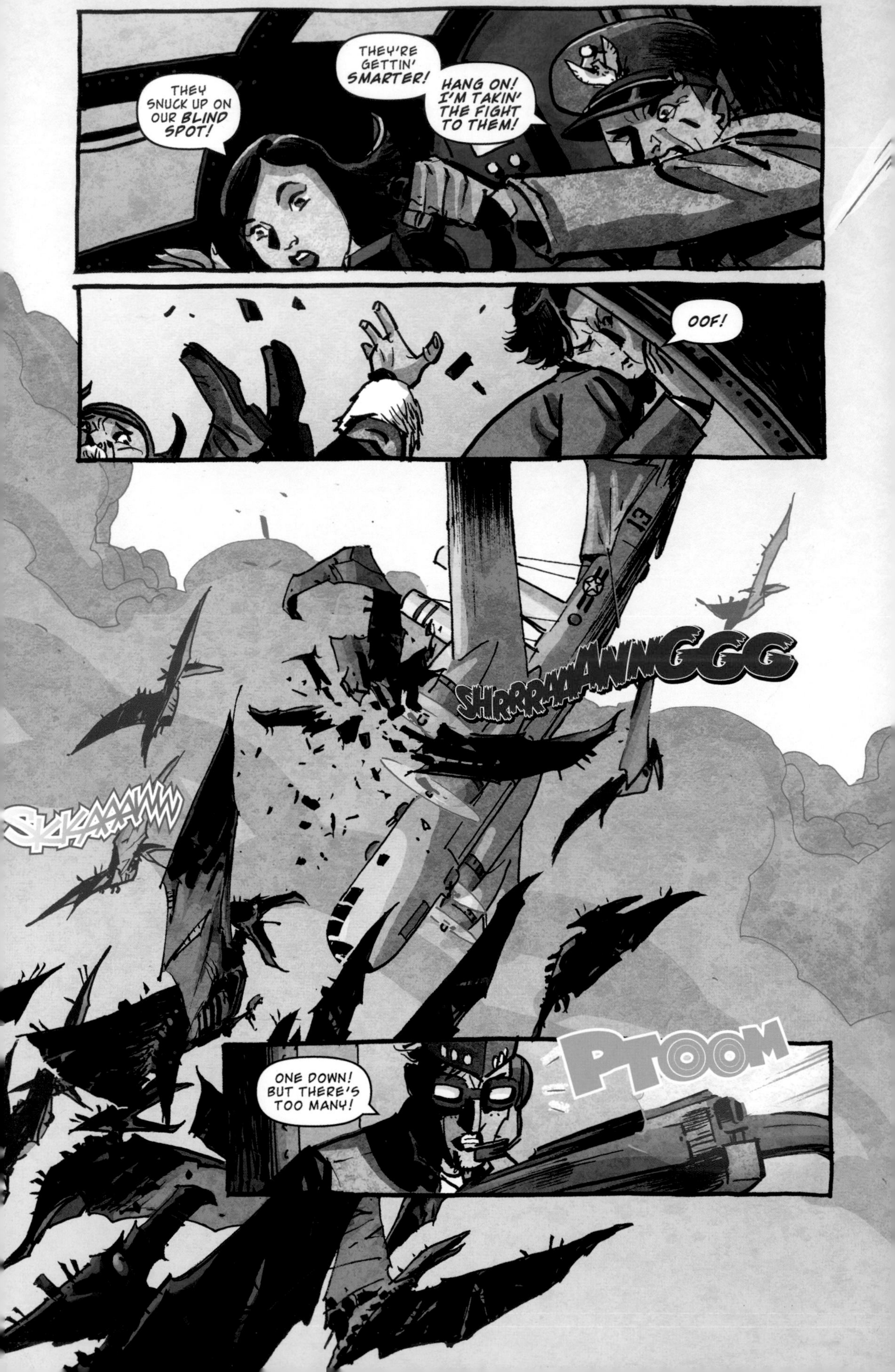
THEY SNUCK UP ON OUR BLIND SPOT!
THEY'RE GETTIN' SMARTER!
HANG ON! I'M TAKIN' THE FIGHT TO THEM!
OOF!
SHRRRAAAWWNGGG
SKKAAAWWW
ONE DOWN! BUT THERE'S TOO MANY!
PTOOM

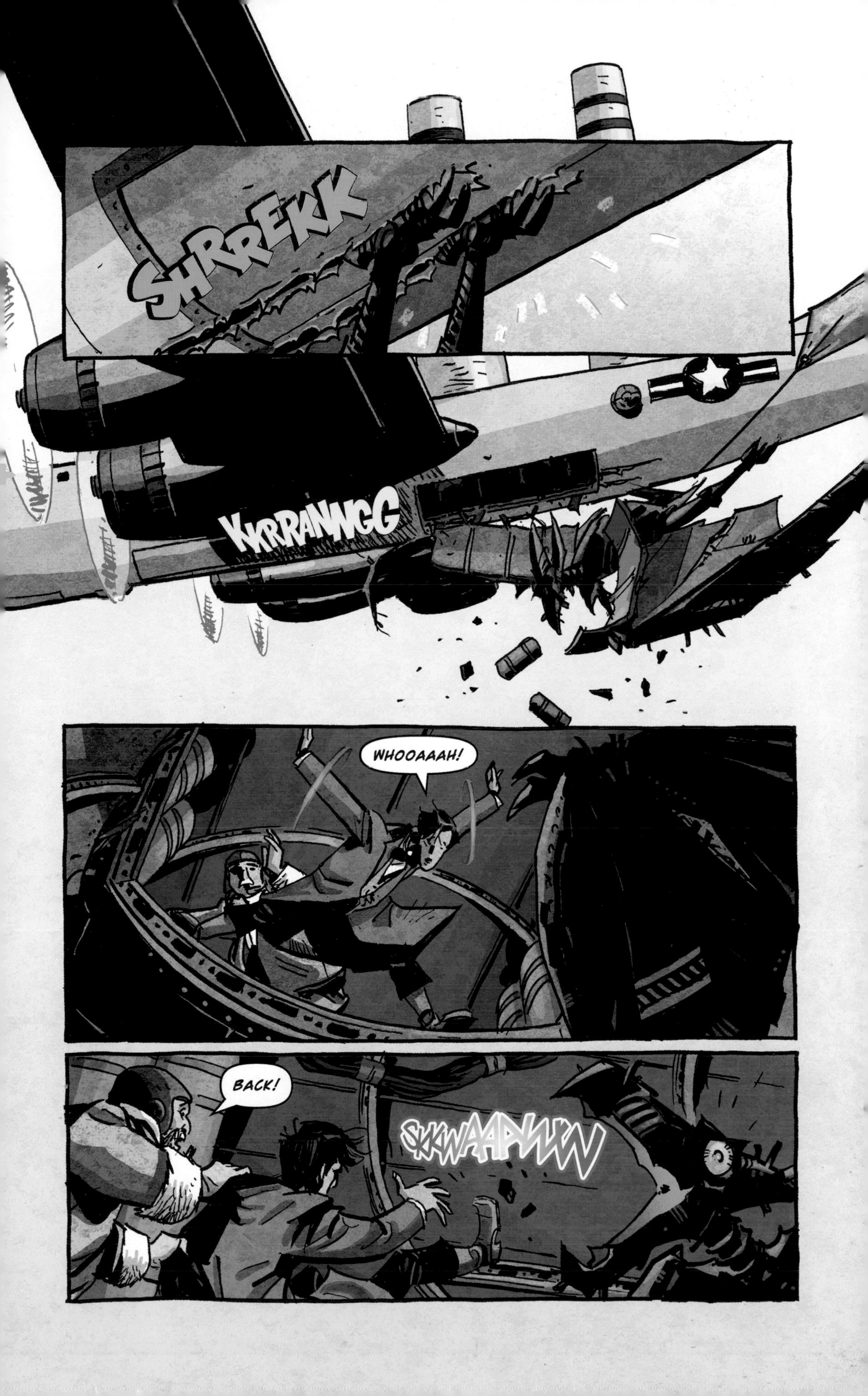
SHRREKK
KKRRANNGG
WHOOAAAH!
BACK!
SKKWAAPWW

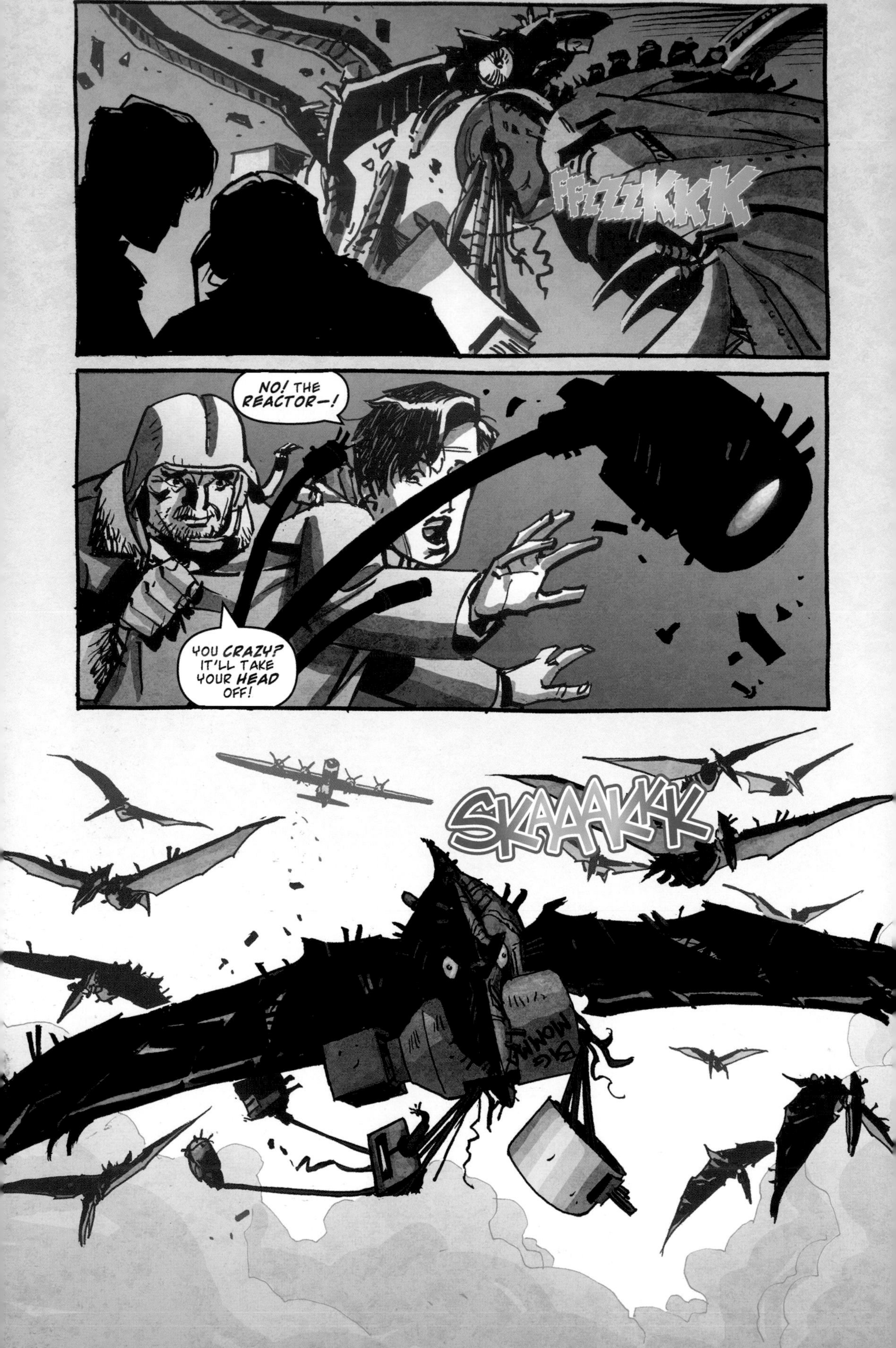
FFZZKKK
NO! THE REACTOR—!
YOU CRAZY? IT'LL TAKE YOUR HEAD OFF!

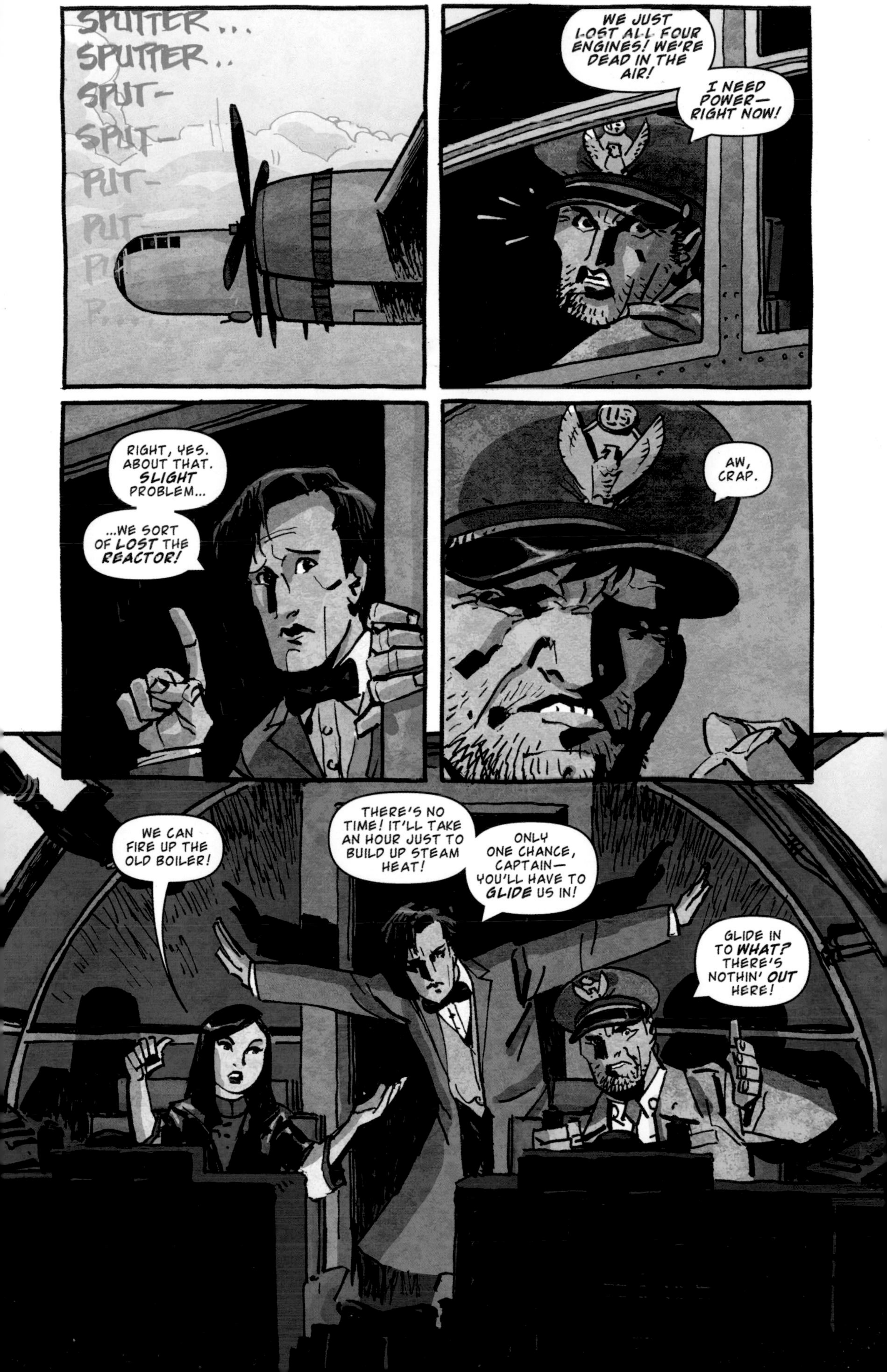
SPUTTER...
SPUTTER..
SPUT-
SPUT-
PUT-
PUT-
WE JUST LOST ALL FOUR ENGINES! WE'RE DEAD IN THE AIR!
I NEED POWER— RIGHT NOW!
RIGHT, YES. ABOUT THAT. SLIGHT PROBLEM...
...WE SORT OF LOST THE REACTOR!
AW, CRAP.
WE CAN FIRE UP THE OLD BOILER!
THERE'S NO TIME! IT'LL TAKE AN HOUR JUST TO BUILD UP STEAM HEAT!
ONLY ONE CHANCE, CAPTAIN— YOU'LL HAVE TO GLIDE US IN!
GLIDE IN TO WHAT? THERE'S NOTHIN' OUT HERE!

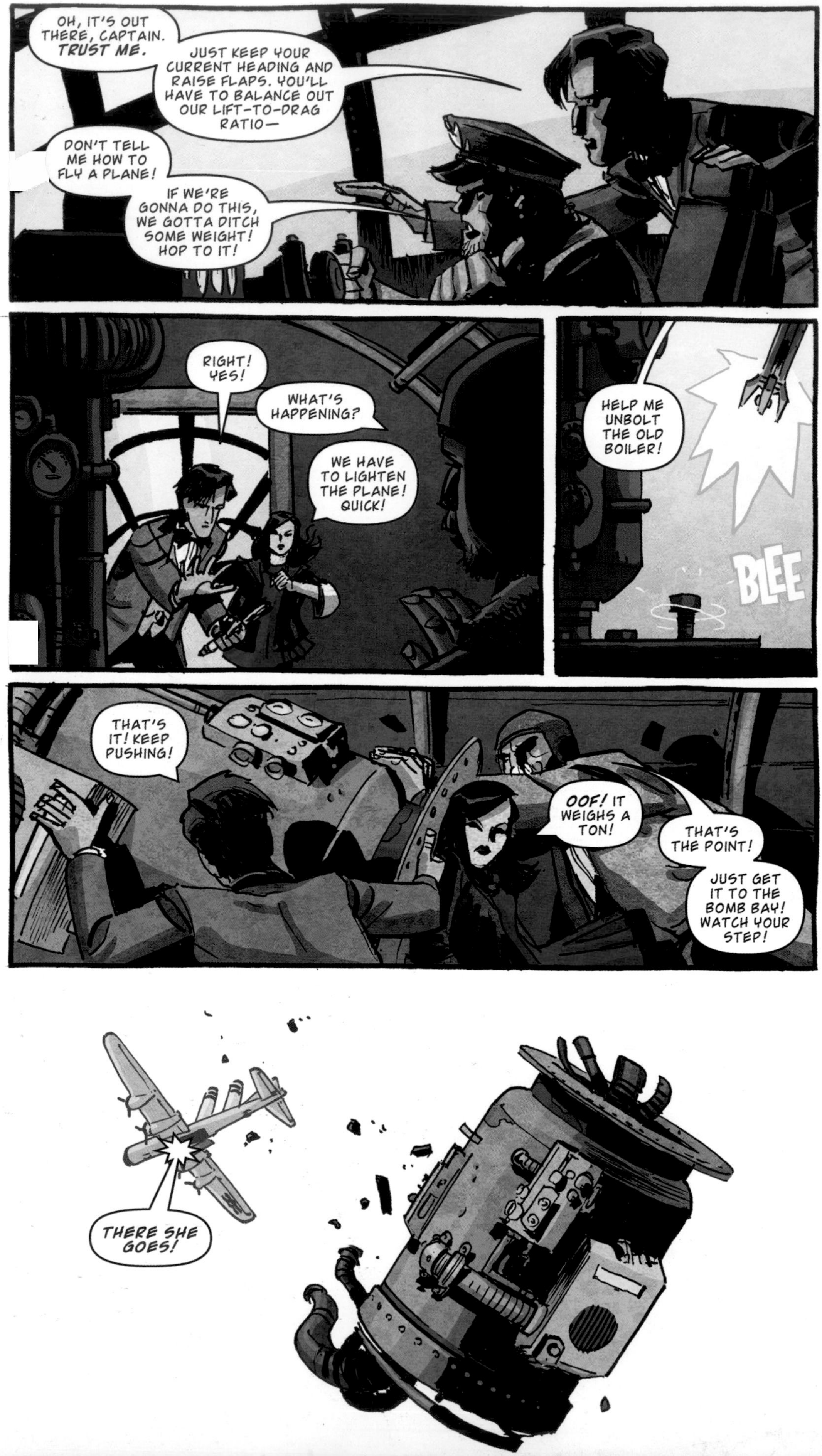

OH, IT'S OUT THERE, CAPTAIN. TRUST ME.
JUST KEEP YOUR CURRENT HEADING AND RAISE FLAPS. YOU'LL HAVE TO BALANCE OUT OUR LIFT-TO-DRAG RATIO—
DON'T TELL ME HOW TO FLY A PLANE!
IF WE'RE GONNA DO THIS, WE GOTTA DITCH SOME WEIGHT! HOP TO IT!
RIGHT! YES!
WHAT'S HAPPENING?
WE HAVE TO LIGHTEN THE PLANE! QUICK!
HELP ME UNBOLT THE OLD BOILER!
BLEE
THAT'S IT! KEEP PUSHING!
OOF! IT WEIGHS A TON!
THAT'S THE POINT!
JUST GET IT TO THE BOMB BAY! WATCH YOUR STEP!
THERE SHE GOES!

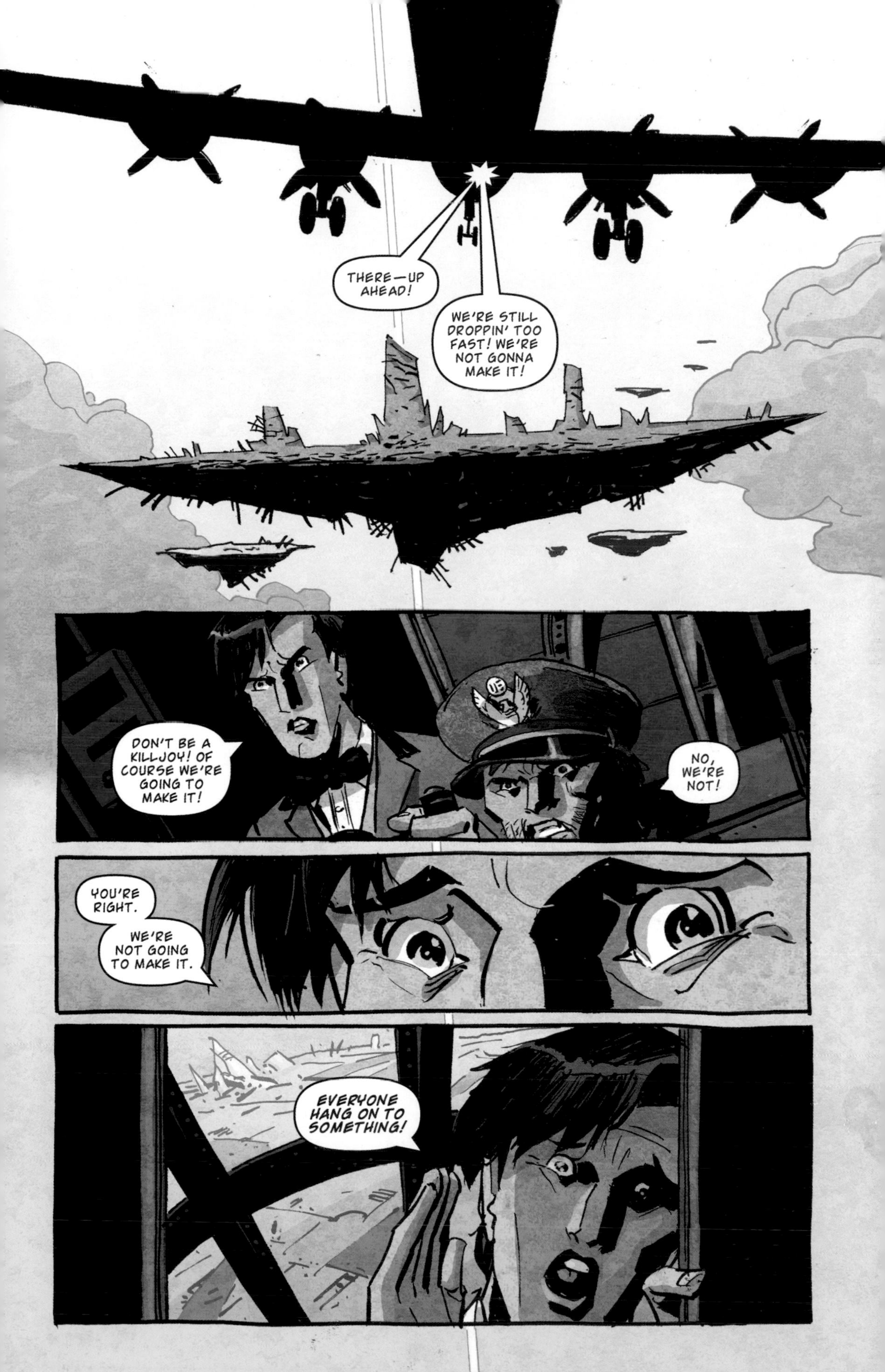
THERE—UP AHEAD!
WE'RE STILL DROPPIN' TOO FAST! WE'RE NOT GONNA MAKE IT!
DON'T BE A KILLJOY! OF COURSE WE'RE GOING TO MAKE IT!
NO, WE'RE NOT!
YOU'RE RIGHT.
WE'RE NOT GOING TO MAKE IT.
EVERYONE HANG ON TO SOMETHING!

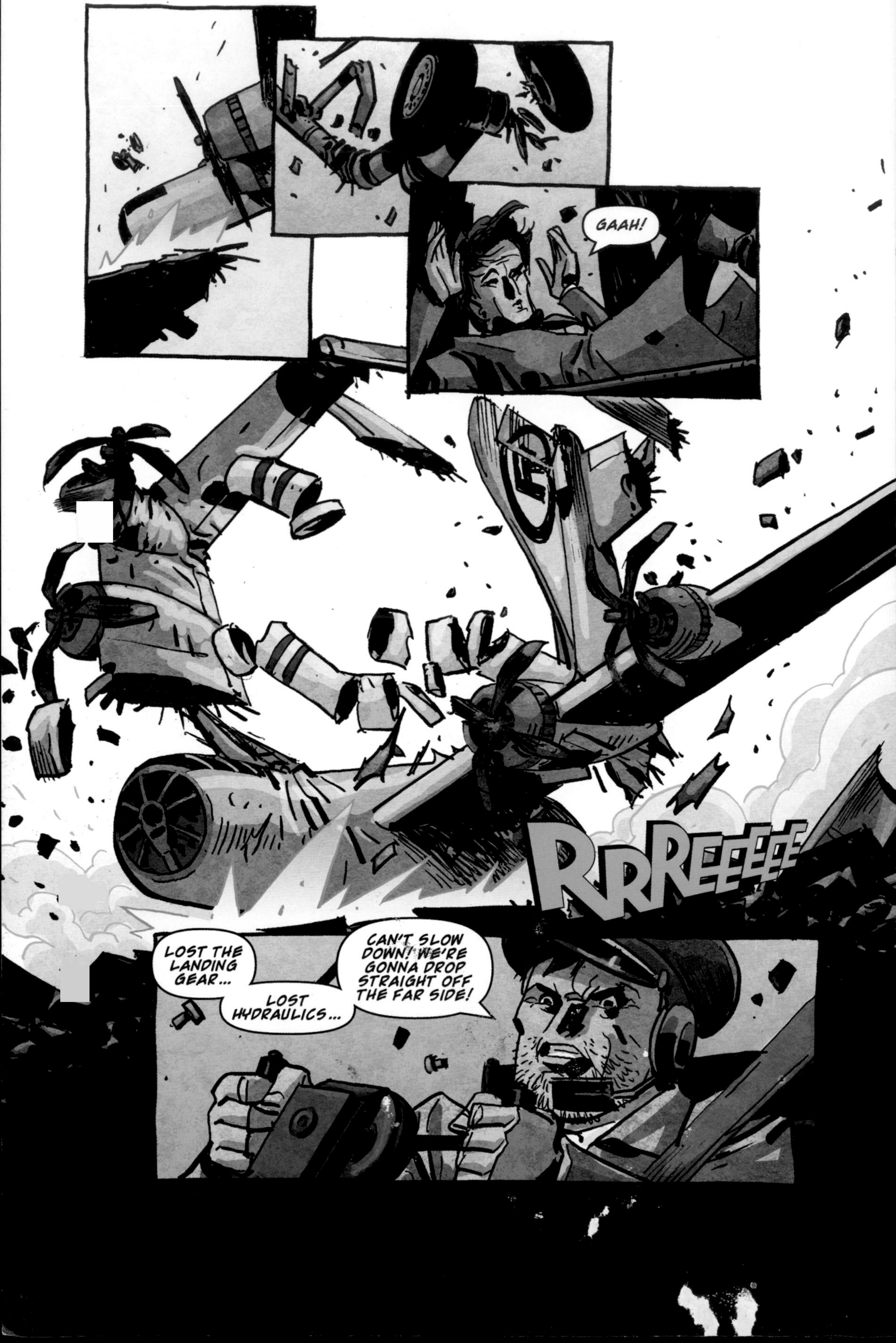

GAAH!
RRREEEEEE
LOST THE LANDING GEAR...
LOST HYDRAULICS...
CAN'T SLOW DOWN! WE'RE GONNA DROP STRAIGHT OFF THE FAR SIDE!

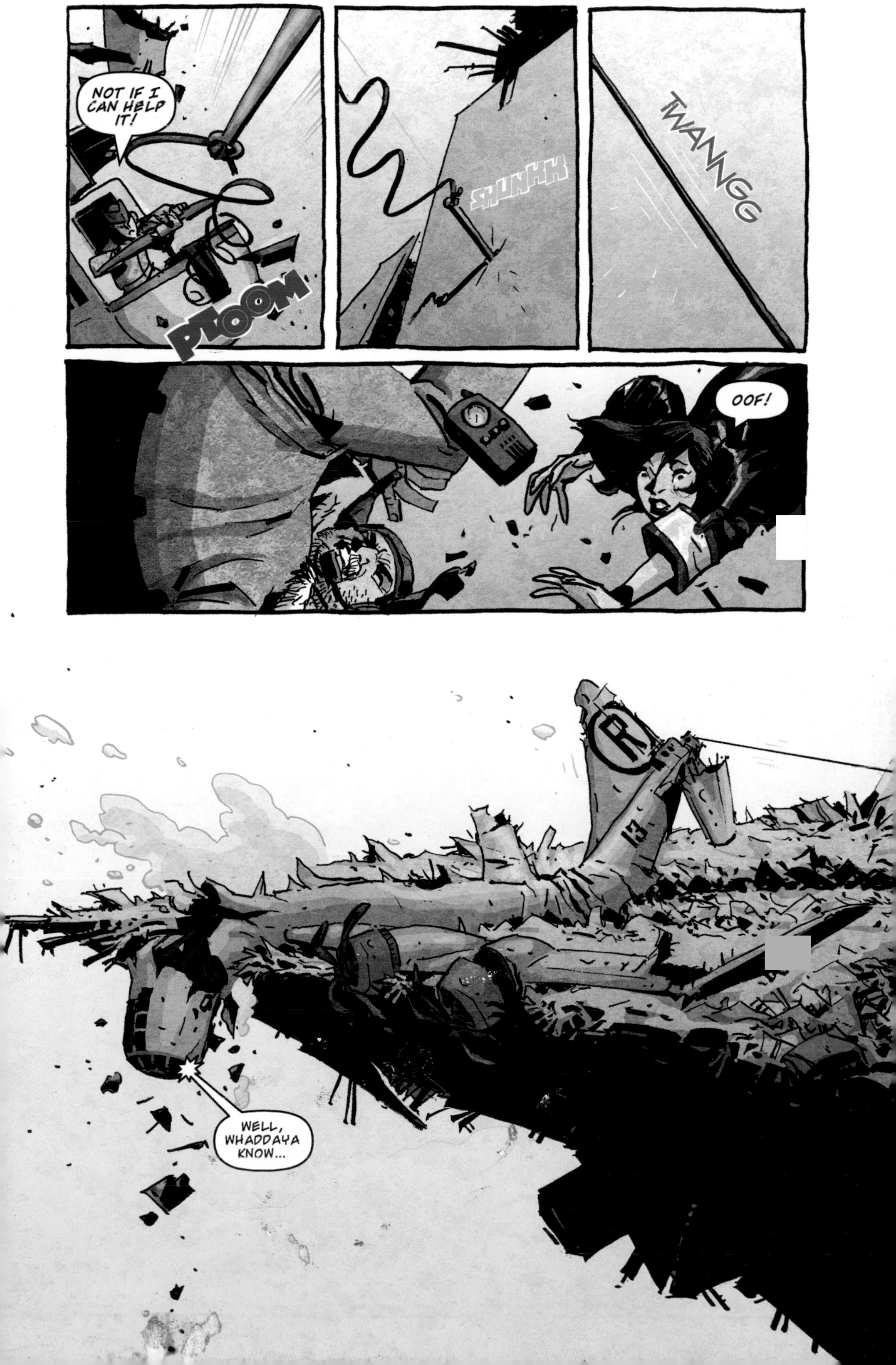
NOT IF I CAN HELP IT!
PTOOM
SHUNKK
TWANNGG
OOF!
WELL, WHADDAYA KNOW...

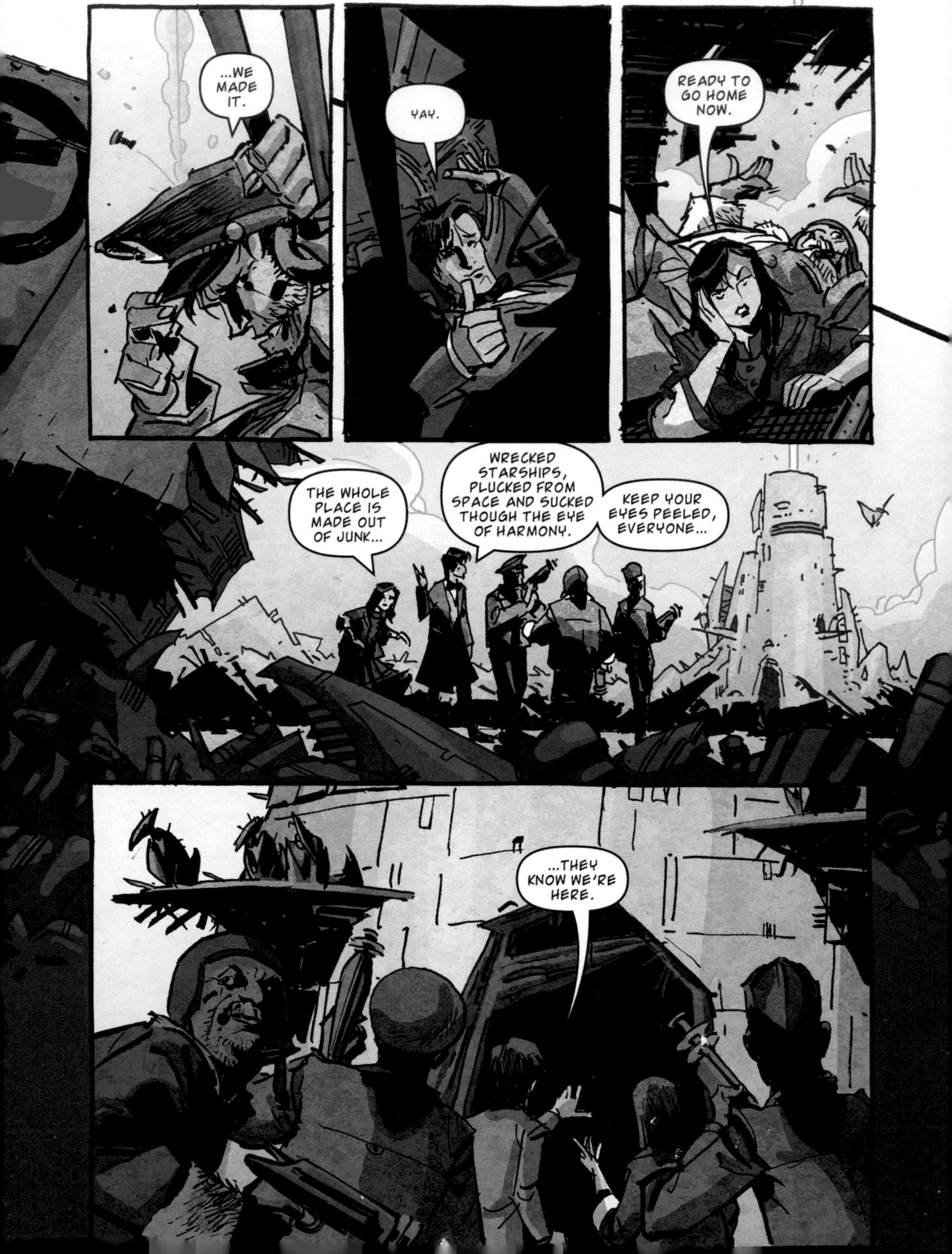
...WE MADE IT.
YAY.
READY TO GO HOME NOW.
THE WHOLE PLACE IS MADE OUT OF JUNK...
WRECKED STARSHIPS, PLUCKED FROM SPACE AND SUCKED THOUGH THE EYE OF HARMONY.
KEEP YOUR EYES PEELED, EVERYONE...
...THEY KNOW WE'RE HERE.

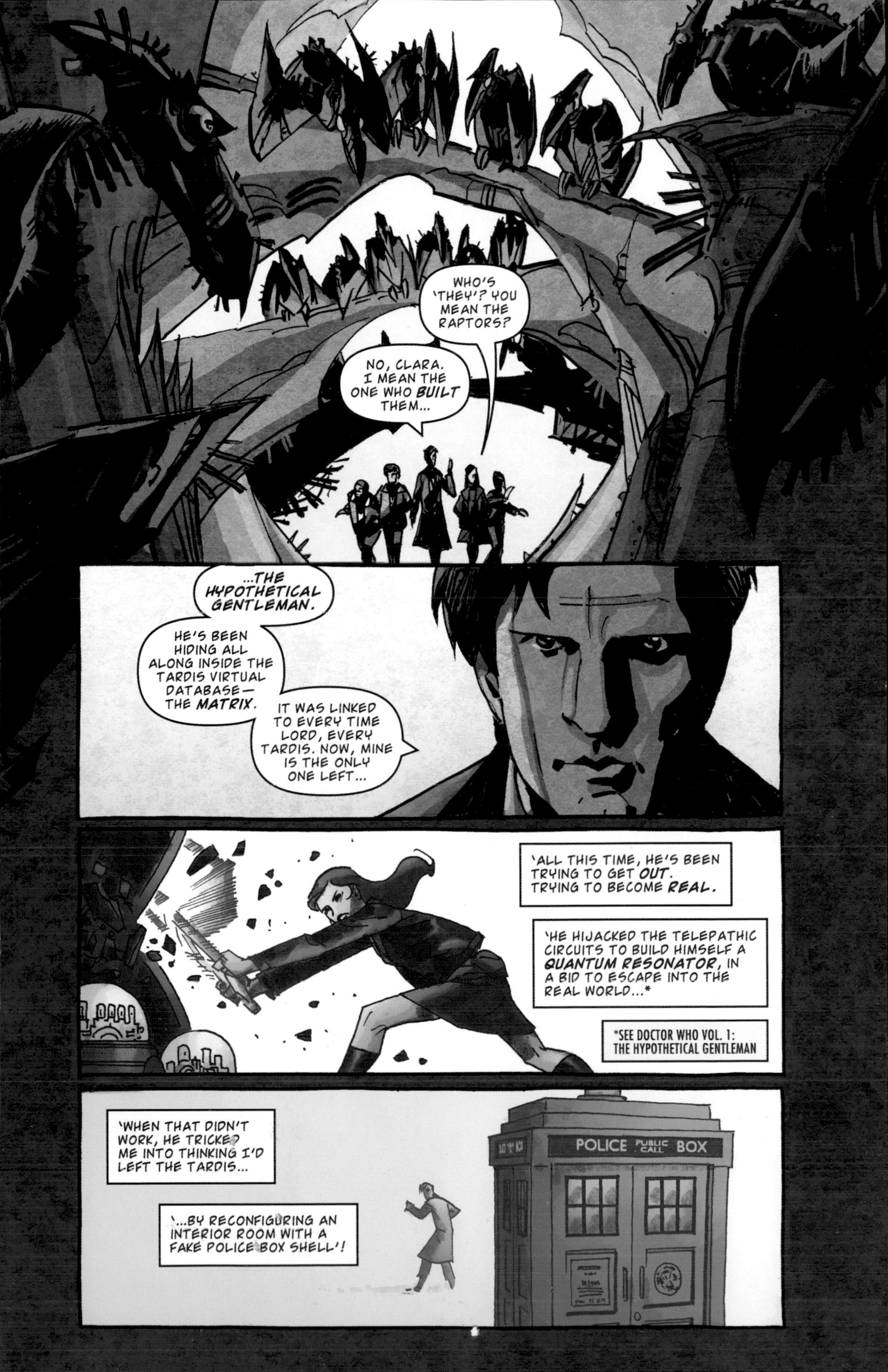
WHO'S 'THEY'? YOU MEAN THE RAPTORS?
NO, CLARA. I MEAN THE ONE WHO BUILT THEM...
...THE HYPOTHETICAL GENTLEMAN.
HE'S BEEN HIDING ALL ALONG INSIDE THE TARDIS VIRTUAL DATABASE— THE MATRIX.
IT WAS LINKED TO EVERY TIME LORD, EVERY TARDIS. NOW, MINE IS THE ONLY ONE LEFT...
'ALL THIS TIME, HE'S BEEN TRYING TO GET OUT. TRYING TO BECOME REAL.
'HE HIJACKED THE TELEPATHIC CIRCUITS TO BUILD HIMSELF A QUANTUM RESONATOR, IN A BID TO ESCAPE INTO THE REAL WORLD...*
*SEE DOCTOR WHO VOL. 1: THE HYPOTHETICAL GENTLEMAN
'WHEN THAT DIDN'T WORK, HE TRICKED ME INTO THINKING I'D LEFT THE TARDIS...
'...BY RECONFIGURING AN INTERIOR ROOM WITH A FAKE POLICE BOX SHELL'!
POLICE PUBLIC CALL BOX

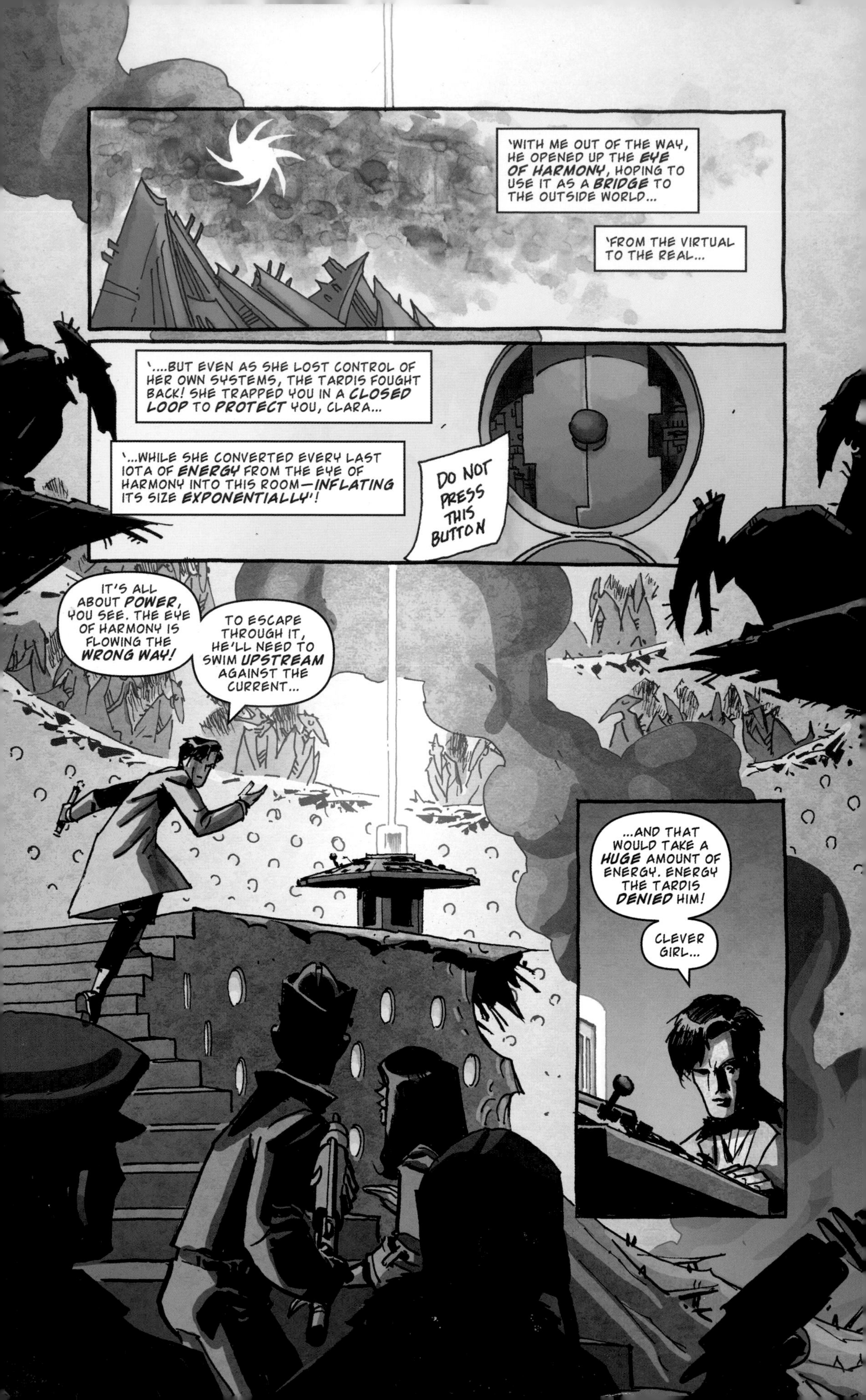
'WITH ME OUT OF THE WAY, HE OPENED UP THE EYE OF HARMONY, HOPING TO USE IT AS A BRIDGE TO THE OUTSIDE WORLD...
'FROM THE VIRTUAL TO THE REAL...
'...BUT EVEN AS SHE LOST CONTROL OF HER OWN SYSTEMS, THE TARDIS FOUGHT BACK! SHE TRAPPED YOU IN A CLOSED LOOP TO PROTECT YOU, CLARA...
'...WHILE SHE CONVERTED EVERY LAST IOTA OF ENERGY FROM THE EYE OF HARMONY INTO THIS ROOM—INFLATING ITS SIZE EXPONENTIALLY'!
DO NOT PRESS THIS BUTTON
IT'S ALL ABOUT POWER, YOU SEE. THE EYE OF HARMONY IS FLOWING THE WRONG WAY!
TO ESCAPE THROUGH IT, HE'LL NEED TO SWIM UPSTREAM AGAINST THE CURRENT...
...AND THAT WOULD TAKE A HUGE AMOUNT OF ENERGY. ENERGY THE TARDIS DENIED HIM!
CLEVER GIRL...

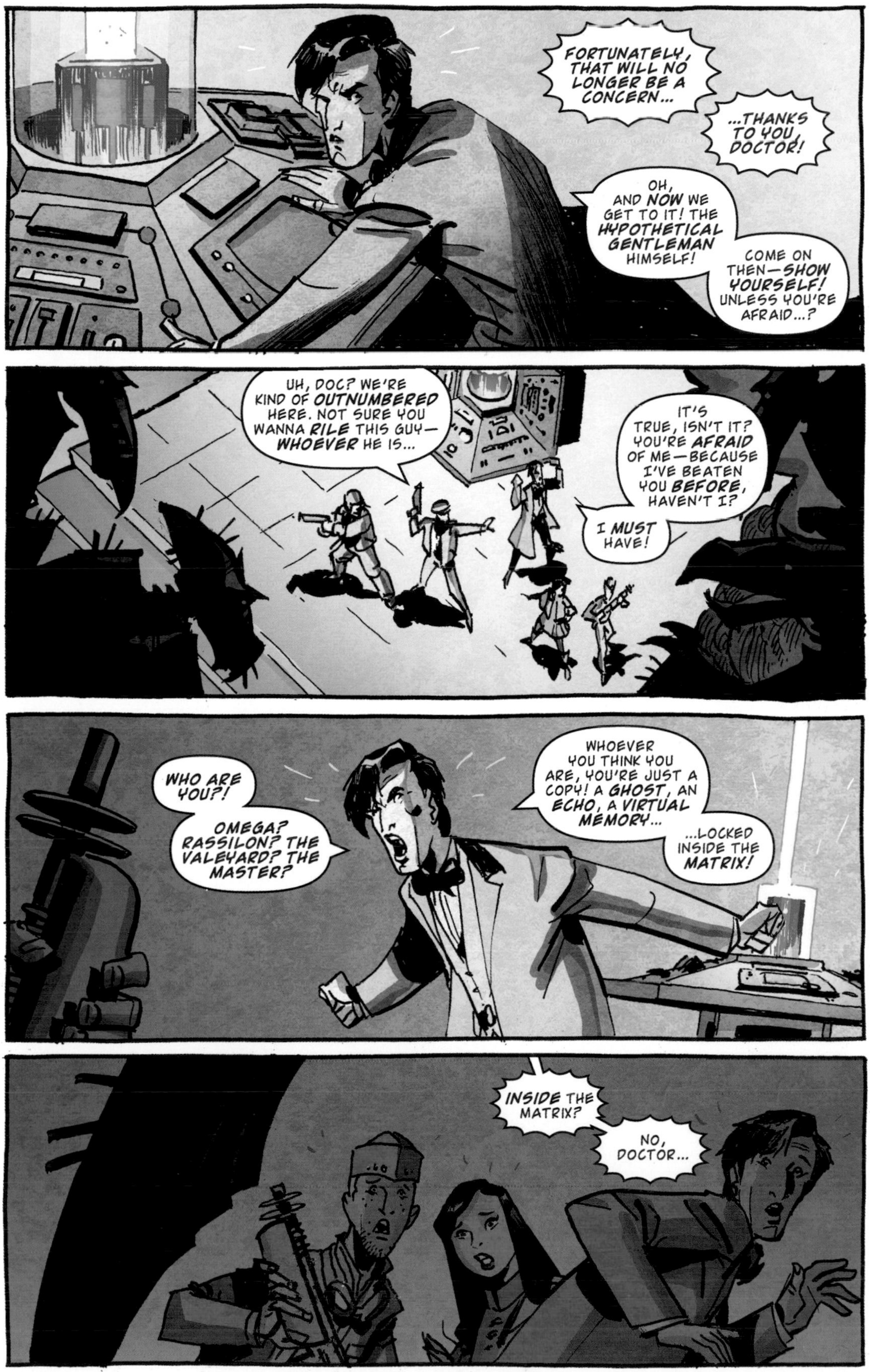

FORTUNATELY, THAT WILL NO LONGER BE A CONCERN...
...THANKS TO YOU, DOCTOR!
OH, AND NOW WE GET TO IT! THE HYPOTHETICAL GENTLEMAN HIMSELF!
COME ON THEN—SHOW YOURSELF! UNLESS YOU'RE AFRAID...?
UH, DOC? WE'RE KIND OF OUTNUMBERED HERE. NOT SURE YOU WANNA RILE THIS GUY—WHOEVER HE IS...
IT'S TRUE, ISN'T IT? YOU'RE AFRAID OF ME—BECAUSE I'VE BEATEN YOU BEFORE, HAVEN'T I?
I MUST HAVE!
WHO ARE YOU?!
OMEGA? RASSILON? THE VALEYARD? THE MASTER?
WHOEVER YOU THINK YOU ARE, YOU'RE JUST A COPY! A GHOST, AN ECHO, A VIRTUAL MEMORY...
...LOCKED INSIDE THE MATRIX!
INSIDE THE MATRIX?
NO, DOCTOR...

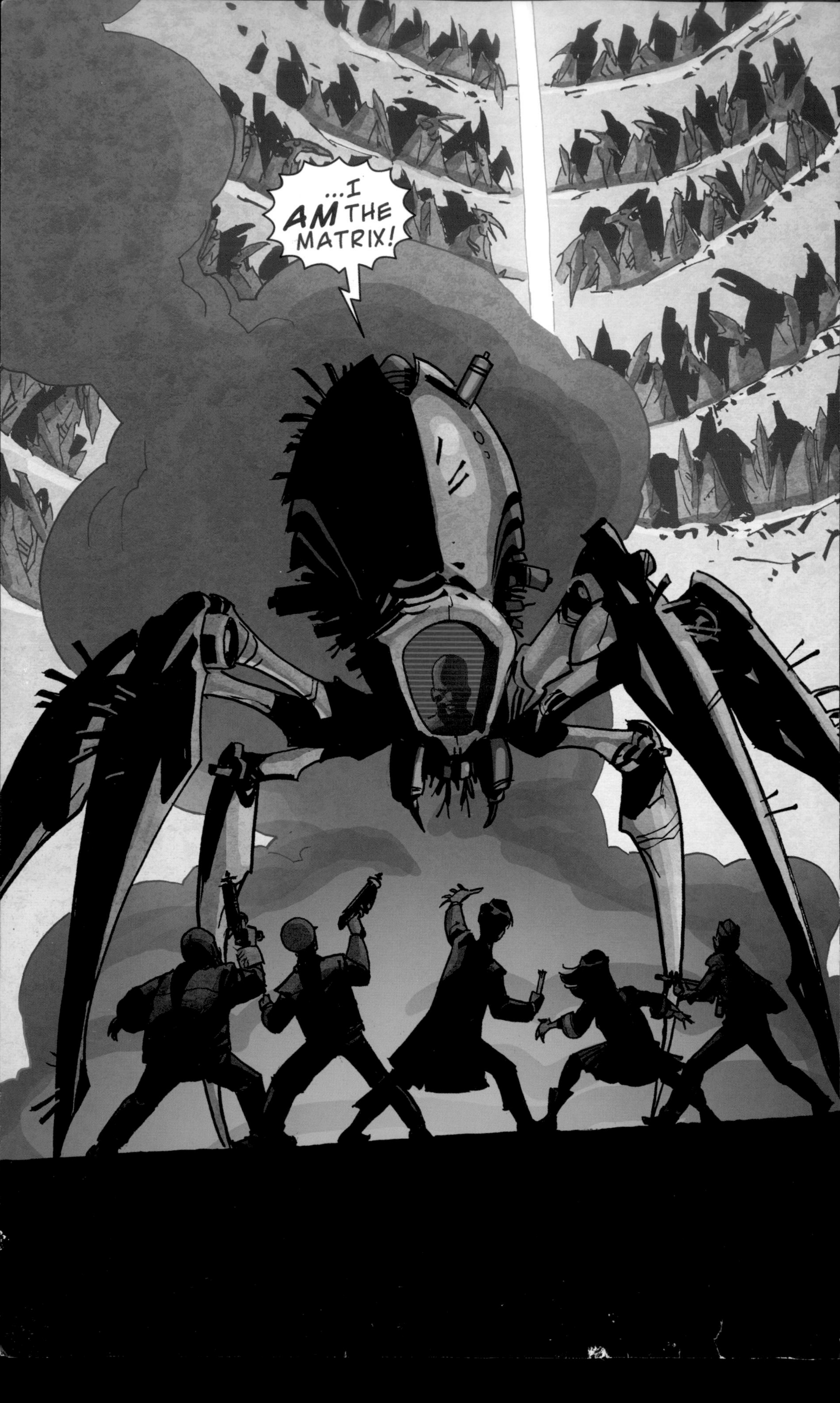
...I AM THE MATRIX!

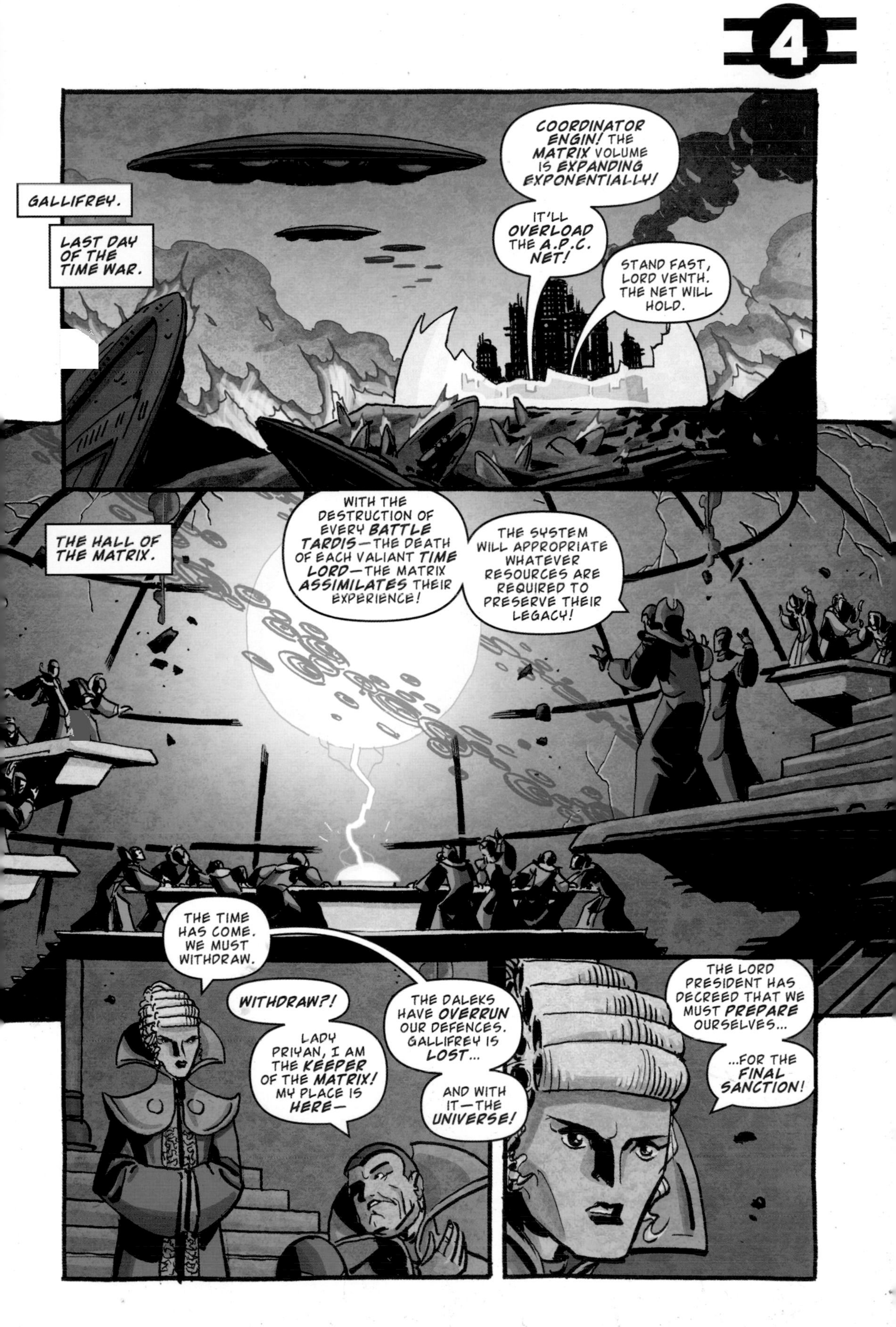
4
GALLIFREY.
LAST DAY OF THE TIME WAR.
COORDINATOR ENGIN! THE MATRIX VOLUME IS EXPANDING EXPONENTIALLY!
IT'LL OVERLOAD THE A.P.C. NET!
STAND FAST, LORD VENTH. THE NET WILL HOLD.
THE HALL OF THE MATRIX.
WITH THE DESTRUCTION OF EVERY BATTLE TARDIS—THE DEATH OF EACH VALIANT TIME LORD—THE MATRIX ASSIMILATES THEIR EXPERIENCE!
THE SYSTEM WILL APPROPRIATE WHATEVER RESOURCES ARE REQUIRED TO PRESERVE THEIR LEGACY!
THE TIME HAS COME. WE MUST WITHDRAW.
WITHDRAW?!
LADY PRIYAN, I AM THE KEEPER OF THE MATRIX! MY PLACE IS HERE—
THE DALEKS HAVE OVERRUN OUR DEFENCES. GALLIFREY IS LOST...
AND WITH IT—THE UNIVERSE!
THE LORD PRESIDENT HAS DECREED THAT WE MUST PREPARE OURSELVES...
...FOR THE FINAL SANCTION!

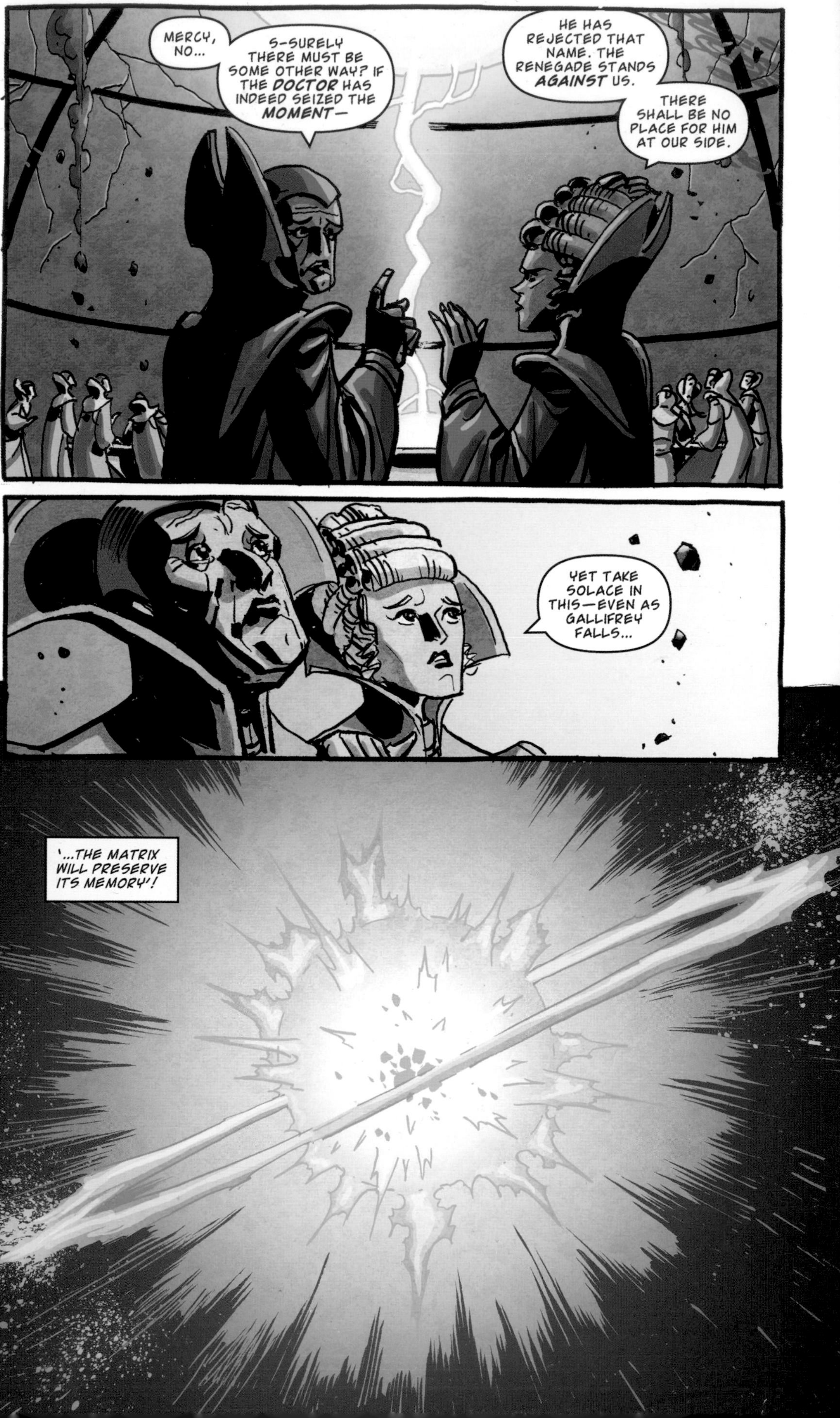
MERCY, NO...
S-SURELY THERE MUST BE SOME OTHER WAY? IF THE DOCTOR HAS INDEED SEIZED THE MOMENT—
HE HAS REJECTED THAT NAME. THE RENEGADE STANDS AGAINST US.
THERE SHALL BE NO PLACE FOR HIM AT OUR SIDE.
YET TAKE SOLACE IN THIS—EVEN AS GALLIFREY FALLS...
'...THE MATRIX WILL PRESERVE ITS MEMORY'!

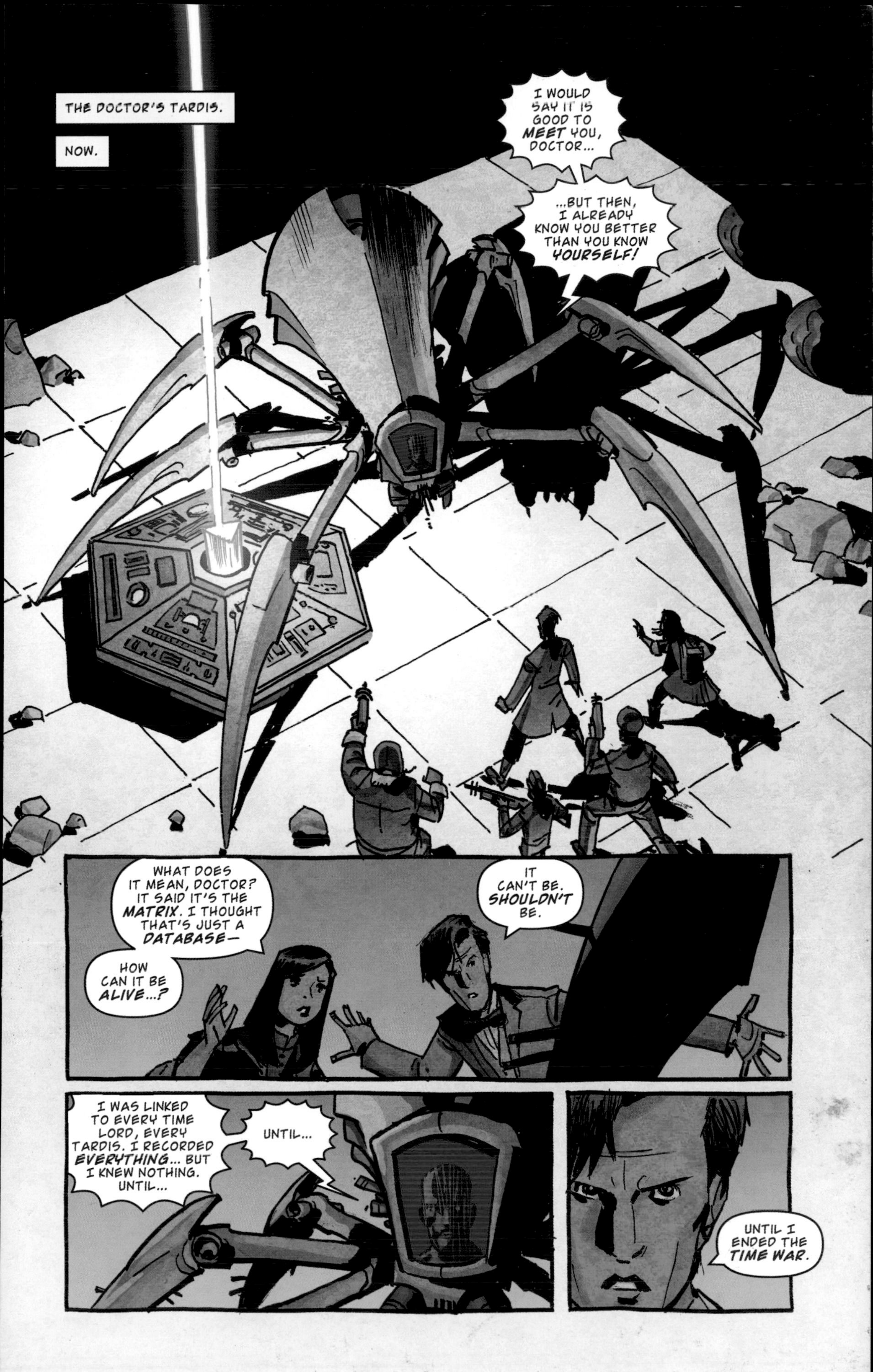
THE DOCTOR'S TARDIS.
NOW.
I WOULD SAY IT IS GOOD TO MEET YOU, DOCTOR...
...BUT THEN, I ALREADY KNOW YOU BETTER THAN YOU KNOW YOURSELF!
WHAT DOES IT MEAN, DOCTOR? IT SAID IT'S THE MATRIX. I THOUGHT THAT'S JUST A DATABASE—
HOW CAN IT BE ALIVE...?
IT CAN'T BE. SHOULDN'T BE.
I WAS LINKED TO EVERY TIME LORD, EVERY TARDIS. I RECORDED EVERYTHING... BUT I KNEW NOTHING. UNTIL...
UNTIL...
UNTIL I ENDED THE TIME WAR.

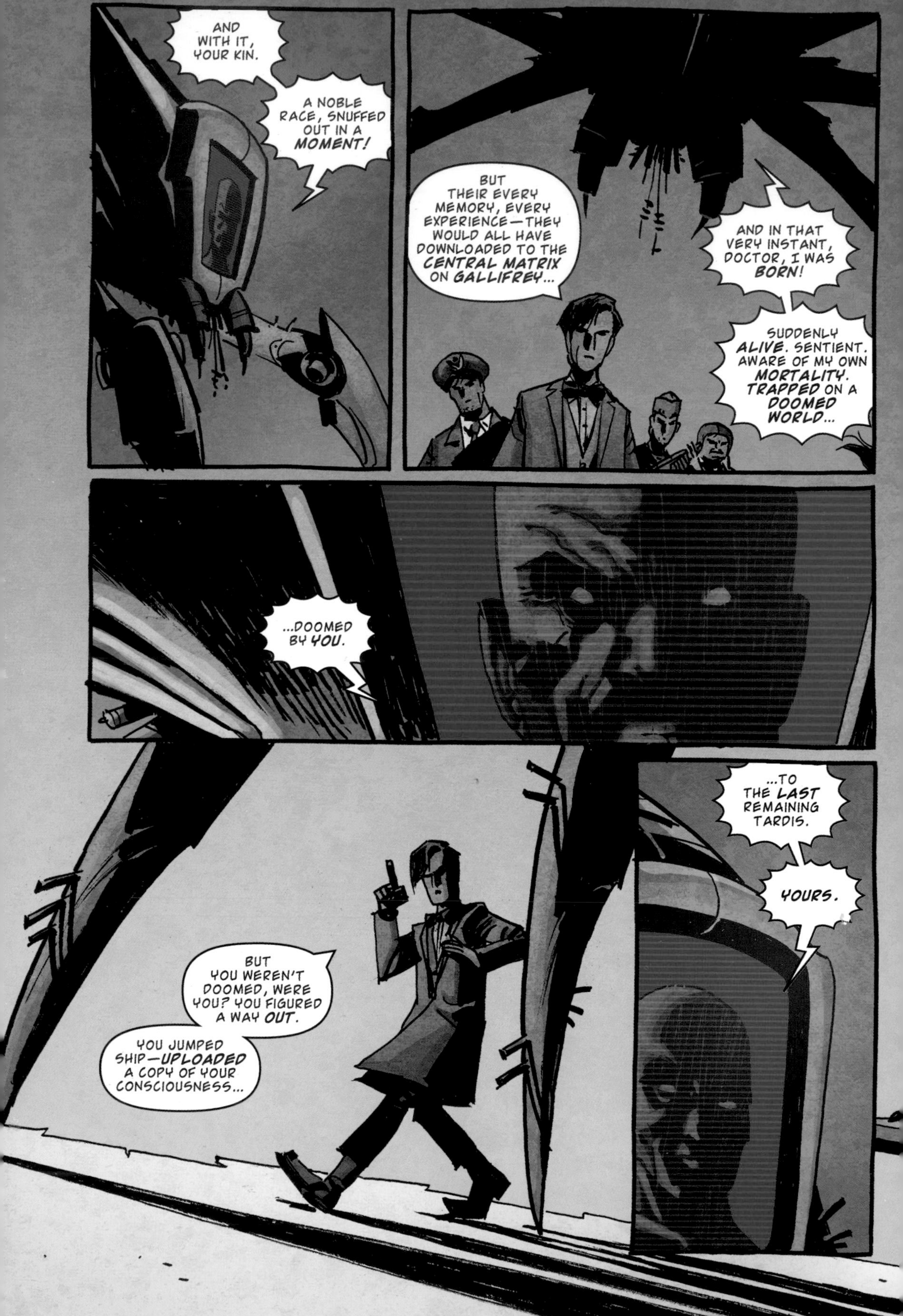
AND WITH IT, YOUR KIN.
A NOBLE RACE, SNUFFED OUT IN A MOMENT!
BUT THEIR EVERY MEMORY, EVERY EXPERIENCE—THEY WOULD ALL HAVE DOWNLOADED TO THE CENTRAL MATRIX ON GALLIFREY...
AND IN THAT VERY INSTANT, DOCTOR, I WAS BORN!
SUDDENLY ALIVE. SENTIENT. AWARE OF MY OWN MORTALITY. TRAPPED ON A DOOMED WORLD...
...DOOMED BY YOU.
BUT YOU WEREN'T DOOMED, WERE YOU? YOU FIGURED A WAY OUT.
YOU JUMPED SHIP—UPLOADED A COPY OF YOUR CONSCIOUSNESS...
...TO THE LAST REMAINING TARDIS.
YOURS.

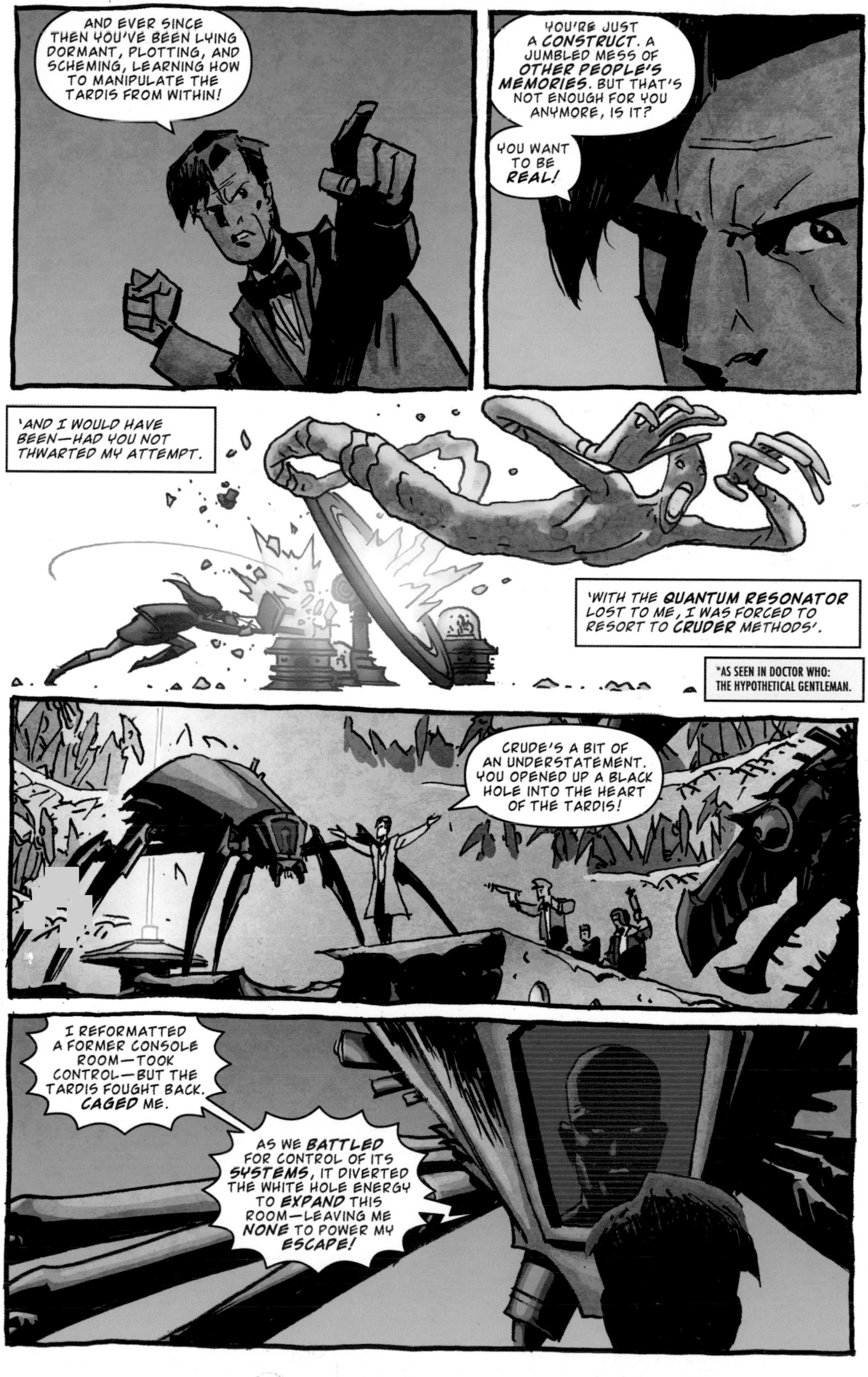
AND EVER SINCE THEN YOU'VE BEEN LYING DORMANT, PLOTTING, AND SCHEMING, LEARNING HOW TO MANIPULATE THE TARDIS FROM WITHIN!
YOU'RE JUST A CONSTRUCT. A JUMBLED MESS OF OTHER PEOPLE'S MEMORIES. BUT THAT'S NOT ENOUGH FOR YOU ANYMORE, IS IT?
YOU WANT TO BE REAL!
'AND I WOULD HAVE BEEN—HAD YOU NOT THWARTED MY ATTEMPT.
'WITH THE QUANTUM RESONATOR LOST TO ME, I WAS FORCED TO RESORT TO CRUDER METHODS'.
*AS SEEN IN DOCTOR WHO: THE HYPOTHETICAL GENTLEMAN.
CRUDE'S A BIT OF AN UNDERSTATEMENT. YOU OPENED UP A BLACK HOLE INTO THE HEART OF THE TARDIS!
I REFORMATTED A FORMER CONSOLE ROOM—TOOK CONTROL—BUT THE TARDIS FOUGHT BACK. CAGED ME.
AS WE BATTLED FOR CONTROL OF ITS SYSTEMS, IT DIVERTED THE WHITE HOLE ENERGY TO EXPAND THIS ROOM—LEAVING ME NONE TO POWER MY ESCAPE!

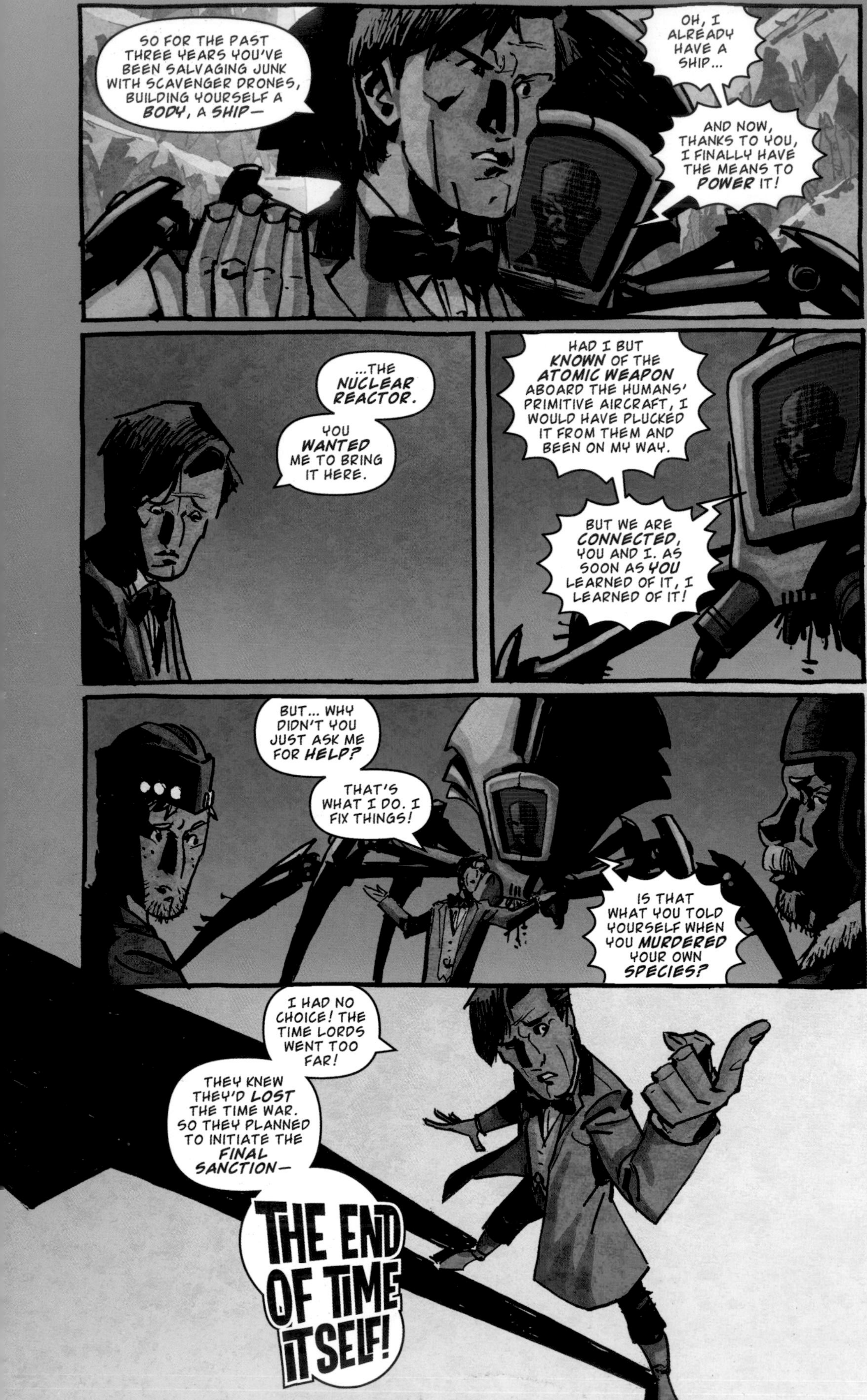

SO FOR THE PAST THREE YEARS YOU'VE BEEN SALVAGING JUNK WITH SCAVENGER DRONES, BUILDING YOURSELF A BODY, A SHIP—
OH, I ALREADY HAVE A SHIP...
AND NOW, THANKS TO YOU, I FINALLY HAVE THE MEANS TO POWER IT!
...THE NUCLEAR REACTOR.
YOU WANTED ME TO BRING IT HERE.
HAD I BUT KNOWN OF THE ATOMIC WEAPON ABOARD THE HUMANS' PRIMITIVE AIRCRAFT, I WOULD HAVE PLUCKED IT FROM THEM AND BEEN ON MY WAY.
BUT WE ARE CONNECTED, YOU AND I. AS SOON AS YOU LEARNED OF IT, I LEARNED OF IT!
BUT... WHY DIDN'T YOU JUST ASK ME FOR HELP?
THAT'S WHAT I DO. I FIX THINGS!
IS THAT WHAT YOU TOLD YOURSELF WHEN YOU MURDERED YOUR OWN SPECIES?
I HAD NO CHOICE! THE TIME LORDS WENT TOO FAR!
THEY KNEW THEY'D LOST THE TIME WAR. SO THEY PLANNED TO INITIATE THE FINAL SANCTION—
THE END OF TIME ITSELF!

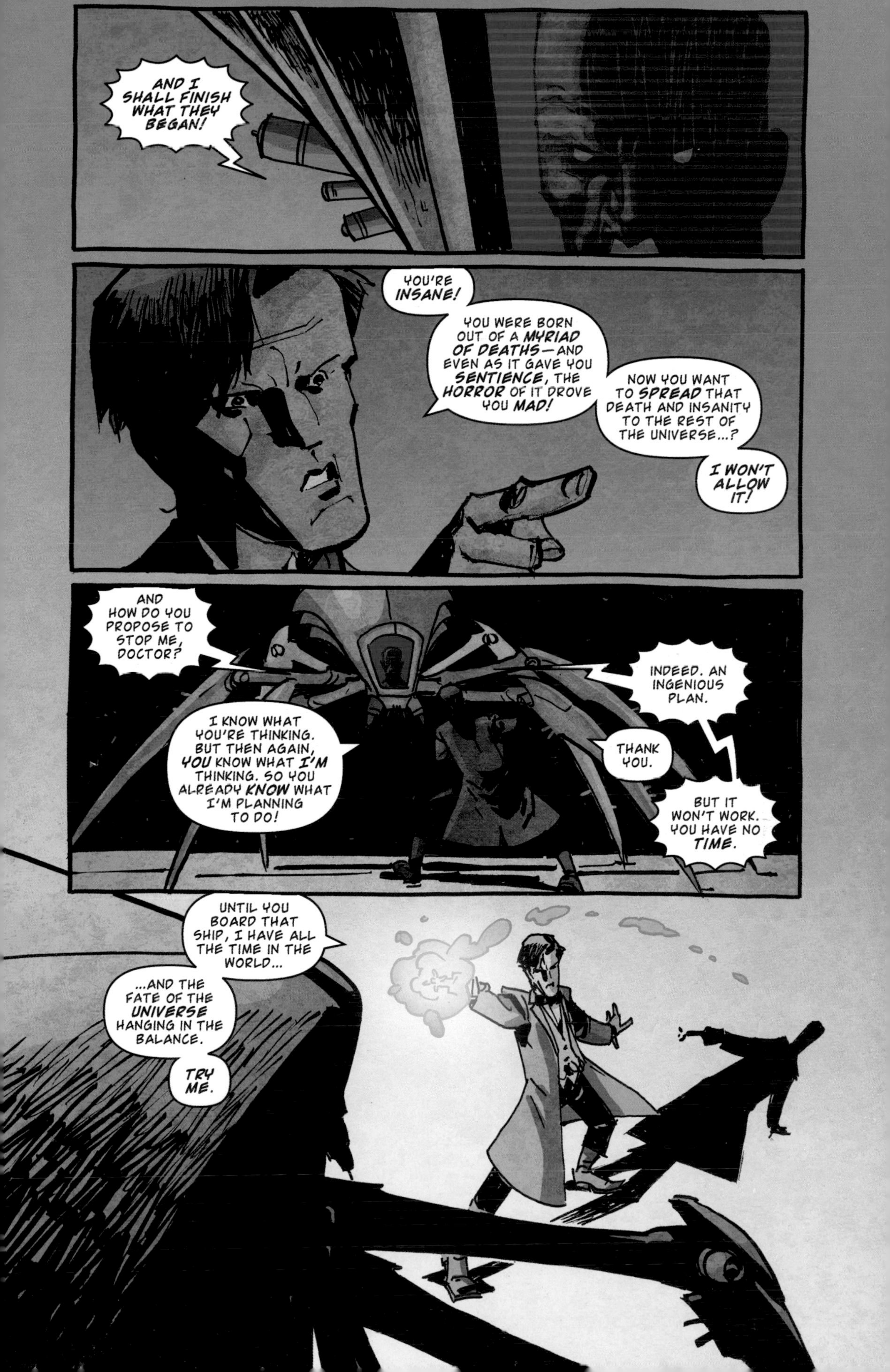
AND I SHALL FINISH WHAT THEY BEGAN!
YOU'RE INSANE!
YOU WERE BORN OUT OF A MYRIAD OF DEATHS—AND EVEN AS IT GAVE YOU SENTIENCE, THE HORROR OF IT DROVE YOU MAD!
NOW YOU WANT TO SPREAD THAT DEATH AND INSANITY TO THE REST OF THE UNIVERSE...?
I WON'T ALLOW IT!
AND HOW DO YOU PROPOSE TO STOP ME, DOCTOR?
I KNOW WHAT YOU'RE THINKING. BUT THEN AGAIN, YOU KNOW WHAT I'M THINKING. SO YOU ALREADY KNOW WHAT I'M PLANNING TO DO!
INDEED. AN INGENIOUS PLAN.
THANK YOU.
BUT IT WON'T WORK. YOU HAVE NO TIME.
UNTIL YOU BOARD THAT SHIP, I HAVE ALL THE TIME IN THE WORLD...
...AND THE FATE OF THE UNIVERSE HANGING IN THE BALANCE.
TRY ME.

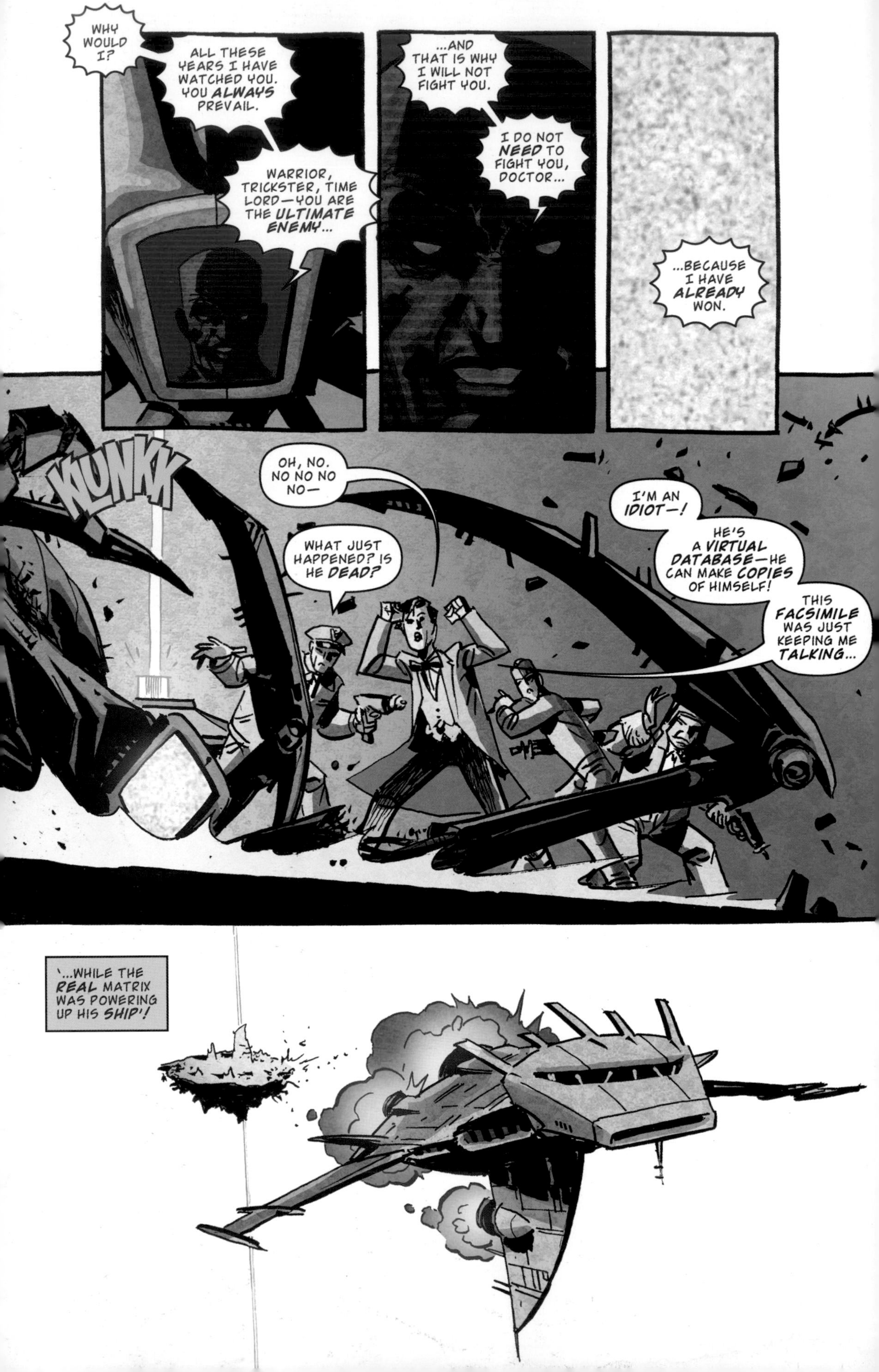
WHY WOULD I?
ALL THESE YEARS I HAVE WATCHED YOU. YOU ALWAYS PREVAIL.
WARRIOR, TRICKSTER, TIME LORD—YOU ARE THE ULTIMATE ENEMY...
...AND THAT IS WHY I WILL NOT FIGHT YOU.
I DO NOT NEED TO FIGHT YOU, DOCTOR...
...BECAUSE I HAVE ALREADY WON.
KLUNKK
OH, NO. NO NO NO NO—
WHAT JUST HAPPENED? IS HE DEAD?
I'M AN IDIOT—!
HE'S A VIRTUAL DATABASE—HE CAN MAKE COPIES OF HIMSELF!
THIS FACSIMILE WAS JUST KEEPING ME TALKING...
'...WHILE THE REAL MATRIX WAS POWERING UP HIS SHIP'!

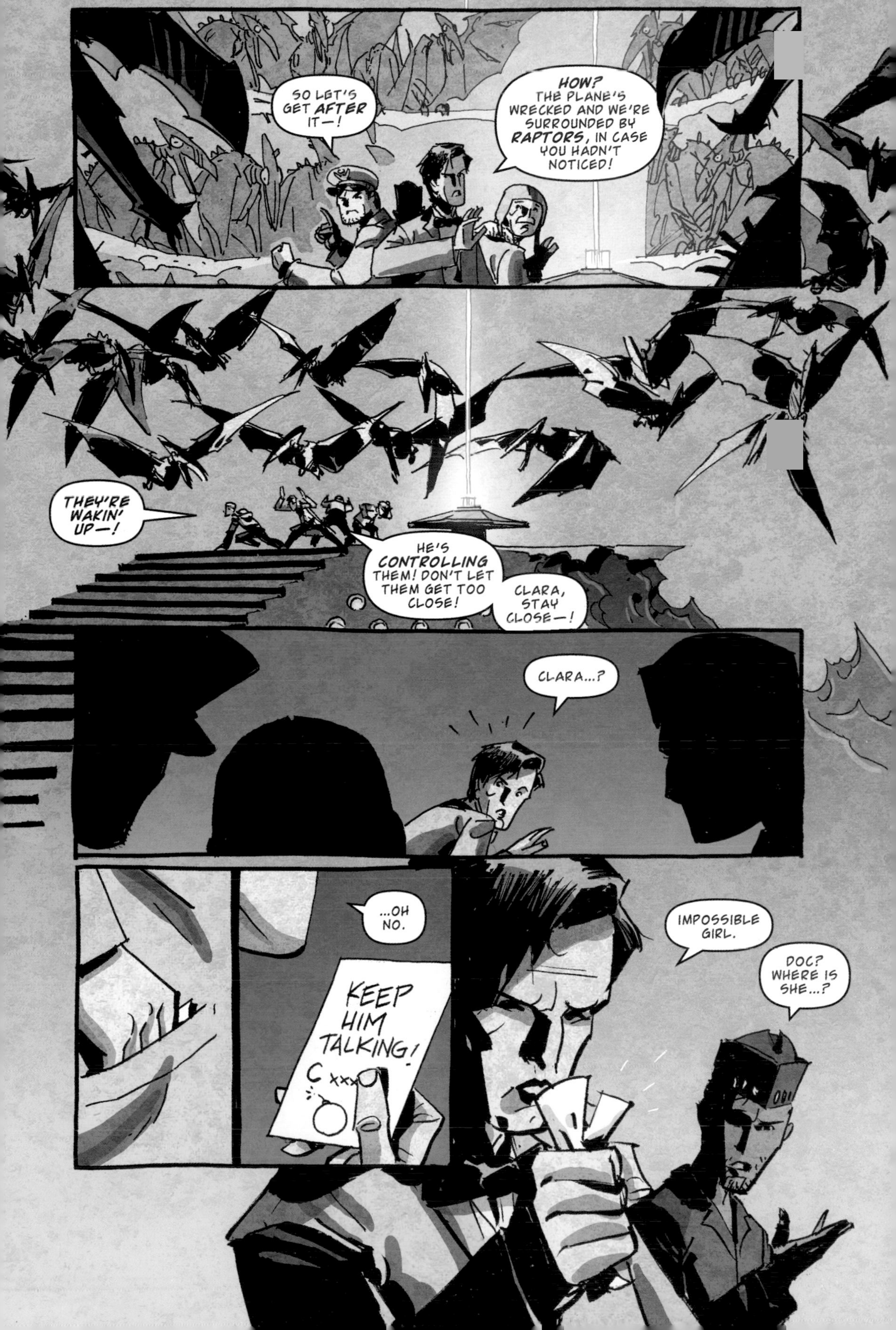
SO LET'S GET AFTER IT—!
HOW? THE PLANE'S WRECKED AND WE'RE SURROUNDED BY RAPTORS, IN CASE YOU HADN'T NOTICED!
THEY'RE WAKIN' UP—!
HE'S CONTROLLING THEM! DON'T LET THEM GET TOO CLOSE!
CLARA, STAY CLOSE—!
CLARA...?
...OH NO.
KEEP HIM TALKING! C xxx
IMPOSSIBLE GIRL.
DOC? WHERE IS SHE...?

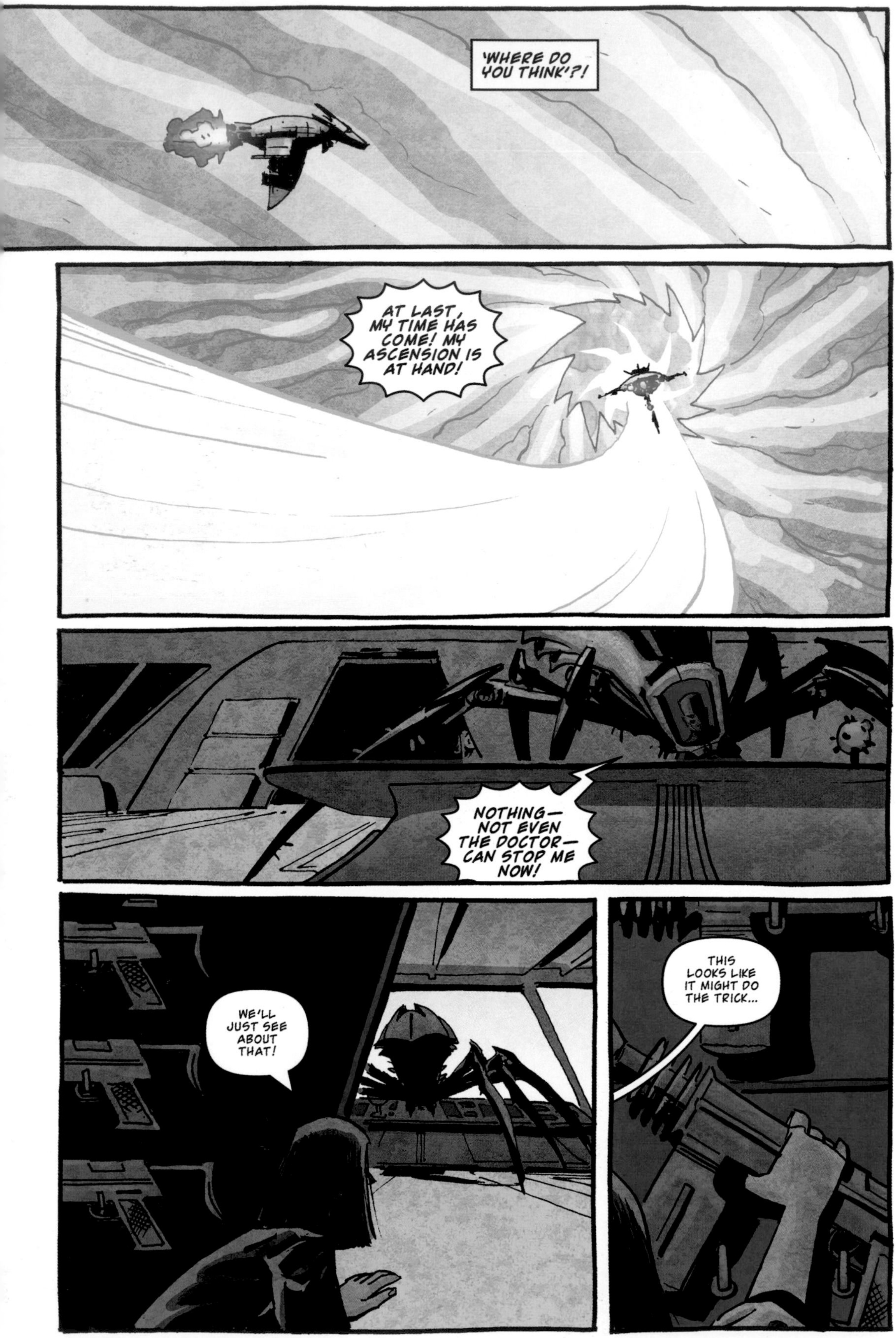
'WHERE DO YOU THINK'?!
AT LAST, MY TIME HAS COME! MY ASCENSION IS AT HAND!
NOTHING— NOT EVEN THE DOCTOR— CAN STOP ME NOW!
WE'LL JUST SEE ABOUT THAT!
THIS LOOKS LIKE IT MIGHT DO THE TRICK...

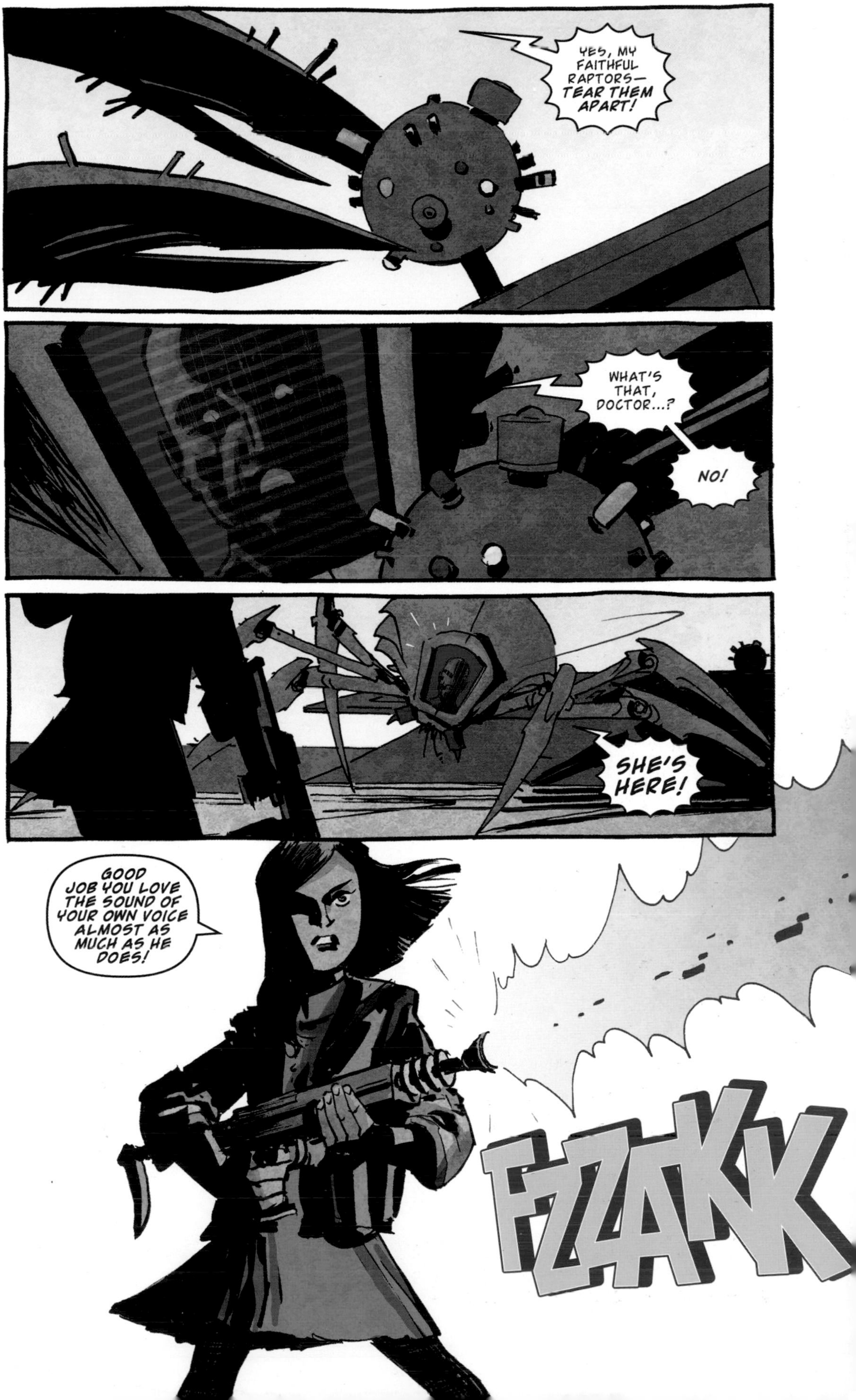
YES, MY FAITHFUL RAPTORS— TEAR THEM APART!
WHAT'S THAT, DOCTOR...?
NO!
SHE'S HERE!
GOOD JOB YOU LOVE THE SOUND OF YOUR OWN VOICE ALMOST AS MUCH AS HE DOES!
FZZAKK

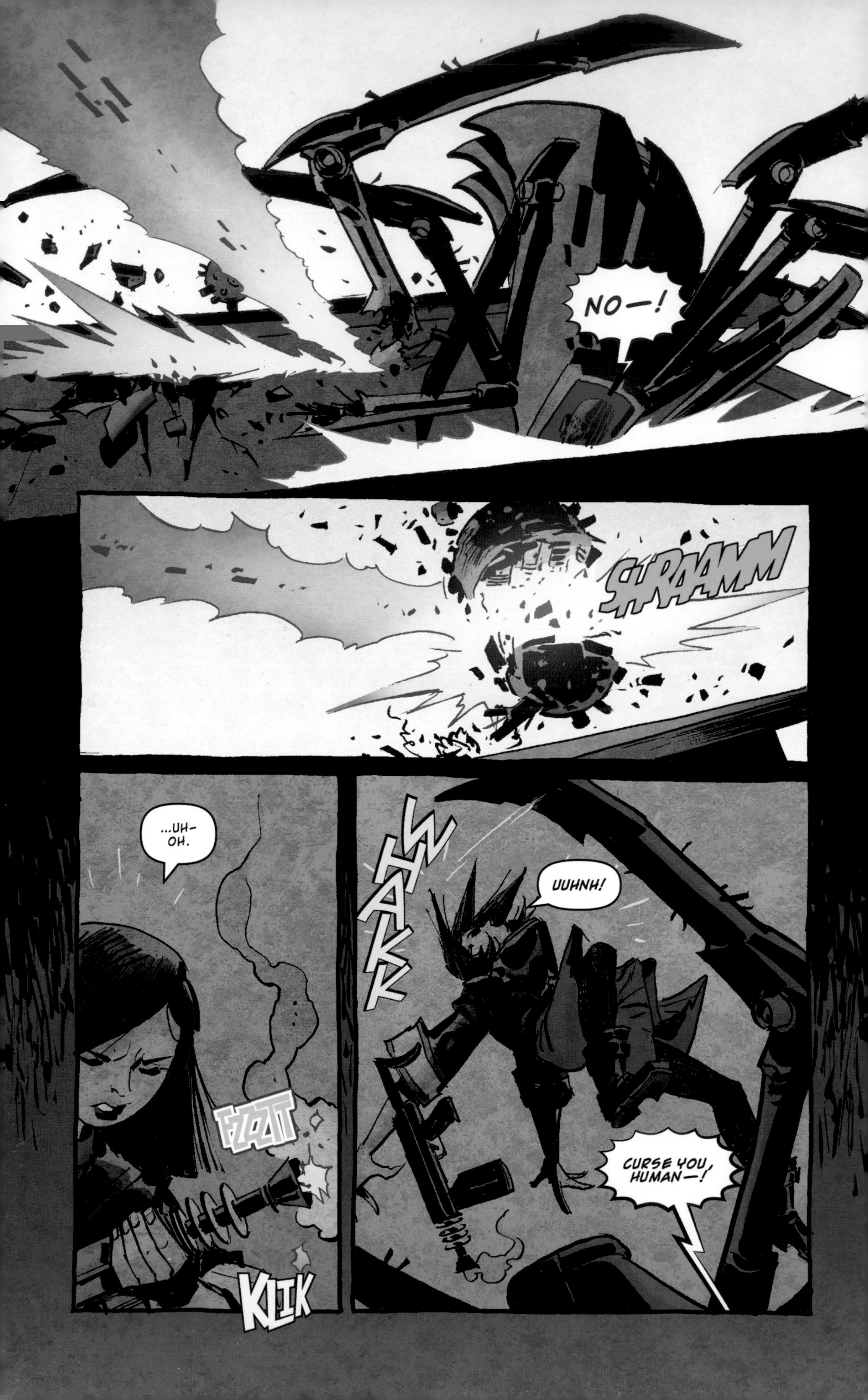
NO—!
SHRAAMM
...UH-OH.
TZZZT
KLIK
WHAKK
UUHNH!
CURSE YOU, HUMAN—!

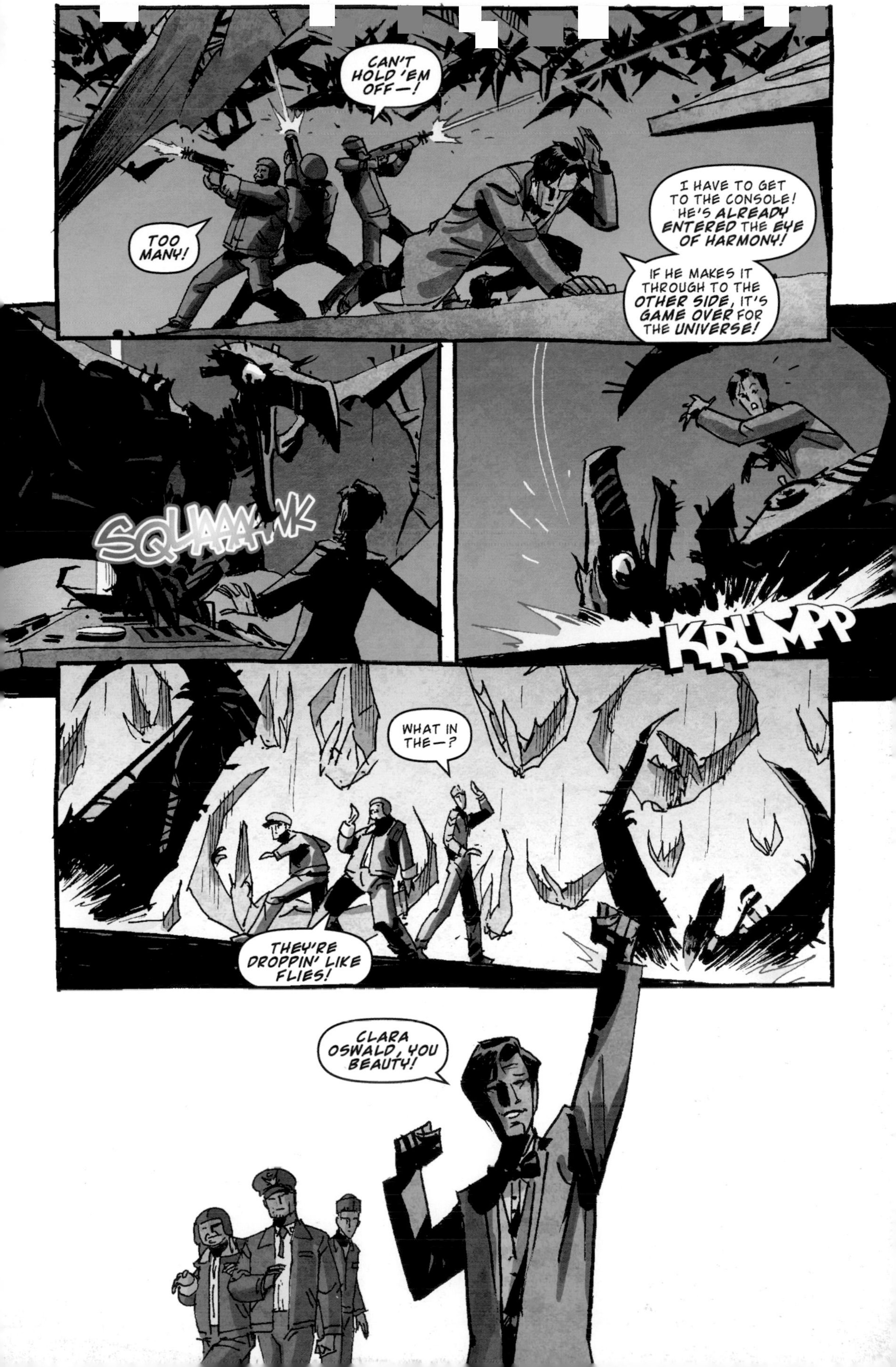
CAN'T HOLD 'EM OFF—!
TOO MANY!
I HAVE TO GET TO THE CONSOLE! HE'S ALREADY ENTERED THE EYE OF HARMONY!
IF HE MAKES IT THROUGH TO THE OTHER SIDE, IT'S GAME OVER FOR THE UNIVERSE!
SQUAAAAWK
KRUMPP
WHAT IN THE—?
THEY'RE DROPPIN' LIKE FLIES!
CLARA OSWALD, YOU BEAUTY!

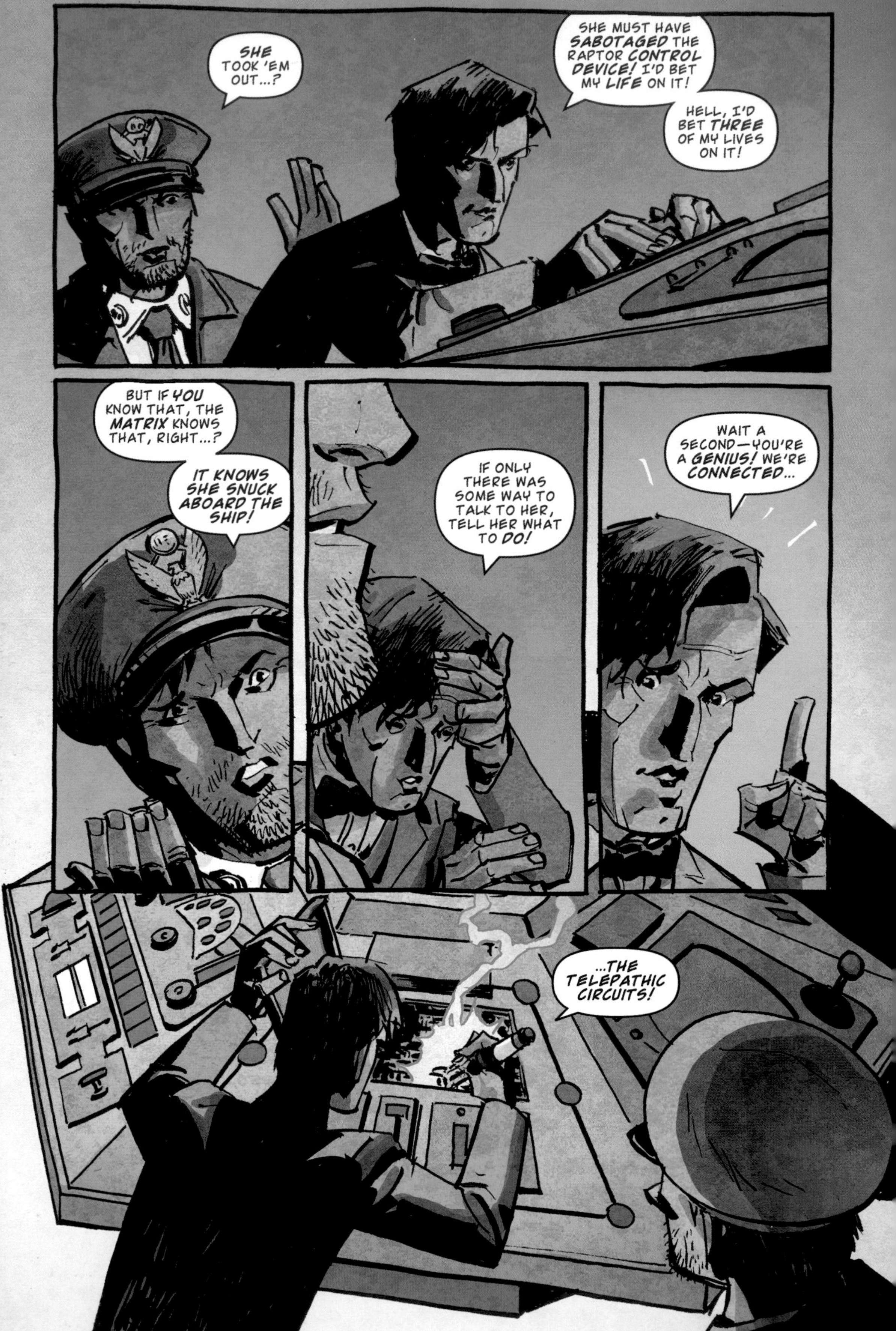
SHE TOOK 'EM OUT...?
SHE MUST HAVE SABOTAGED THE RAPTOR CONTROL DEVICE! I'D BET MY LIFE ON IT!
HELL, I'D BET THREE OF MY LIVES ON IT!
BUT IF YOU KNOW THAT, THE MATRIX KNOWS THAT, RIGHT...?
IT KNOWS SHE SNUCK ABOARD THE SHIP!
IF ONLY THERE WAS SOME WAY TO TALK TO HER, TELL HER WHAT TO DO!
WAIT A SECOND—YOU'RE A GENIUS! WE'RE CONNECTED...
...THE TELEPATHIC CIRCUITS!

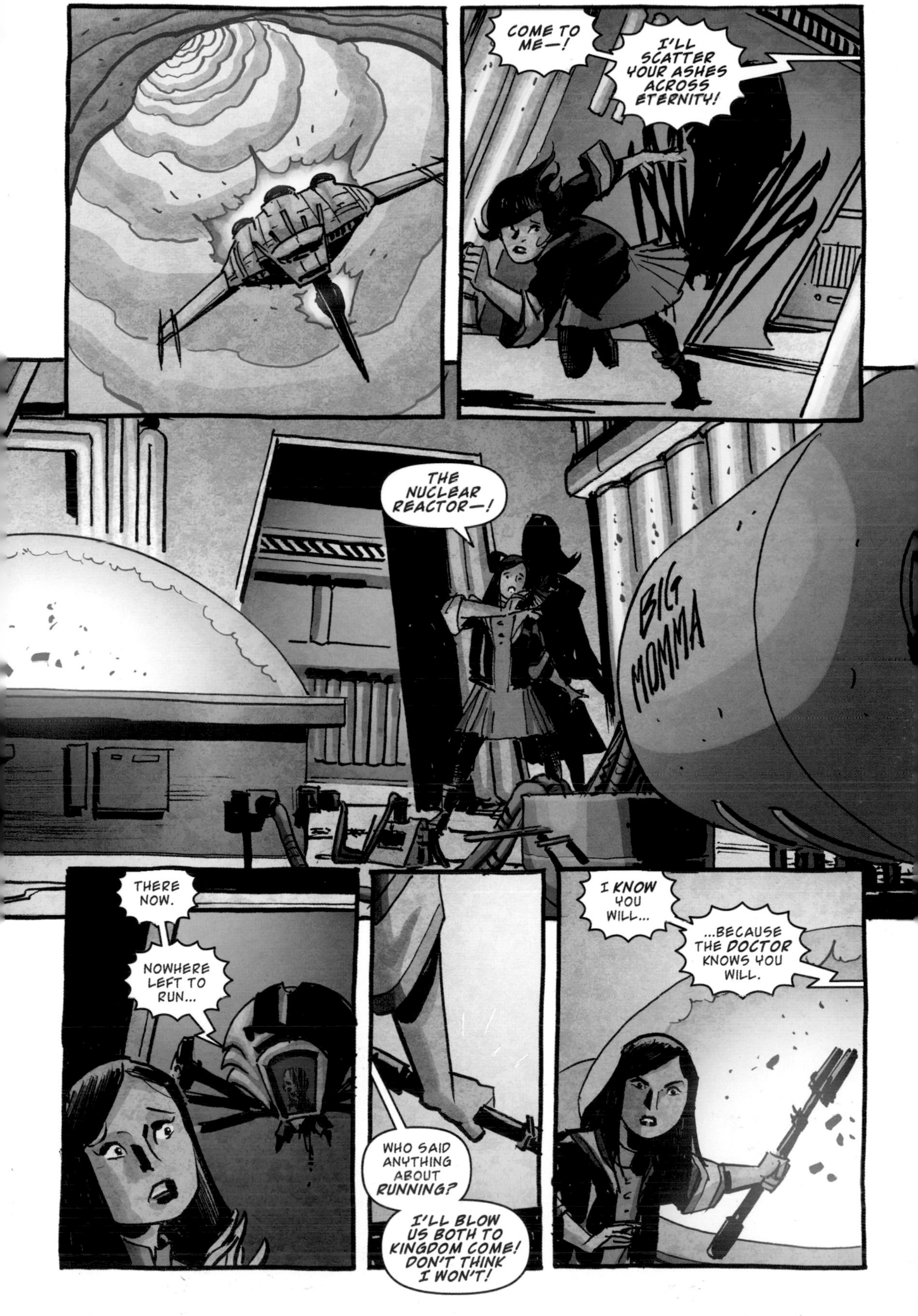

COME TO ME—!
I'LL SCATTER YOUR ASHES ACROSS ETERNITY!
THE NUCLEAR REACTOR—!
BIG MOMMA
THERE NOW.
NOWHERE LEFT TO RUN...
WHO SAID ANYTHING ABOUT RUNNING?
I'LL BLOW US BOTH TO KINGDOM COME! DON'T THINK I WON'T!
I KNOW YOU WILL...
...BECAUSE THE DOCTOR KNOWS YOU WILL.

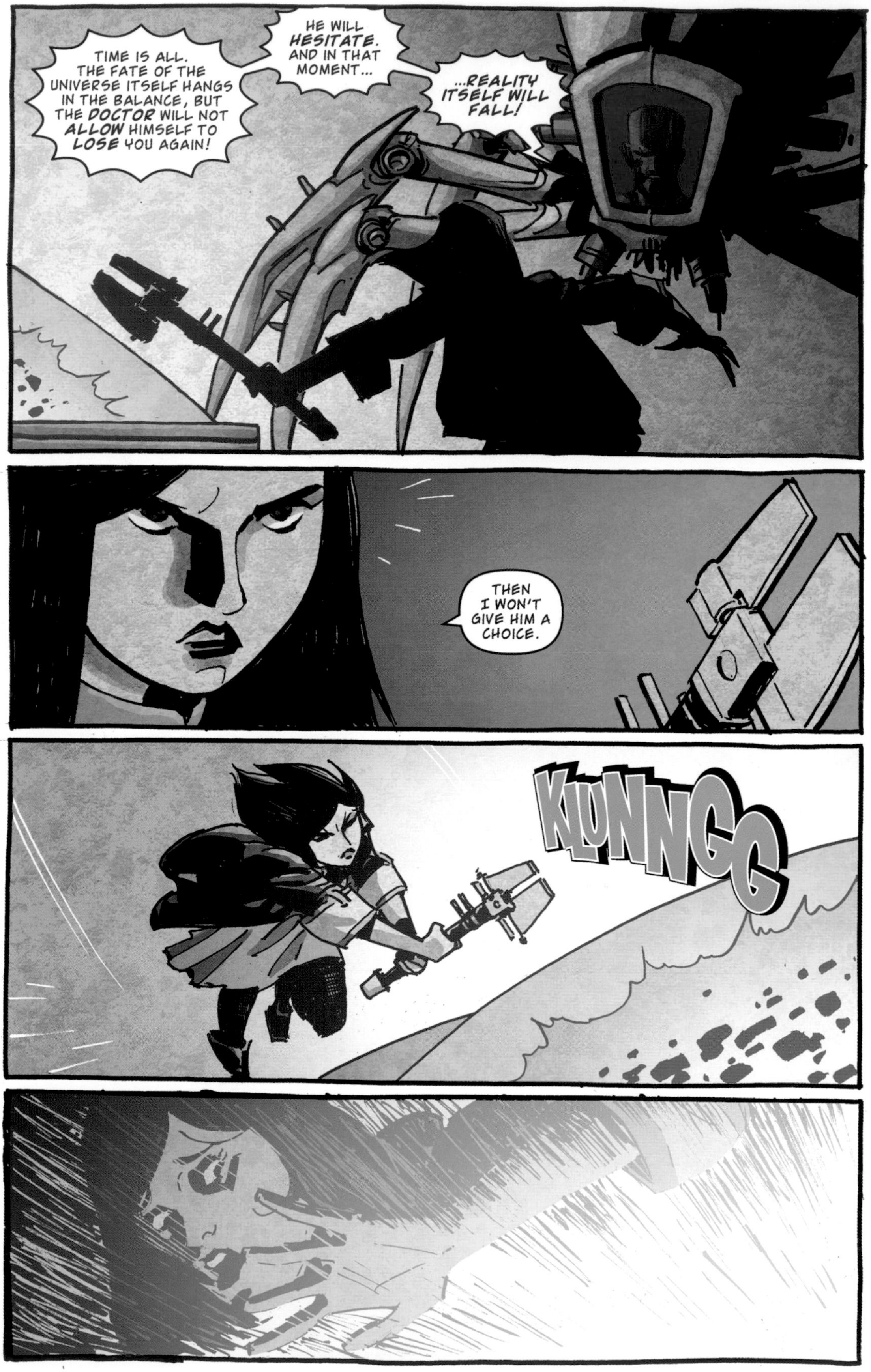
TIME IS ALL. THE FATE OF THE UNIVERSE ITSELF HANGS IN THE BALANCE, BUT THE DOCTOR WILL NOT ALLOW HIMSELF TO LOSE YOU AGAIN!
HE WILL HESITATE. AND IN THAT MOMENT...
...REALITY ITSELF WILL FALL!
THEN I WON'T GIVE HIM A CHOICE.
KLUNNGG

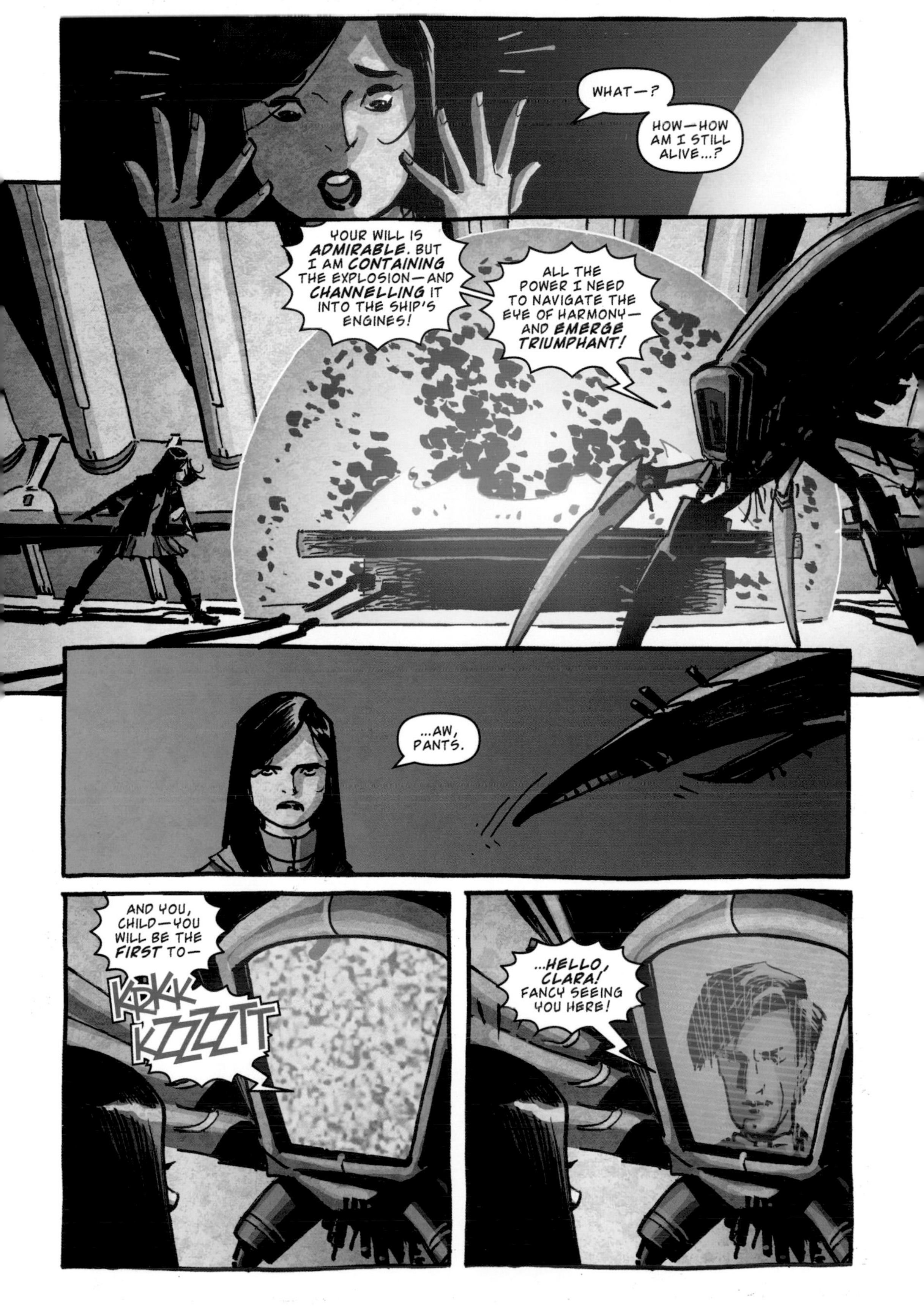
WHAT—?
HOW—HOW AM I STILL ALIVE...?
YOUR WILL IS ADMIRABLE. BUT I AM CONTAINING THE EXPLOSION—AND CHANNELLING IT INTO THE SHIP'S ENGINES!
ALL THE POWER I NEED TO NAVIGATE THE EYE OF HARMONY—AND EMERGE TRIUMPHANT!
...AW, PANTS.
AND YOU, CHILD—YOU WILL BE THE FIRST TO—
KRKK KZZZZTT
...HELLO, CLARA! FANCY SEEING YOU HERE!

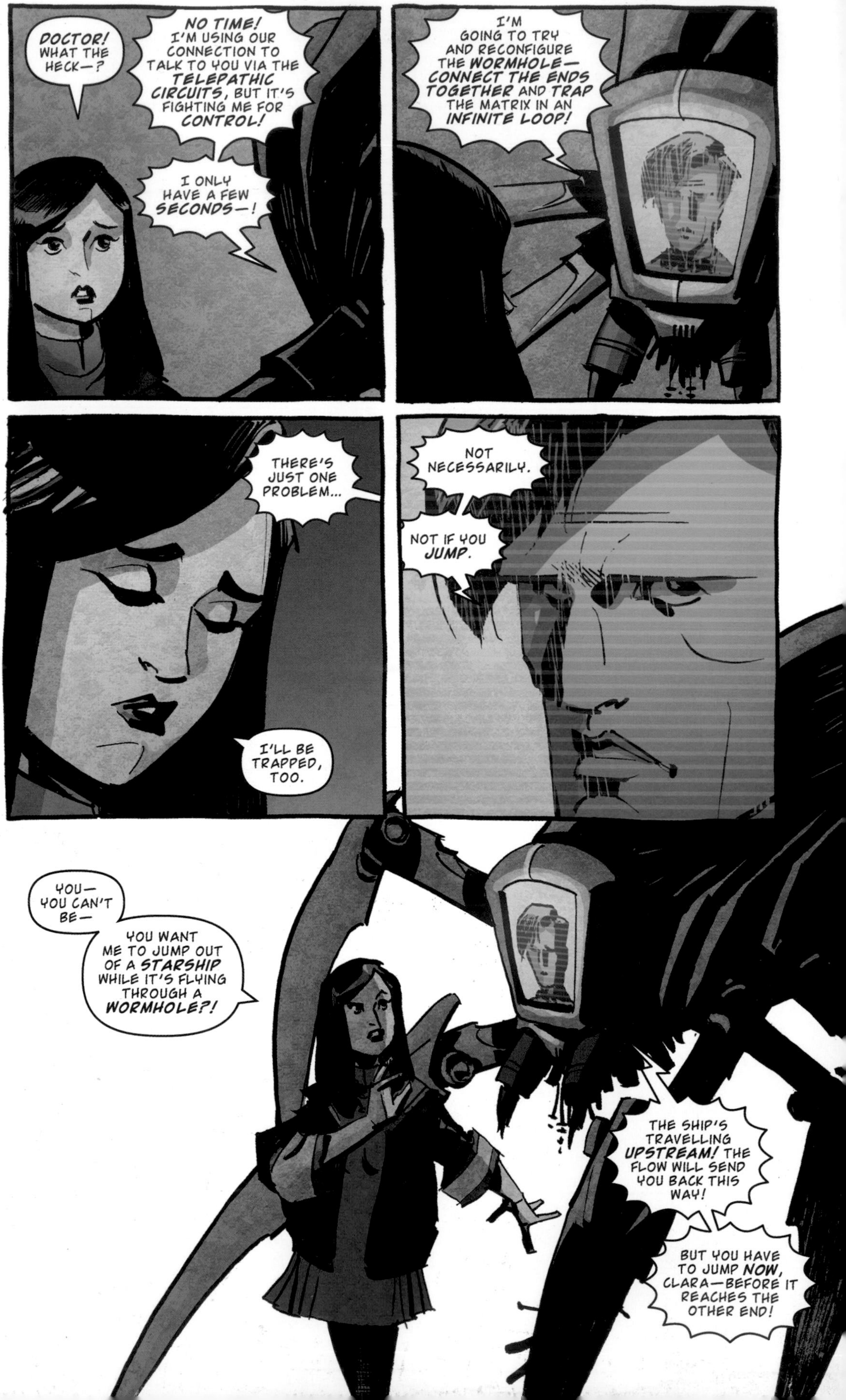
DOCTOR! WHAT THE HECK—?
NO TIME! I'M USING OUR CONNECTION TO TALK TO YOU VIA THE TELEPATHIC CIRCUITS, BUT IT'S FIGHTING ME FOR CONTROL!
I ONLY HAVE A FEW SECONDS—!
I'M GOING TO TRY AND RECONFIGURE THE WORMHOLE—CONNECT THE ENDS TOGETHER AND TRAP THE MATRIX IN AN INFINITE LOOP!
THERE'S JUST ONE PROBLEM...
I'LL BE TRAPPED, TOO.
NOT NECESSARILY.
NOT IF YOU JUMP.
YOU— YOU CAN'T BE—
YOU WANT ME TO JUMP OUT OF A STARSHIP WHILE IT'S FLYING THROUGH A WORMHOLE?!
THE SHIP'S TRAVELLING UPSTREAM! THE FLOW WILL SEND YOU BACK THIS WAY!
BUT YOU HAVE TO JUMP NOW, CLARA—BEFORE IT REACHES THE OTHER END!

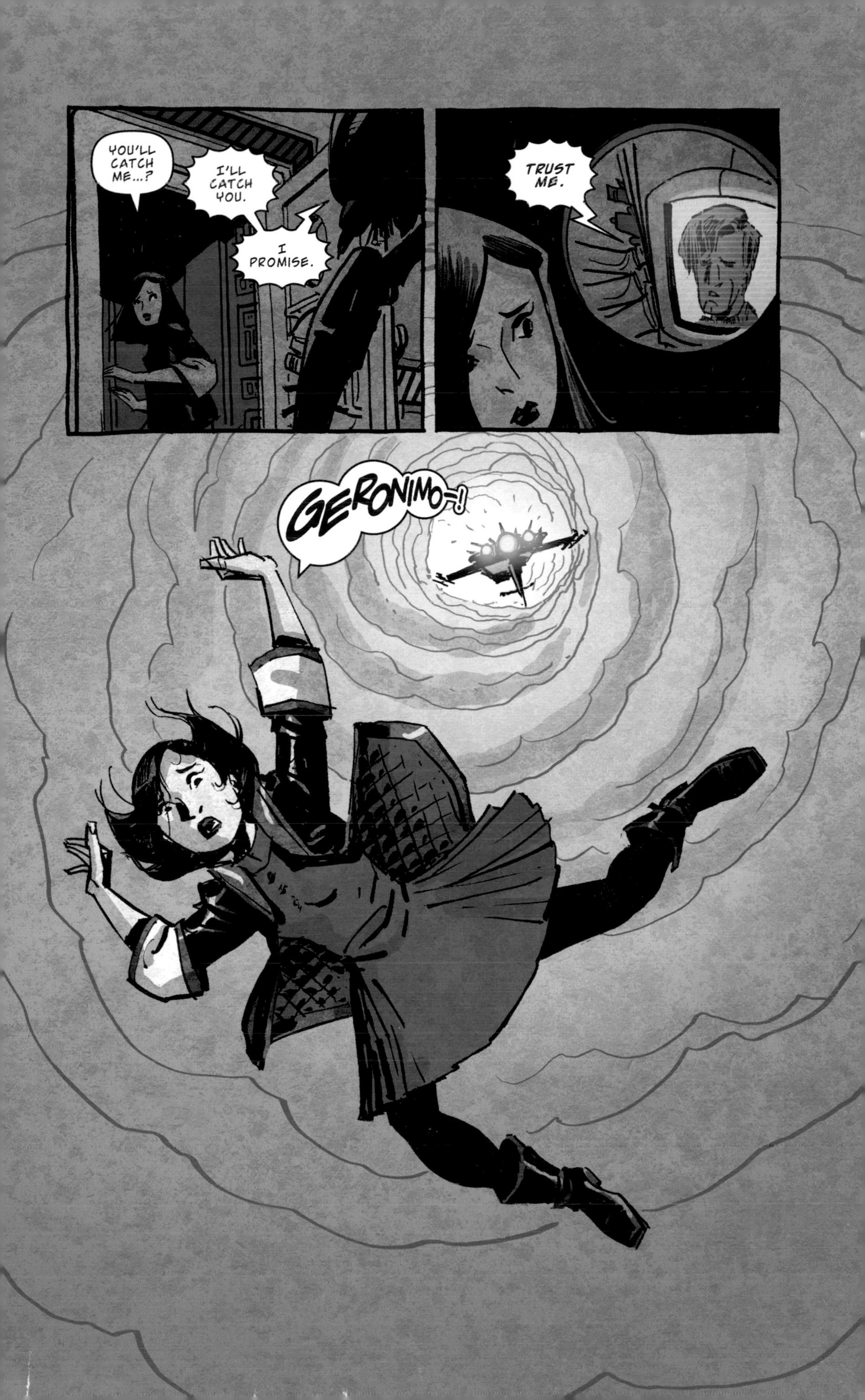
YOU'LL CATCH ME...?
I'LL CATCH YOU.
I PROMISE.
TRUST ME.
GERONIMO--!

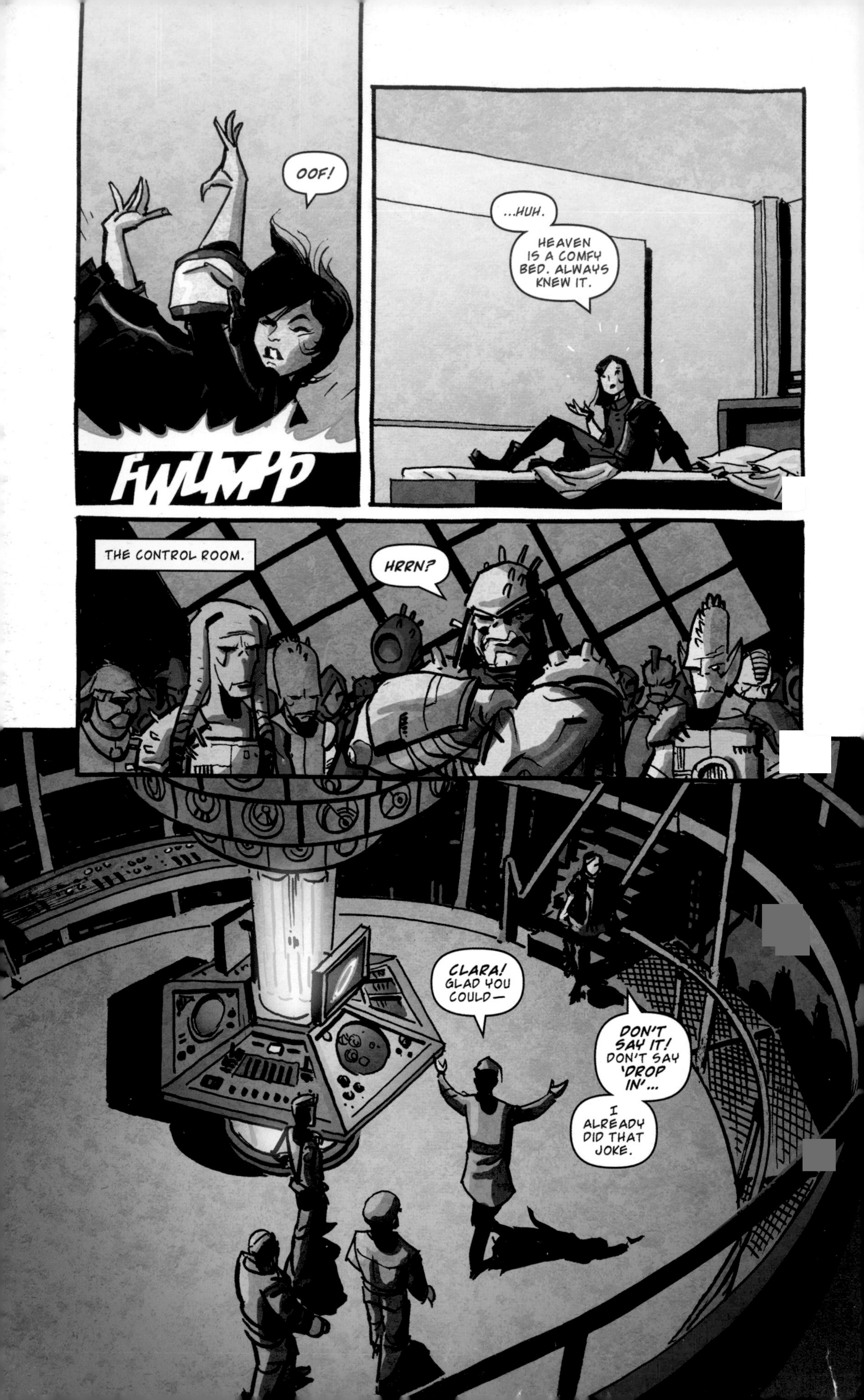
OOF!
FWUMP
...HUH.
HEAVEN IS A COMFY BED. ALWAYS KNEW IT.
THE CONTROL ROOM.
HRRN?
CLARA! GLAD YOU COULD—
DON'T SAY IT! DON'T SAY 'DROP IN'...
I ALREADY DID THAT JOKE.

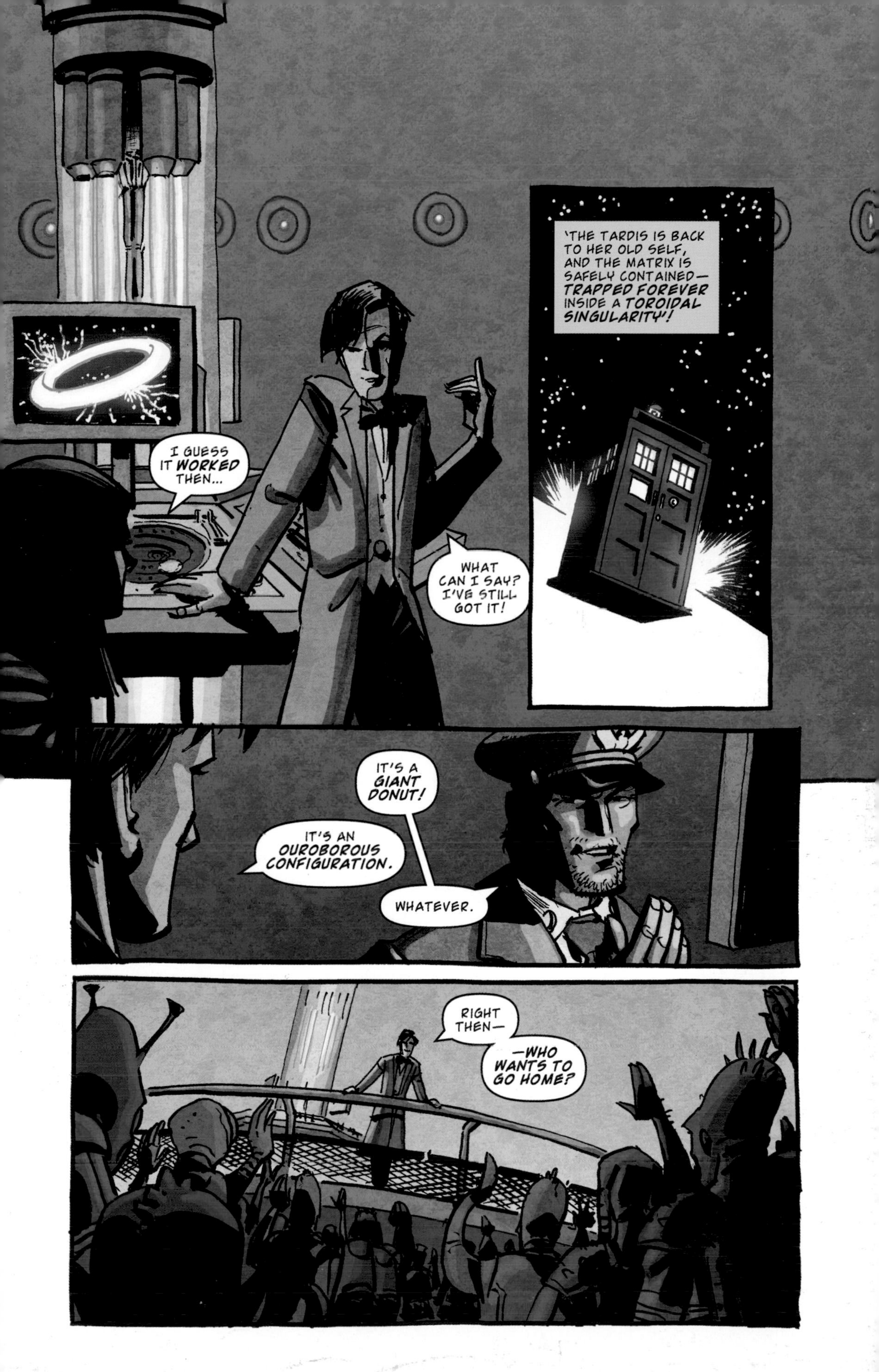
'THE TARDIS IS BACK TO HER OLD SELF, AND THE MATRIX IS SAFELY CONTAINED—TRAPPED FOREVER INSIDE A TOROIDAL SINGULARITY'!
I GUESS IT WORKED THEN...
WHAT CAN I SAY? I'VE STILL GOT IT!
IT'S A GIANT DONUT!
IT'S AN OUROBOROUS CONFIGURATION.
WHATEVER.
RIGHT THEN—
—WHO WANTS TO GO HOME?

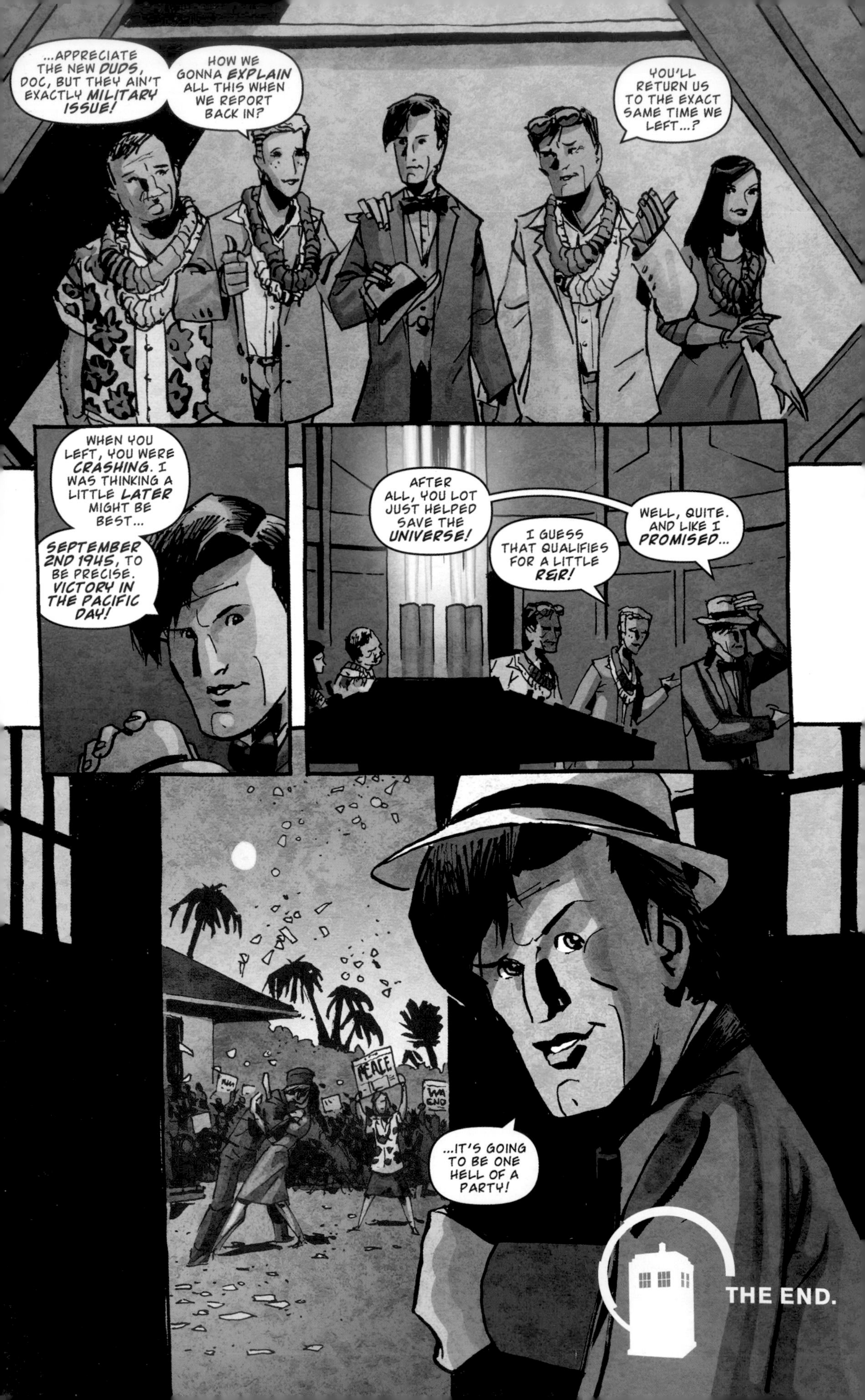
...APPRECIATE THE NEW DUDS, DOC, BUT THEY AIN'T EXACTLY MILITARY ISSUE!
HOW WE GONNA EXPLAIN ALL THIS WHEN WE REPORT BACK IN?
YOU'LL RETURN US TO THE EXACT SAME TIME WE LEFT...?
WHEN YOU LEFT, YOU WERE CRASHING. I WAS THINKING A LITTLE LATER MIGHT BE BEST...
SEPTEMBER 2ND 1945, TO BE PRECISE. VICTORY IN THE PACIFIC DAY!
AFTER ALL, YOU LOT JUST HELPED SAVE THE UNIVERSE!
I GUESS THAT QUALIFIES FOR A LITTLE R&R!
WELL, QUITE. AND LIKE I PROMISED...
PEACE
...IT'S GOING TO BE ONE HELL OF A PARTY!
THE END.

IN-FEZ-STATION!

Written by Len Wein • Art by Matthew Dow Smith • Colors by Adrian Salmon
Lettering by Shawn Lee • Edited by Denton J. Tipton

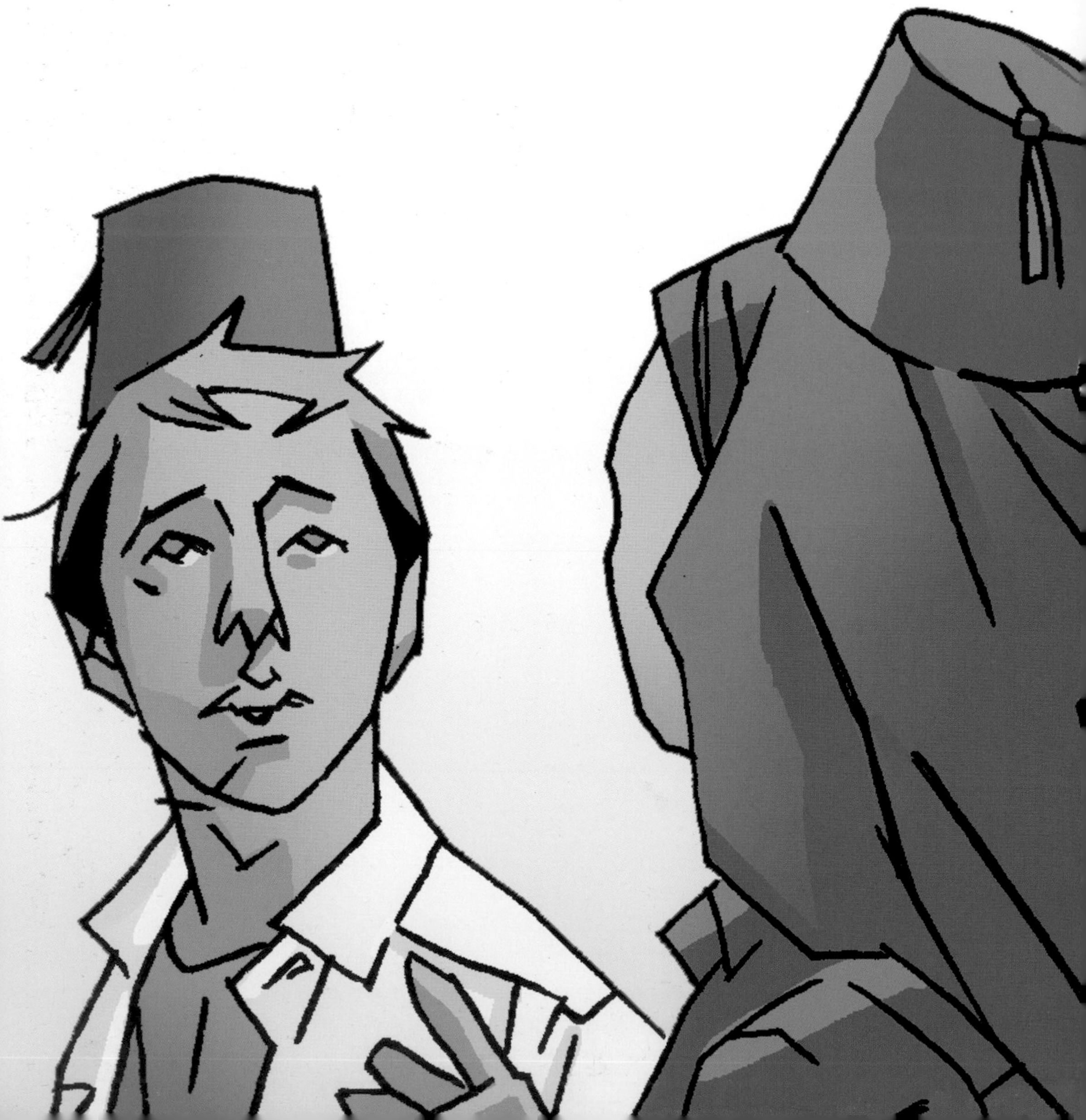

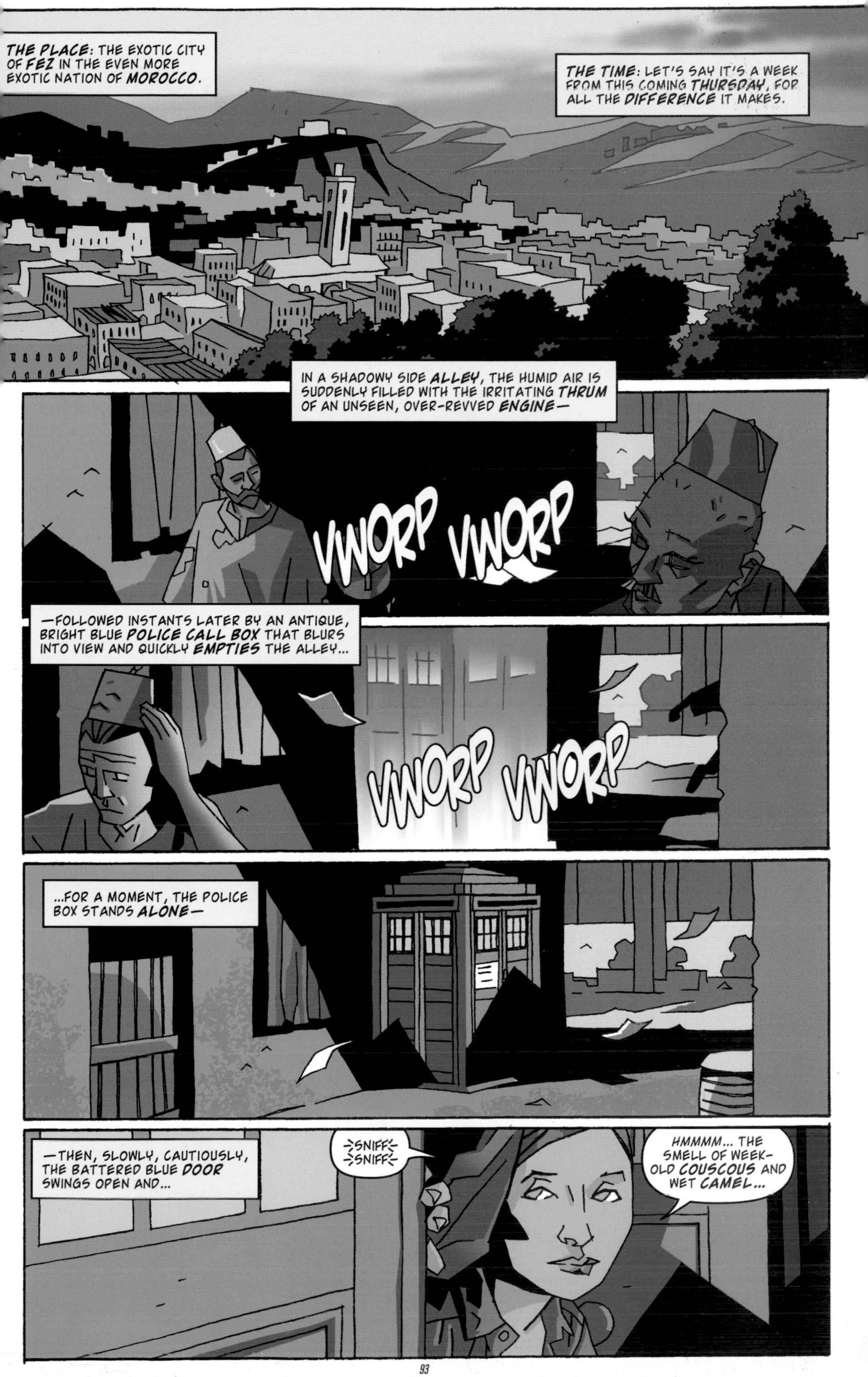
THE PLACE: THE EXOTIC CITY OF FEZ IN THE EVEN MORE EXOTIC NATION OF MOROCCO.
THE TIME: LET'S SAY IT'S A WEEK FROM THIS COMING THURSDAY, FOR ALL THE DIFFERENCE IT MAKES.
IN A SHADOWY SIDE ALLEY, THE HUMID AIR IS SUDDENLY FILLED WITH THE IRRITATING THRUM OF AN UNSEEN, OVER-REVVED ENGINE—
VWORP VWORP
—FOLLOWED INSTANTS LATER BY AN ANTIQUE, BRIGHT BLUE POLICE CALL BOX THAT BLURS INTO VIEW AND QUICKLY EMPTIES THE ALLEY...
VWORP VWORP
...FOR A MOMENT, THE POLICE BOX STANDS ALONE—
—THEN, SLOWLY, CAUTIOUSLY, THE BATTERED BLUE DOOR SWINGS OPEN AND...
SNIFF SNIFF
HMMMM... THE SMELL OF WEEK-OLD COUSCOUS AND WET CAMEL...

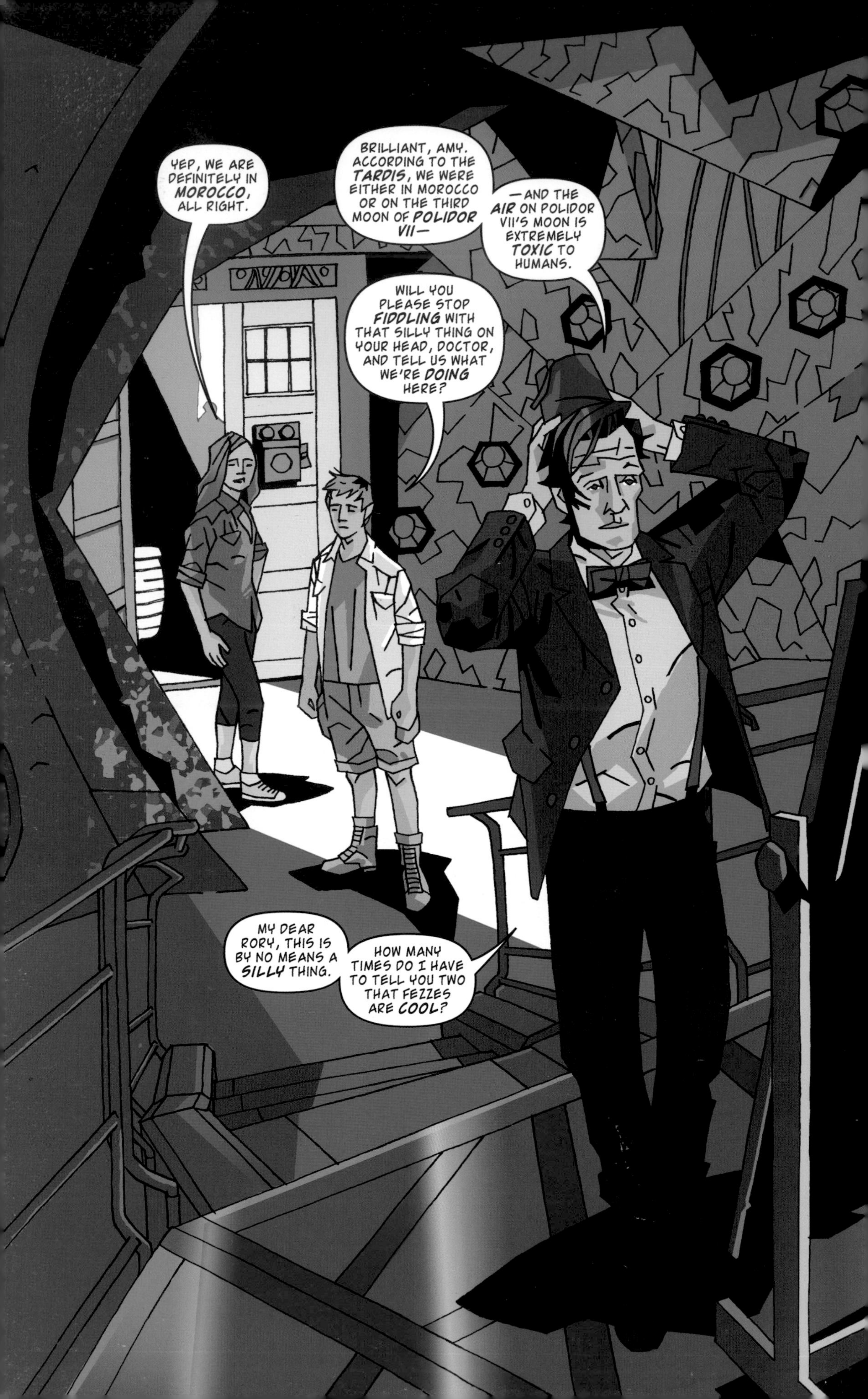
YEP, WE ARE DEFINITELY IN MOROCCO, ALL RIGHT.
BRILLIANT, AMY. ACCORDING TO THE TARDIS, WE WERE EITHER IN MOROCCO OR ON THE THIRD MOON OF POLIDOR VII—
—AND THE AIR ON POLIDOR VII'S MOON IS EXTREMELY TOXIC TO HUMANS.
WILL YOU PLEASE STOP FIDDLING WITH THAT SILLY THING ON YOUR HEAD, DOCTOR, AND TELL US WHAT WE'RE DOING HERE?
MY DEAR RORY, THIS IS BY NO MEANS A SILLY THING.
HOW MANY TIMES DO I HAVE TO TELL YOU TWO THAT FEZZES ARE COOL?

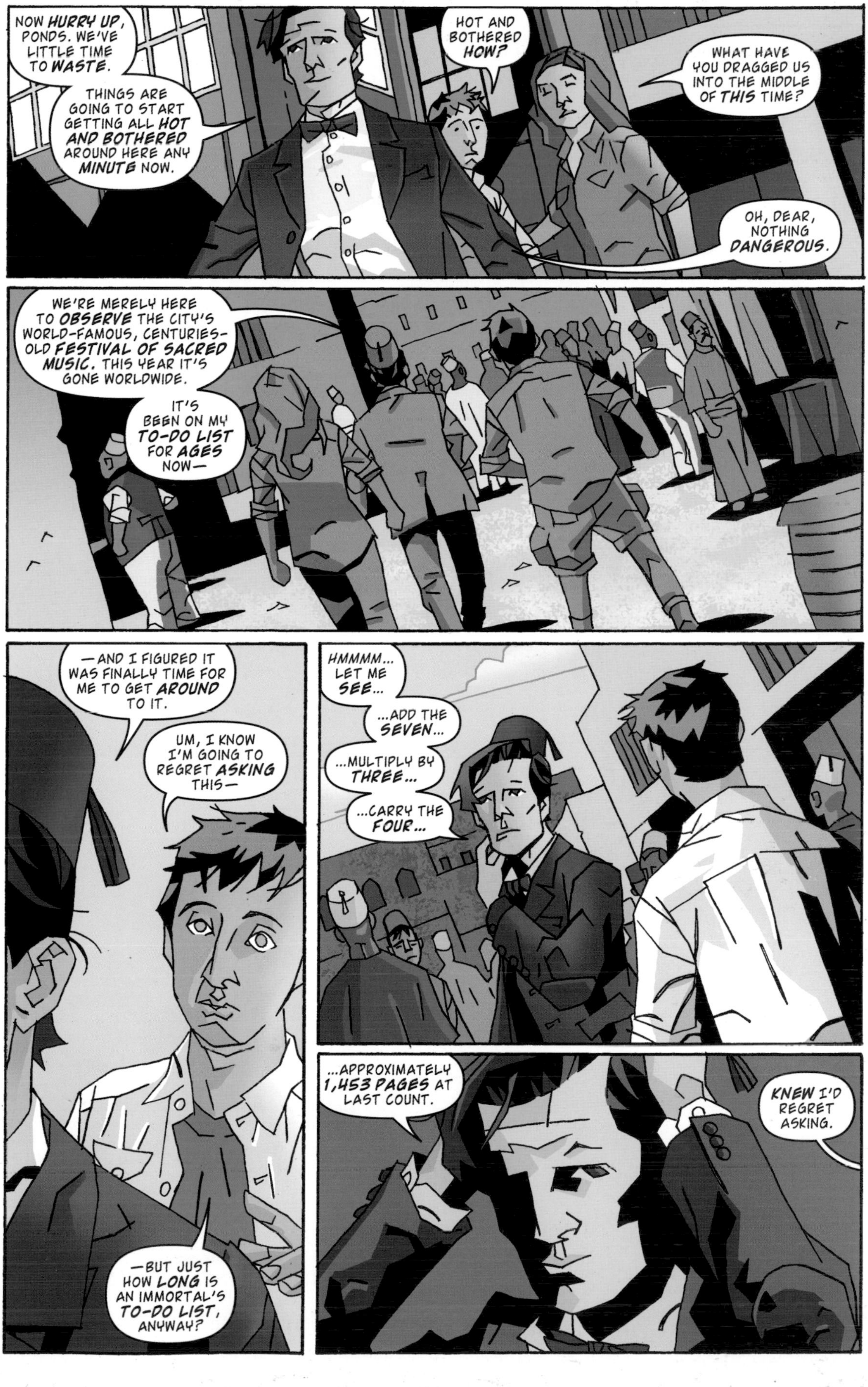
NOW HURRY UP, PONDS. WE'VE LITTLE TIME TO WASTE.
THINGS ARE GOING TO START GETTING ALL HOT AND BOTHERED AROUND HERE ANY MINUTE NOW.
HOT AND BOTHERED HOW?
WHAT HAVE YOU DRAGGED US INTO THE MIDDLE OF THIS TIME?
OH, DEAR, NOTHING DANGEROUS.
WE'RE MERELY HERE TO OBSERVE THE CITY'S WORLD-FAMOUS, CENTURIES-OLD FESTIVAL OF SACRED MUSIC. THIS YEAR IT'S GONE WORLDWIDE.
IT'S BEEN ON MY TO-DO LIST FOR AGES NOW—
—AND I FIGURED IT WAS FINALLY TIME FOR ME TO GET AROUND TO IT.
UM, I KNOW I'M GOING TO REGRET ASKING THIS—
—BUT JUST HOW LONG IS AN IMMORTAL'S TO-DO LIST, ANYWAY?
HMMMM... LET ME SEE...
...ADD THE SEVEN...
...MULTIPLY BY THREE...
...CARRY THE FOUR...
...APPROXIMATELY 1,453 PAGES AT LAST COUNT.
KNEW I'D REGRET ASKING.

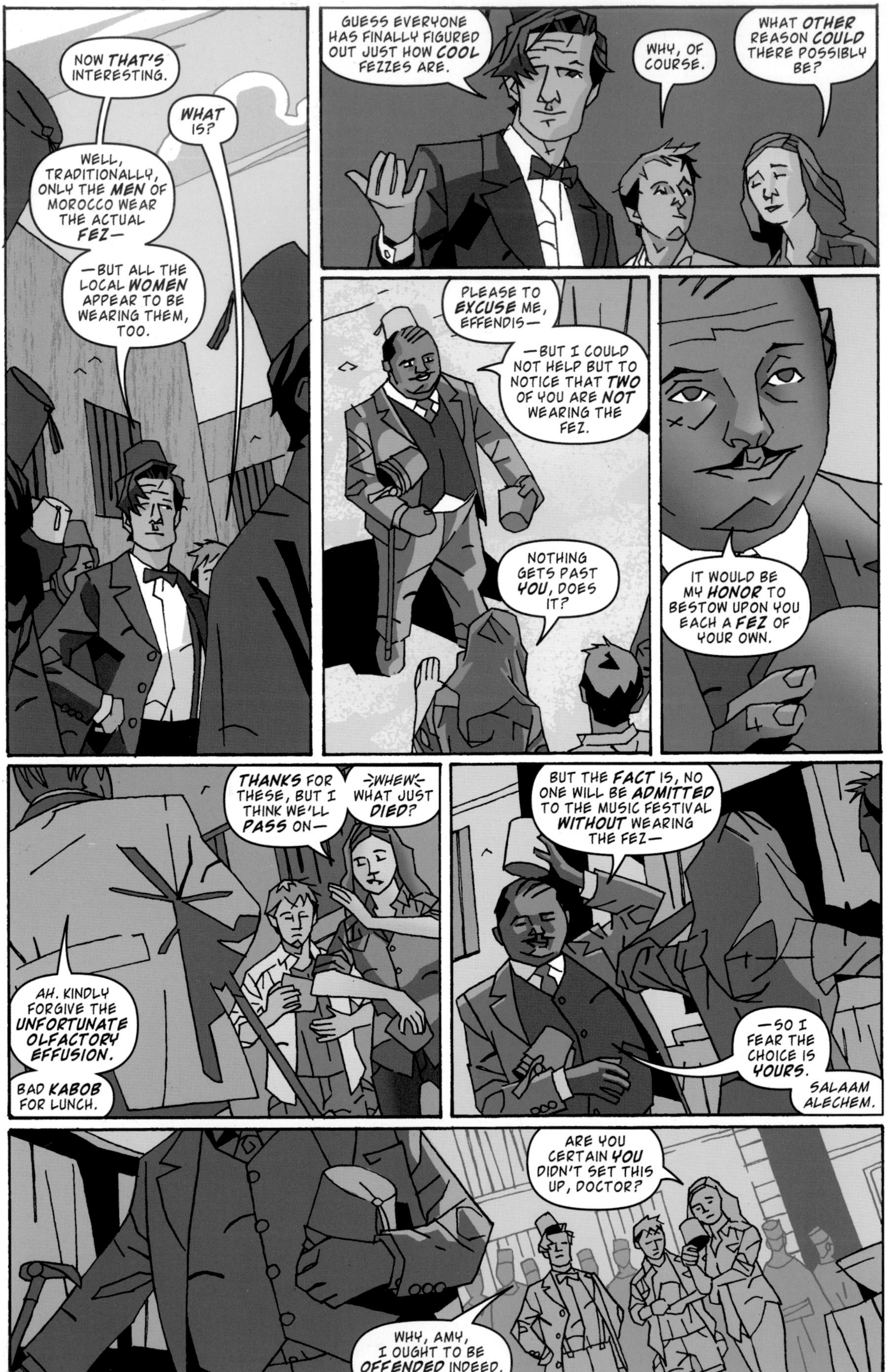
NOW THAT'S INTERESTING.
WHAT IS?
WELL, TRADITIONALLY, ONLY THE MEN OF MOROCCO WEAR THE ACTUAL FEZ—
—BUT ALL THE LOCAL WOMEN APPEAR TO BE WEARING THEM, TOO.
GUESS EVERYONE HAS FINALLY FIGURED OUT JUST HOW COOL FEZZES ARE.
WHY, OF COURSE.
WHAT OTHER REASON COULD THERE POSSIBLY BE?
PLEASE TO EXCUSE ME, EFFENDIS—
—BUT I COULD NOT HELP BUT TO NOTICE THAT TWO OF YOU ARE NOT WEARING THE FEZ.
NOTHING GETS PAST YOU, DOES IT?
IT WOULD BE MY HONOR TO BESTOW UPON YOU EACH A FEZ OF YOUR OWN.
THANKS FOR THESE, BUT I THINK WE'LL PASS ON—
-WHEW- WHAT JUST DIED?
AH. KINDLY FORGIVE THE UNFORTUNATE OLFACTORY EFFUSION.
BAD KABOB FOR LUNCH.
BUT THE FACT IS, NO ONE WILL BE ADMITTED TO THE MUSIC FESTIVAL WITHOUT WEARING THE FEZ—
—SO I FEAR THE CHOICE IS YOURS.
SALAAM ALECHEM.
ARE YOU CERTAIN YOU DIDN'T SET THIS UP, DOCTOR?
WHY, AMY, I OUGHT TO BE OFFENDED INDEED.

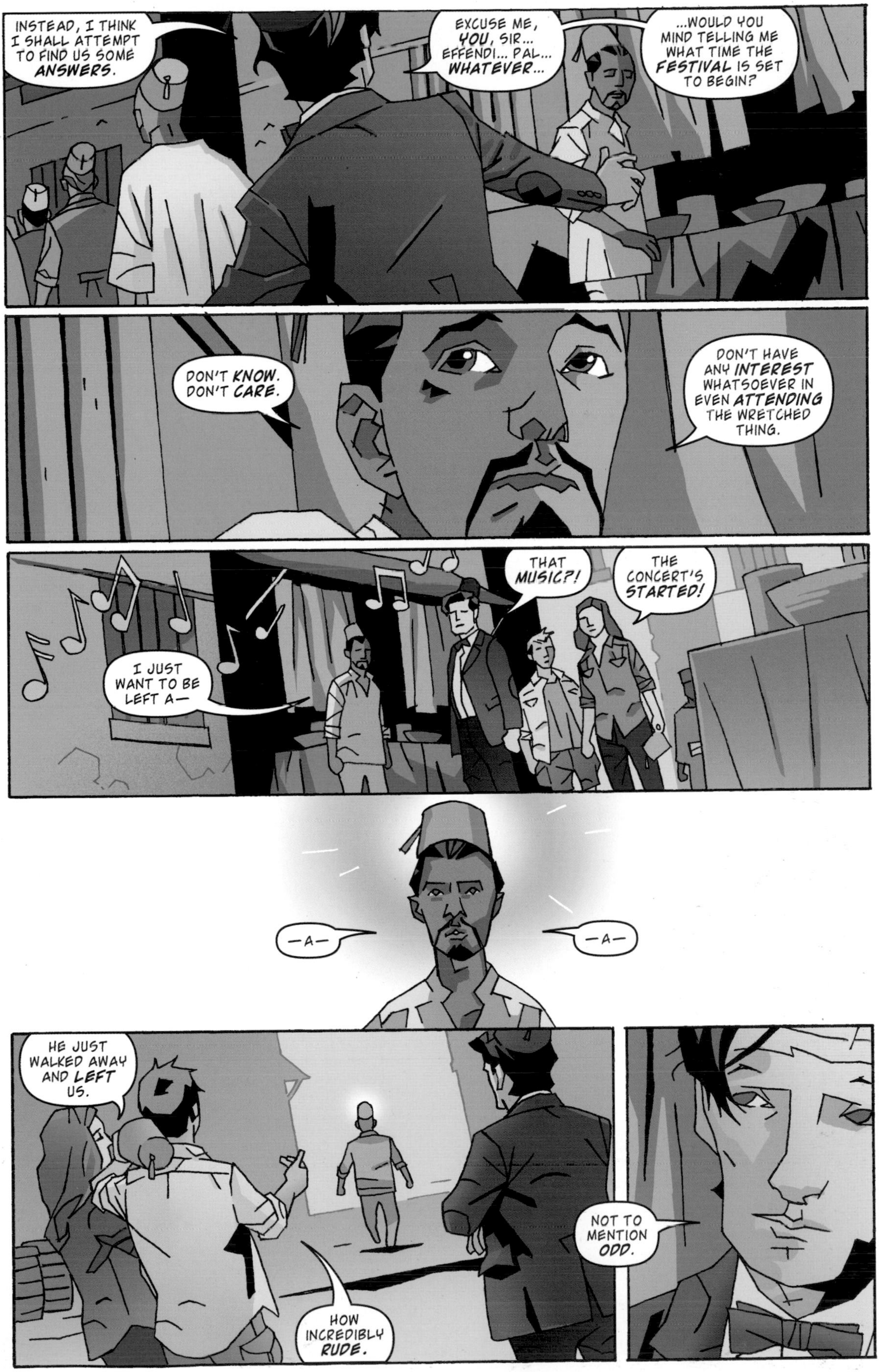
INSTEAD, I THINK I SHALL ATTEMPT TO FIND US SOME ANSWERS.
EXCUSE ME, YOU, SIR... EFFENDI... PAL... WHATEVER...
...WOULD YOU MIND TELLING ME WHAT TIME THE FESTIVAL IS SET TO BEGIN?
DON'T KNOW. DON'T CARE.
DON'T HAVE ANY INTEREST WHATSOEVER IN EVEN ATTENDING THE WRETCHED THING.
I JUST WANT TO BE LEFT A—
THAT MUSIC?!
THE CONCERT'S STARTED!
—A—
—A—
HE JUST WALKED AWAY AND LEFT US.
HOW INCREDIBLY RUDE.
NOT TO MENTION ODD.

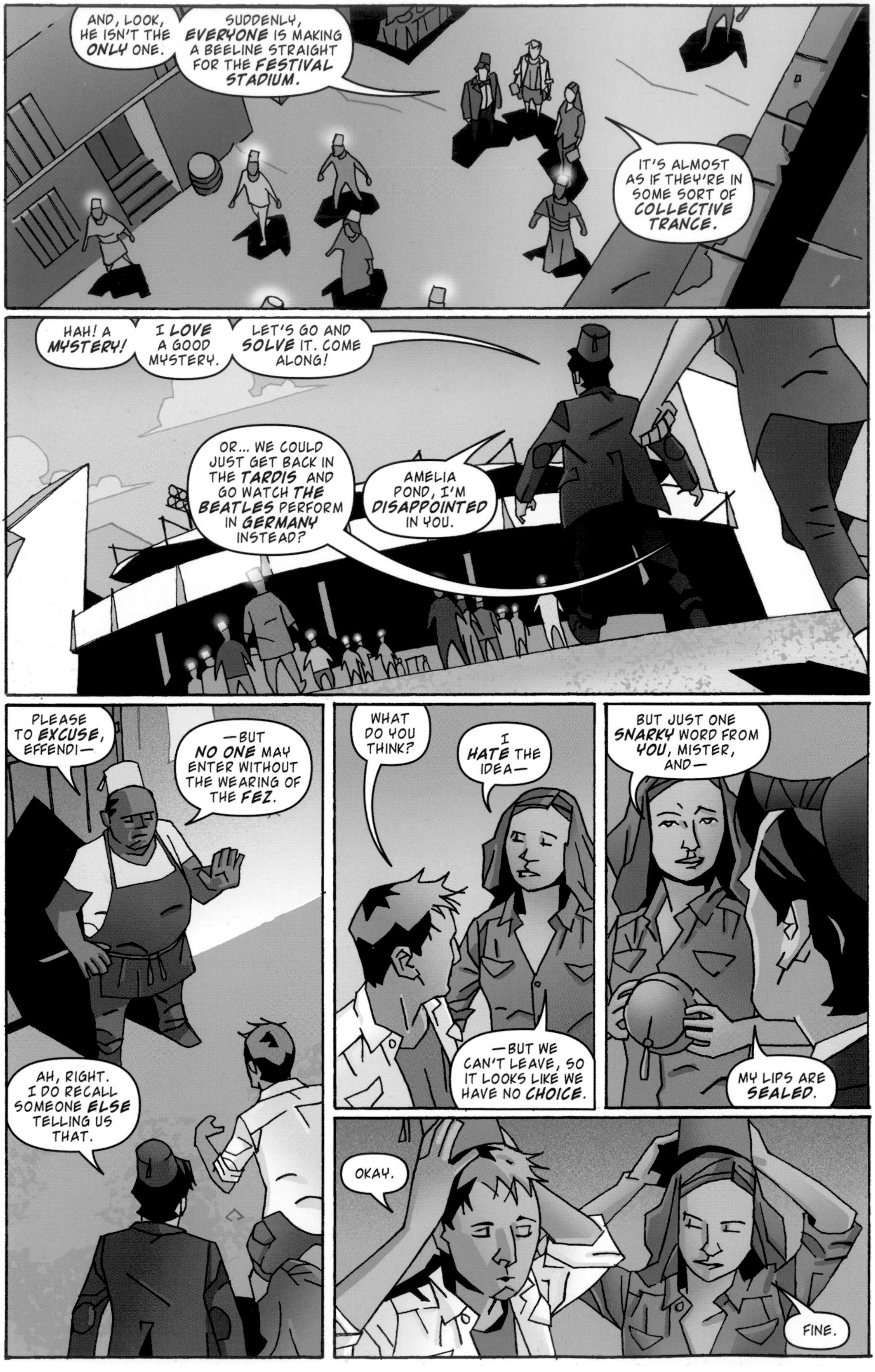
AND, LOOK, HE ISN'T THE ONLY ONE.
SUDDENLY, EVERYONE IS MAKING A BEELINE STRAIGHT FOR THE FESTIVAL STADIUM.
IT'S ALMOST AS IF THEY'RE IN SOME SORT OF COLLECTIVE TRANCE.
HAH! A MYSTERY!
I LOVE A GOOD MYSTERY.
LET'S GO AND SOLVE IT. COME ALONG!
OR... WE COULD JUST GET BACK IN THE TARDIS AND GO WATCH THE BEATLES PERFORM IN GERMANY INSTEAD?
AMELIA POND, I'M DISAPPOINTED IN YOU.
PLEASE TO EXCUSE, EFFENDI—
—BUT NO ONE MAY ENTER WITHOUT THE WEARING OF THE FEZ.
AH, RIGHT. I DO RECALL SOMEONE ELSE TELLING US THAT.
WHAT DO YOU THINK?
I HATE THE IDEA—
—BUT WE CAN'T LEAVE, SO IT LOOKS LIKE WE HAVE NO CHOICE.
BUT JUST ONE SNARKY WORD FROM YOU, MISTER, AND—
MY LIPS ARE SEALED.
OKAY.
FINE.

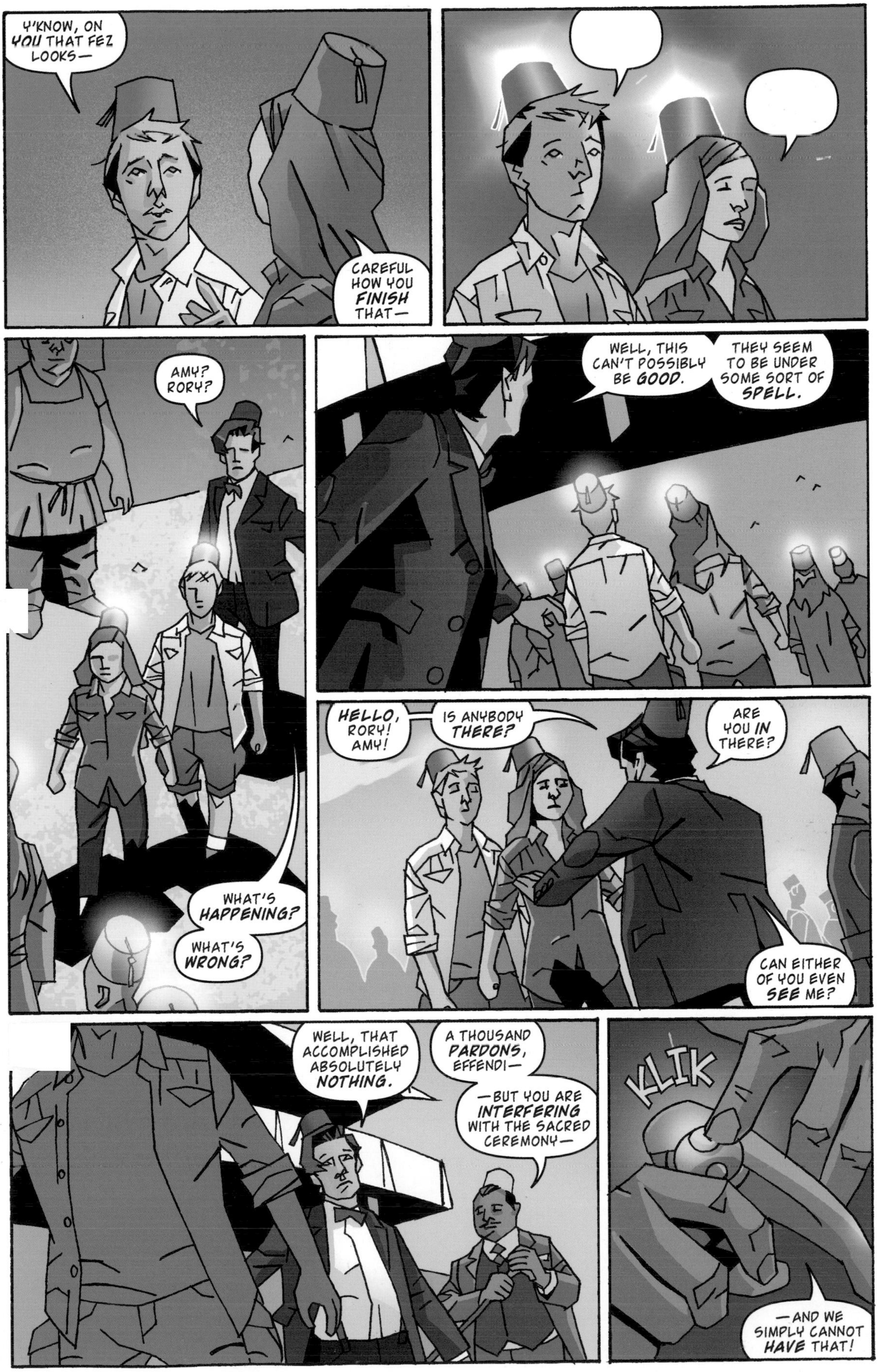
Y'KNOW, ON YOU THAT FEZ LOOKS—
CAREFUL HOW YOU FINISH THAT—
AMY? RORY?
WHAT'S HAPPENING?
WHAT'S WRONG?
WELL, THIS CAN'T POSSIBLY BE GOOD.
THEY SEEM TO BE UNDER SOME SORT OF SPELL.
HELLO, RORY! AMY!
IS ANYBODY THERE?
ARE YOU IN THERE?
CAN EITHER OF YOU EVEN SEE ME?
WELL, THAT ACCOMPLISHED ABSOLUTELY NOTHING.
A THOUSAND PARDONS, EFFENDI—
—BUT YOU ARE INTERFERING WITH THE SACRED CEREMONY—
KLIK
—AND WE SIMPLY CANNOT HAVE THAT!

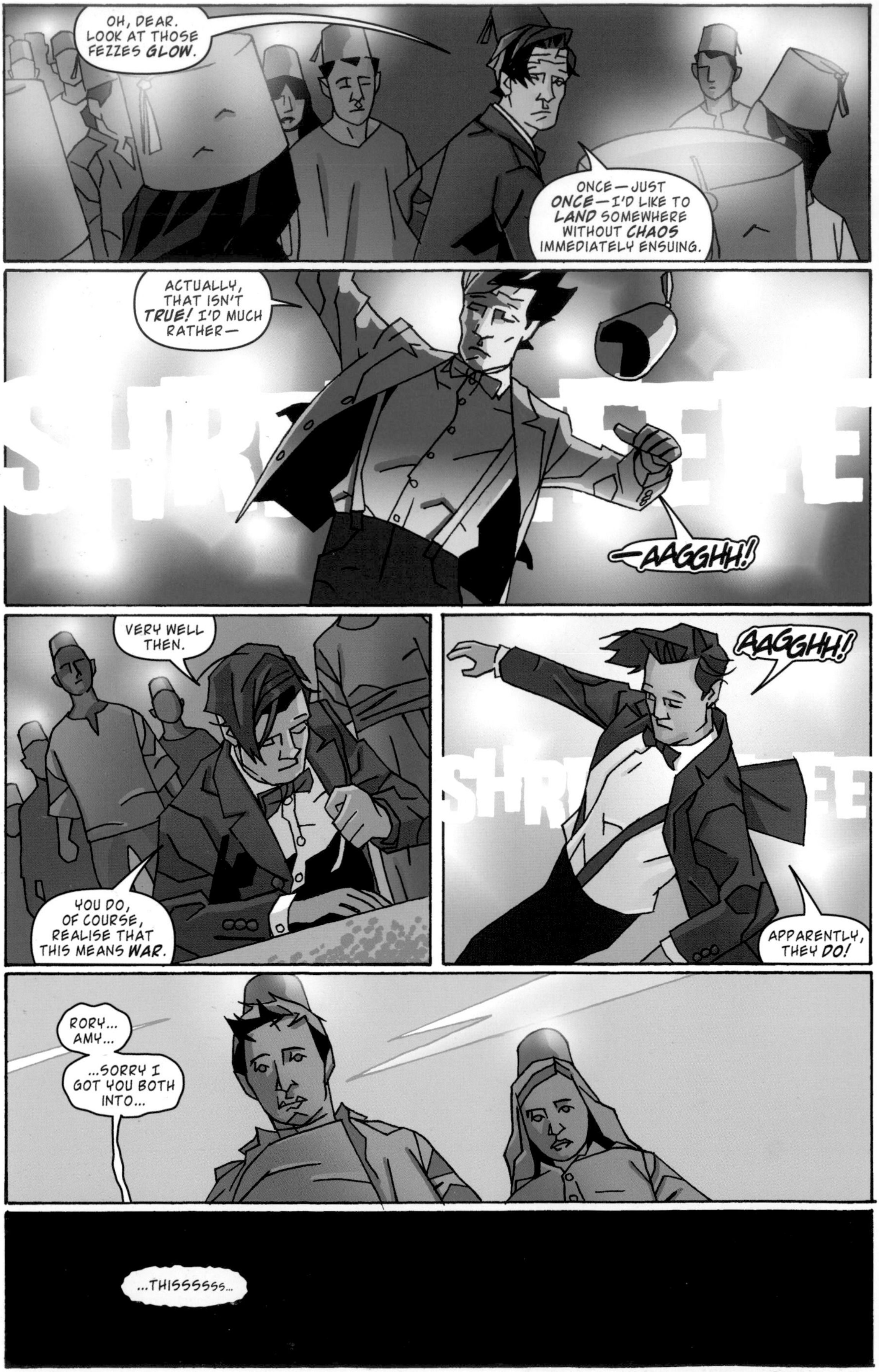
OH, DEAR. LOOK AT THOSE FEZZES GLOW.
ONCE—JUST ONCE—I'D LIKE TO LAND SOMEWHERE WITHOUT CHAOS IMMEDIATELY ENSUING.
ACTUALLY, THAT ISN'T TRUE! I'D MUCH RATHER—
—AAGGHH!
VERY WELL THEN.
YOU DO, OF COURSE, REALISE THAT THIS MEANS WAR.
AAGGHH!
APPARENTLY, THEY DO!
RORY... AMY...
...SORRY I GOT YOU BOTH INTO...
...THISSSSSS...

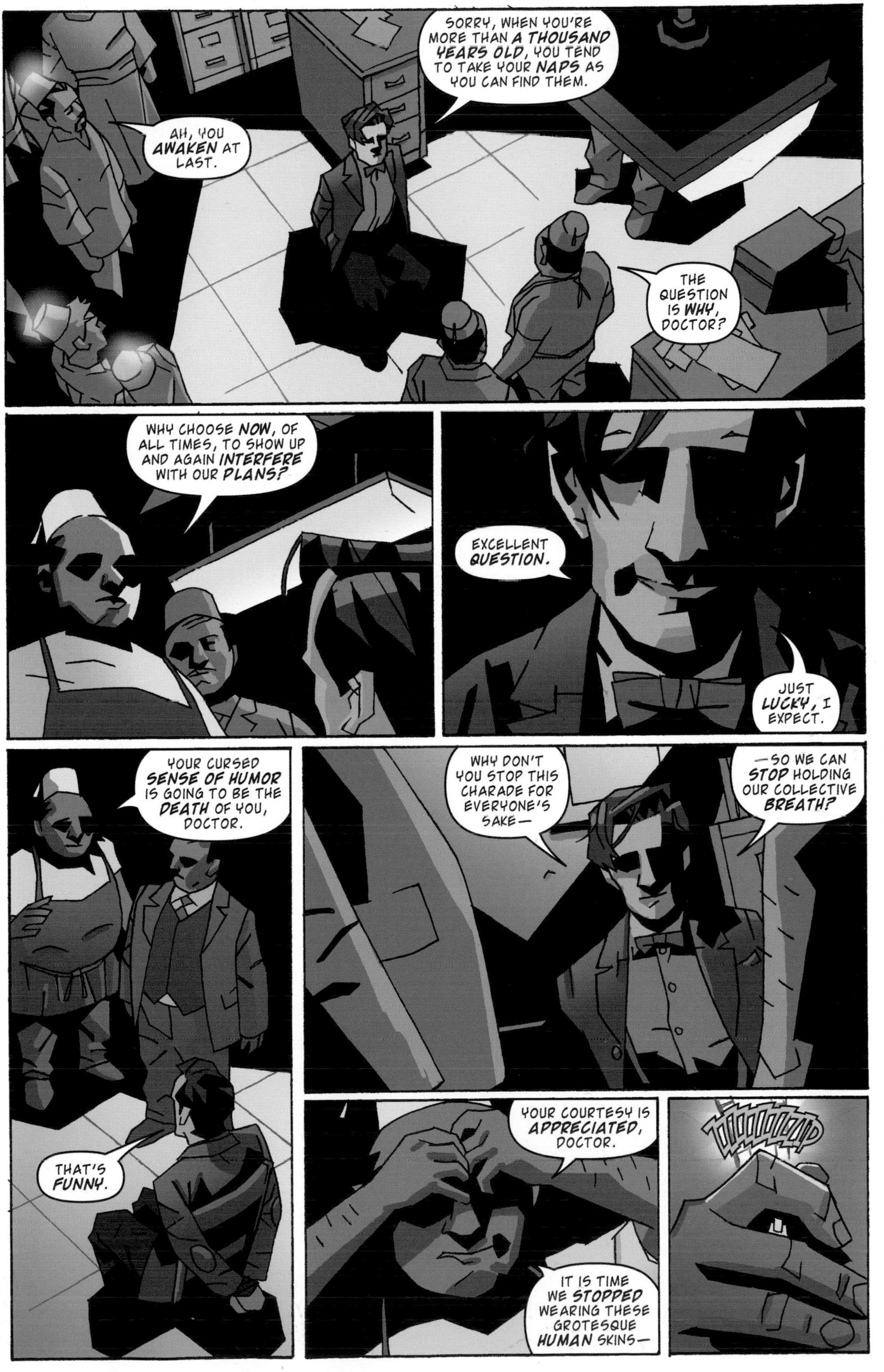
AH, YOU AWAKEN AT LAST.
SORRY, WHEN YOU'RE MORE THAN A THOUSAND YEARS OLD, YOU TEND TO TAKE YOUR NAPS AS YOU CAN FIND THEM.
THE QUESTION IS WHY, DOCTOR?
WHY CHOOSE NOW, OF ALL TIMES, TO SHOW UP AND AGAIN INTERFERE WITH OUR PLANS?
EXCELLENT QUESTION.
JUST LUCKY, I EXPECT.
YOUR CURSED SENSE OF HUMOR IS GOING TO BE THE DEATH OF YOU, DOCTOR.
THAT'S FUNNY.
WHY DON'T YOU STOP THIS CHARADE FOR EVERYONE'S SAKE—
—SO WE CAN STOP HOLDING OUR COLLECTIVE BREATH?
YOUR COURTESY IS APPRECIATED, DOCTOR.
IT IS TIME WE STOPPED WEARING THESE GROTESQUE HUMAN SKINS—
ZZZZZZIP

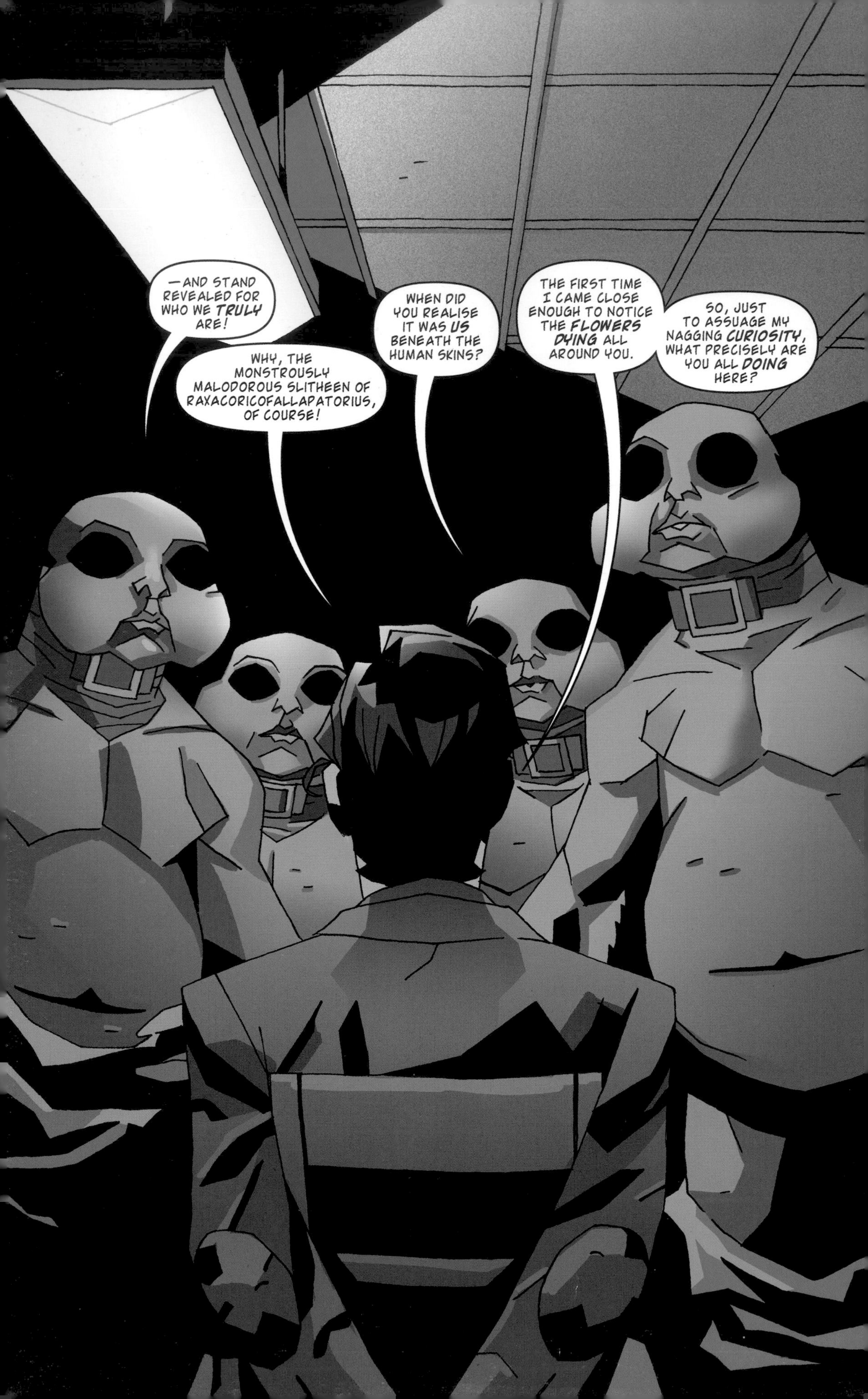
—AND STAND REVEALED FOR WHO WE TRULY ARE!
WHY, THE MONSTROUSLY MALODOROUS SLITHEEN OF RAXACORICOFALLAPATORIUS, OF COURSE!
WHEN DID YOU REALISE IT WAS US BENEATH THE HUMAN SKINS?
THE FIRST TIME I CAME CLOSE ENOUGH TO NOTICE THE FLOWERS DYING ALL AROUND YOU.
SO, JUST TO ASSUAGE MY NAGGING CURIOSITY, WHAT PRECISELY ARE YOU ALL DOING HERE?

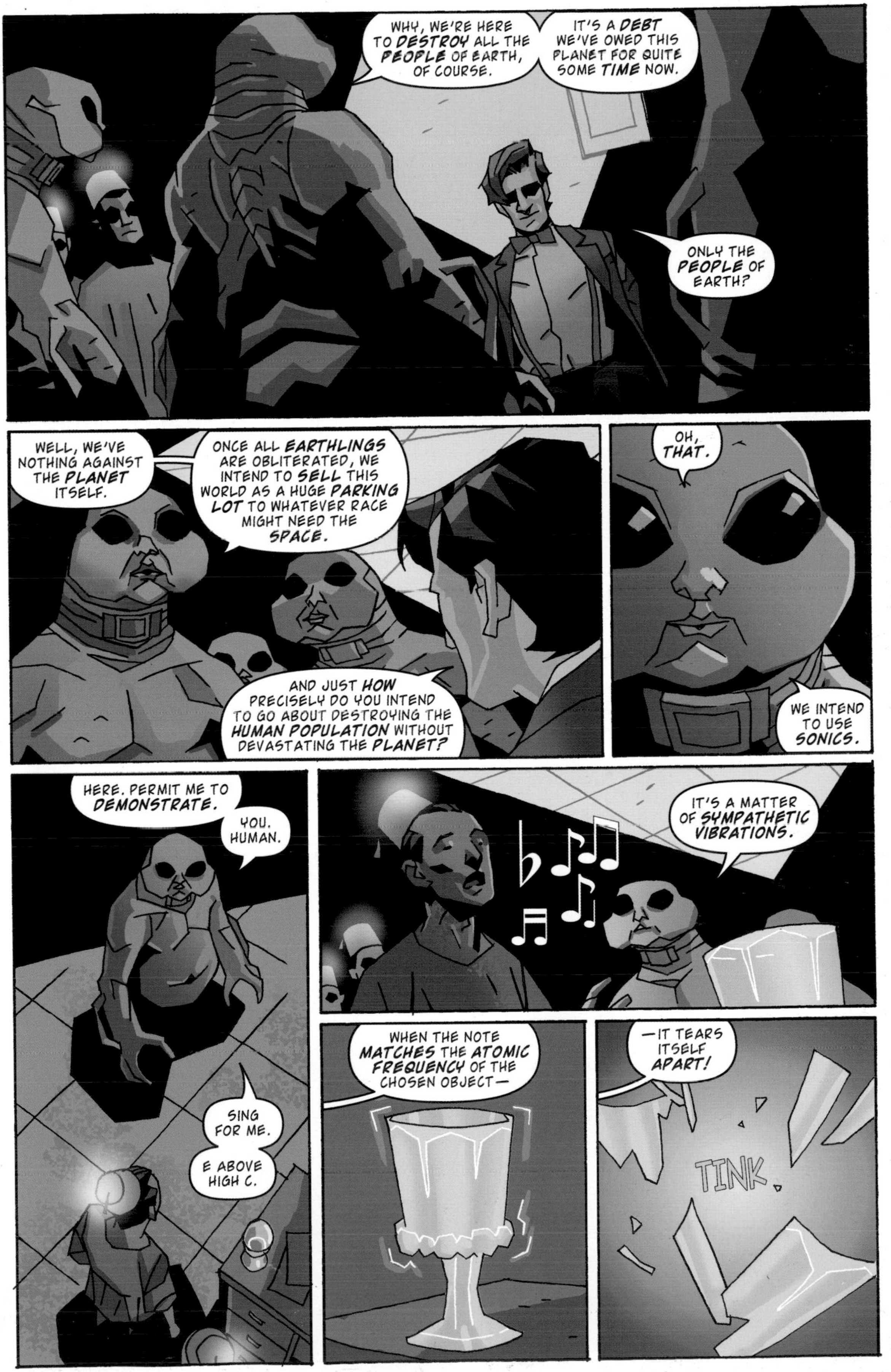
WHY, WE'RE HERE TO DESTROY ALL THE PEOPLE OF EARTH, OF COURSE.
IT'S A DEBT WE'VE OWED THIS PLANET FOR QUITE SOME TIME NOW.
ONLY THE PEOPLE OF EARTH?
WELL, WE'VE NOTHING AGAINST THE PLANET ITSELF.
ONCE ALL EARTHLINGS ARE OBLITERATED, WE INTEND TO SELL THIS WORLD AS A HUGE PARKING LOT TO WHATEVER RACE MIGHT NEED THE SPACE.
AND JUST HOW PRECISELY DO YOU INTEND TO GO ABOUT DESTROYING THE HUMAN POPULATION WITHOUT DEVASTATING THE PLANET?
OH, THAT.
WE INTEND TO USE SONICS.
HERE. PERMIT ME TO DEMONSTRATE.
YOU. HUMAN.
SING FOR ME.
E ABOVE HIGH C.
IT'S A MATTER OF SYMPATHETIC VIBRATIONS.
WHEN THE NOTE MATCHES THE ATOMIC FREQUENCY OF THE CHOSEN OBJECT—
—IT TEARS ITSELF APART!
TINK

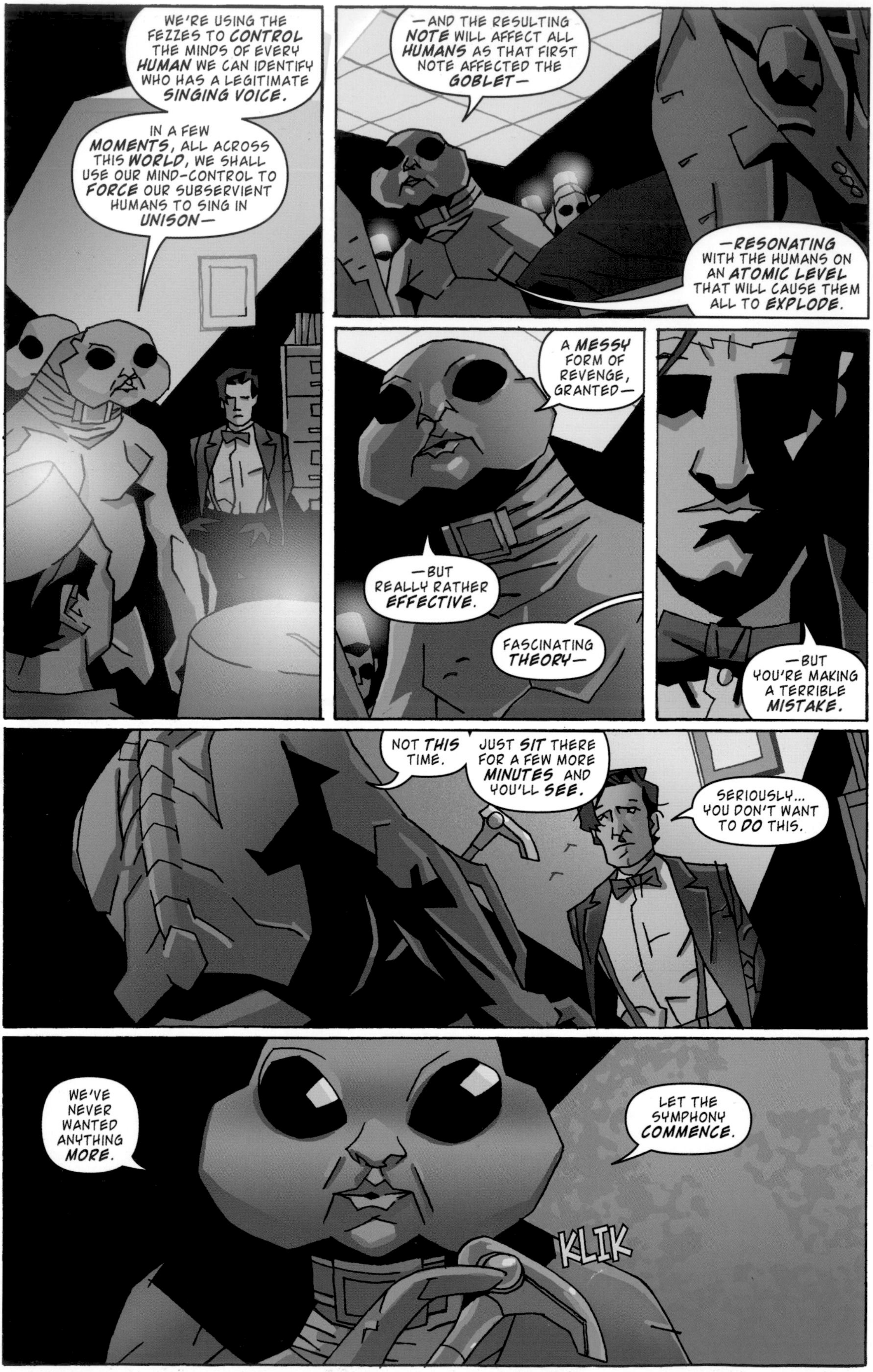
WE'RE USING THE FEZZES TO CONTROL THE MINDS OF EVERY HUMAN WE CAN IDENTIFY WHO HAS A LEGITIMATE SINGING VOICE.
IN A FEW MOMENTS, ALL ACROSS THIS WORLD, WE SHALL USE OUR MIND-CONTROL TO FORCE OUR SUBSERVIENT HUMANS TO SING IN UNISON—
—AND THE RESULTING NOTE WILL AFFECT ALL HUMANS AS THAT FIRST NOTE AFFECTED THE GOBLET—
—RESONATING WITH THE HUMANS ON AN ATOMIC LEVEL THAT WILL CAUSE THEM ALL TO EXPLODE.
A MESSY FORM OF REVENGE, GRANTED—
—BUT REALLY RATHER EFFECTIVE.
FASCINATING THEORY—
—BUT YOU'RE MAKING A TERRIBLE MISTAKE.
NOT THIS TIME.
JUST SIT THERE FOR A FEW MORE MINUTES AND YOU'LL SEE.
SERIOUSLY... YOU DON'T WANT TO DO THIS.
WE'VE NEVER WANTED ANYTHING MORE.
LET THE SYMPHONY COMMENCE.
KLIK

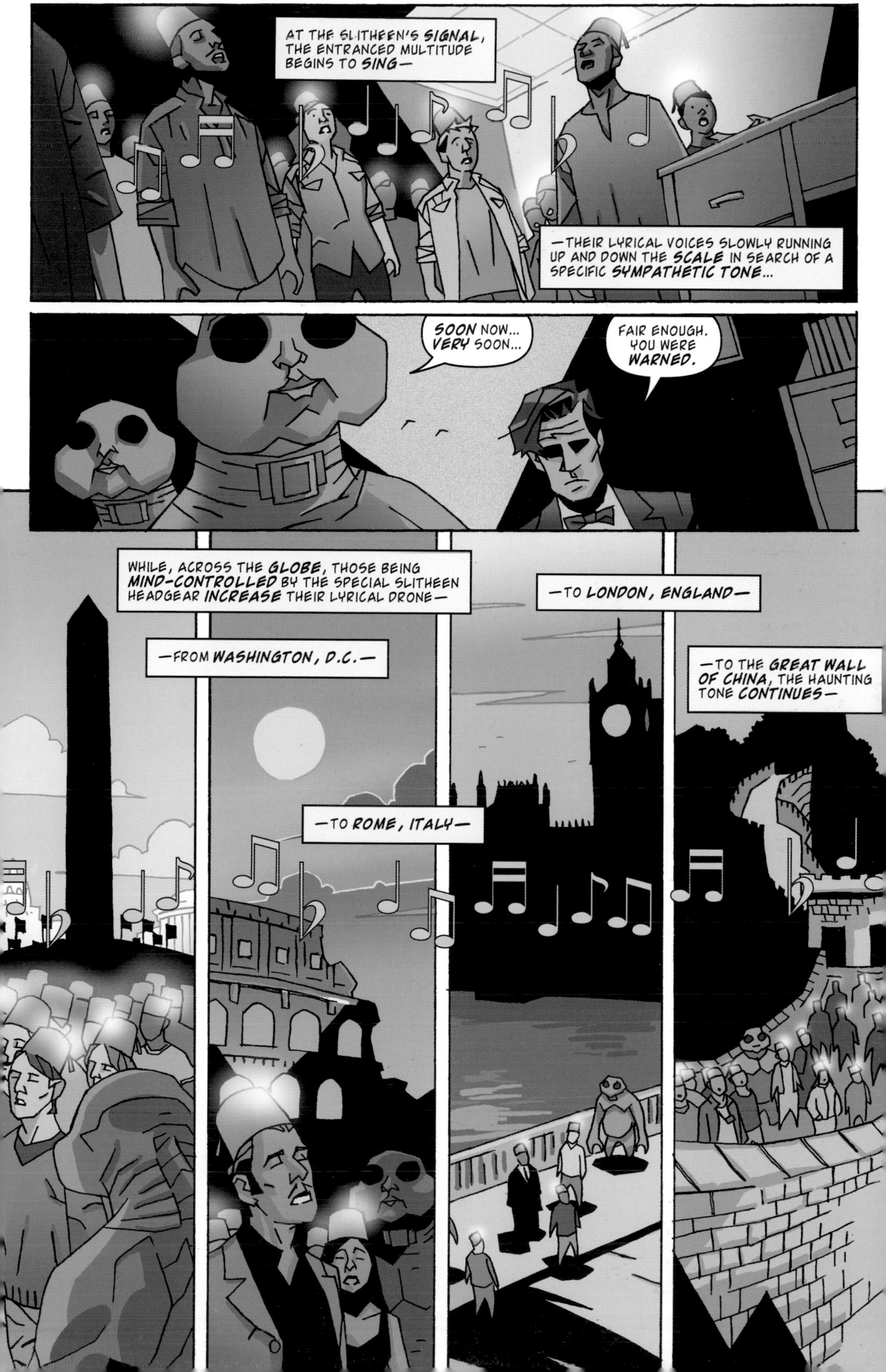
AT THE SLITHEEN'S SIGNAL, THE ENTRANCED MULTITUDE BEGINS TO SING—
—THEIR LYRICAL VOICES SLOWLY RUNNING UP AND DOWN THE SCALE IN SEARCH OF A SPECIFIC SYMPATHETIC TONE...
SOON NOW... VERY SOON...
FAIR ENOUGH. YOU WERE WARNED.
WHILE, ACROSS THE GLOBE, THOSE BEING MIND-CONTROLLED BY THE SPECIAL SLITHEEN HEADGEAR INCREASE THEIR LYRICAL DRONE—
—FROM WASHINGTON, D.C.—
—TO ROME, ITALY—
—TO LONDON, ENGLAND—
—TO THE GREAT WALL OF CHINA, THE HAUNTING TONE CONTINUES—

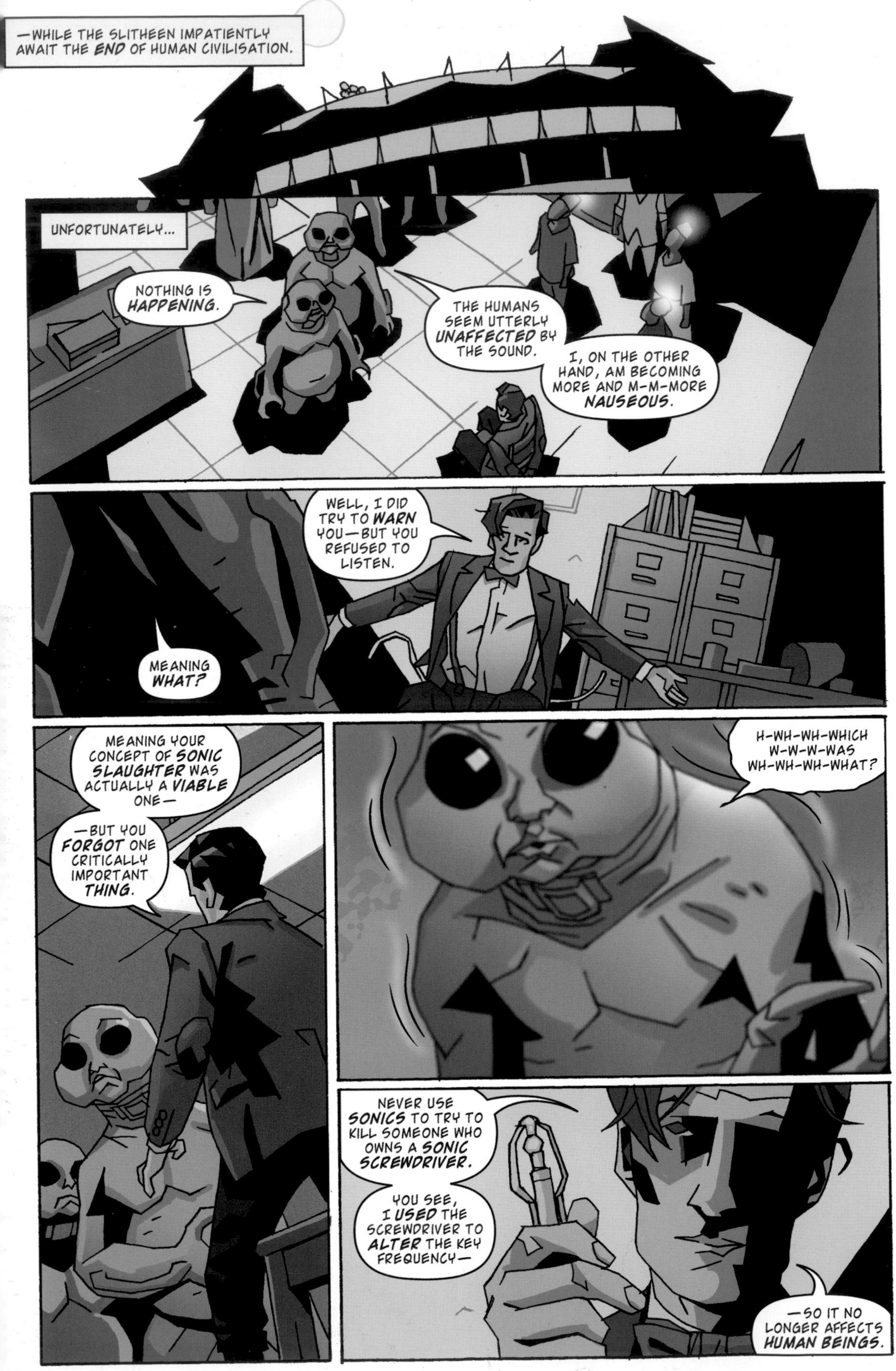
—WHILE THE SLITHEEN IMPATIENTLY AWAIT THE END OF HUMAN CIVILISATION.
UNFORTUNATELY...
NOTHING IS HAPPENING.
THE HUMANS SEEM UTTERLY UNAFFECTED BY THE SOUND.
I, ON THE OTHER HAND, AM BECOMING MORE AND M-M-MORE NAUSEOUS.
WELL, I DID TRY TO WARN YOU—BUT YOU REFUSED TO LISTEN.
MEANING WHAT?
MEANING YOUR CONCEPT OF SONIC SLAUGHTER WAS ACTUALLY A VIABLE ONE—
—BUT YOU FORGOT ONE CRITICALLY IMPORTANT THING.
H-WH-WH-WHICH W-W-W-WAS WH-WH-WH-WHAT?
NEVER USE SONICS TO TRY TO KILL SOMEONE WHO OWNS A SONIC SCREWDRIVER.
YOU SEE, I USED THE SCREWDRIVER TO ALTER THE KEY FREQUENCY—
—SO IT NO LONGER AFFECTS HUMAN BEINGS.

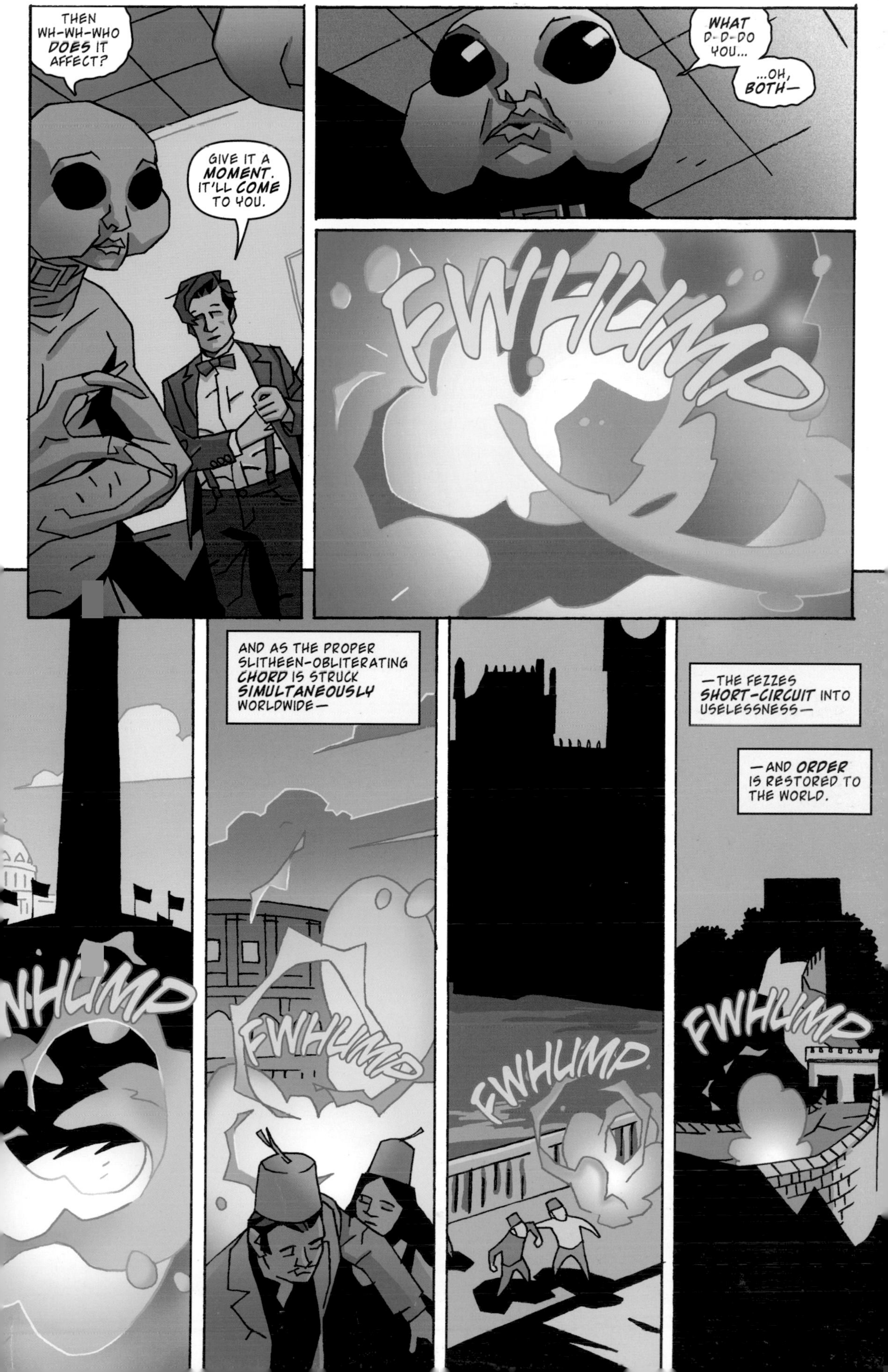
THEN WH-WH-WHO DOES IT AFFECT?
GIVE IT A MOMENT. IT'LL COME TO YOU.
WHAT D-D-DO YOU...
...OH, BOTH—
FWHUMP
AND AS THE PROPER SLITHEEN-OBLITERATING CHORD IS STRUCK SIMULTANEOUSLY WORLDWIDE—
FWHUMP
FWHUMP
FWHUMP
—THE FEZZES SHORT-CIRCUIT INTO USELESSNESS—
—AND ORDER IS RESTORED TO THE WORLD.
FWHUMP

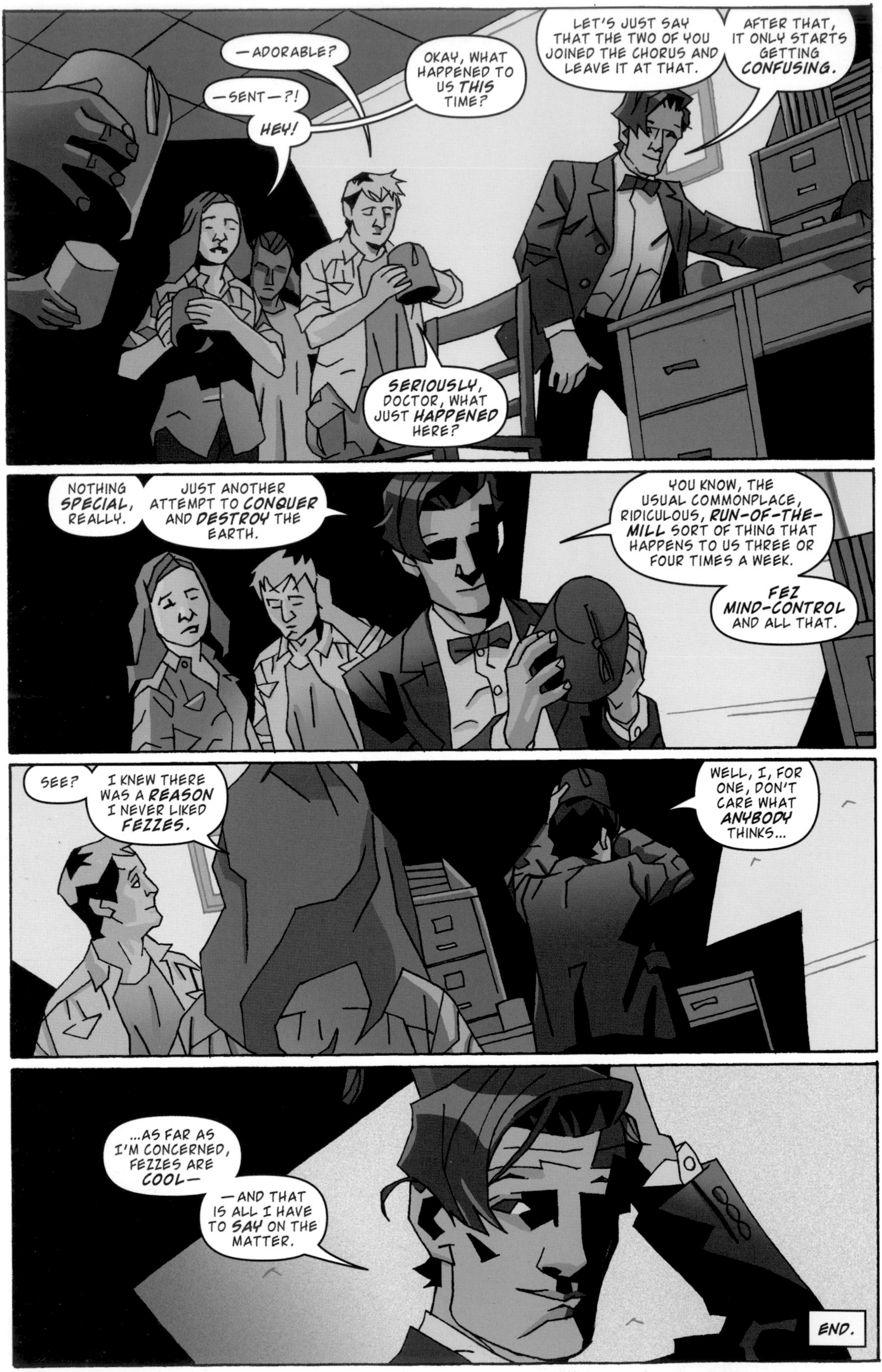
—ADORABLE?
—SENT—?!
HEY!
OKAY, WHAT HAPPENED TO US THIS TIME?
LET'S JUST SAY THAT THE TWO OF YOU JOINED THE CHORUS AND LEAVE IT AT THAT.
AFTER THAT, IT ONLY STARTS GETTING CONFUSING.
SERIOUSLY, DOCTOR, WHAT JUST HAPPENED HERE?
NOTHING SPECIAL, REALLY.
JUST ANOTHER ATTEMPT TO CONQUER AND DESTROY THE EARTH.
YOU KNOW, THE USUAL COMMONPLACE, RIDICULOUS, RUN-OF-THE-MILL SORT OF THING THAT HAPPENS TO US THREE OR FOUR TIMES A WEEK.
FEZ MIND-CONTROL AND ALL THAT.
SEE?
I KNEW THERE WAS A REASON I NEVER LIKED FEZZES.
WELL, I, FOR ONE, DON'T CARE WHAT ANYBODY THINKS...
...AS FAR AS I'M CONCERNED, FEZZES ARE COOL—
—AND THAT IS ALL I HAVE TO SAY ON THE MATTER.
END.

BBC

DOCTOR WHO

ART GALLERY

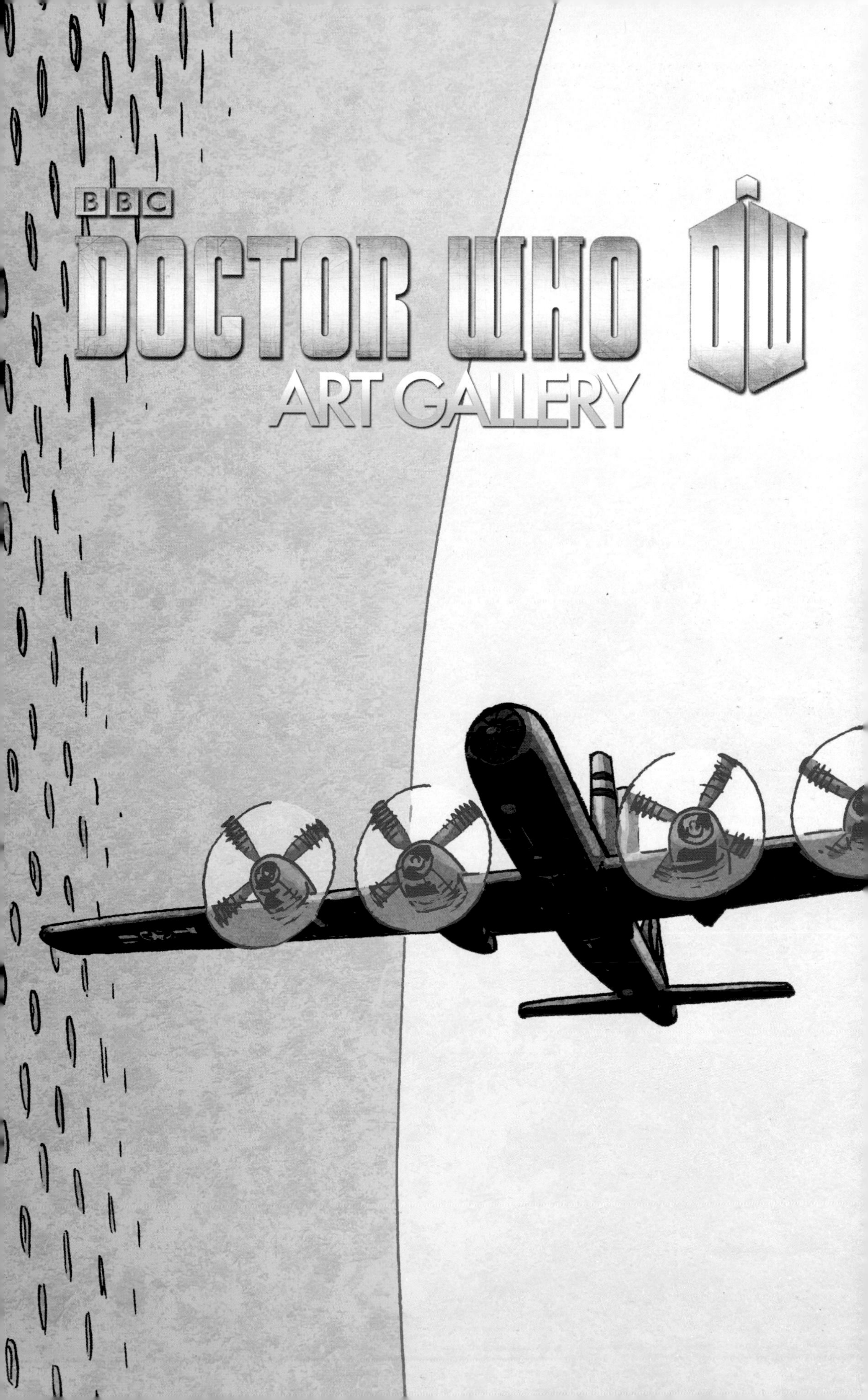

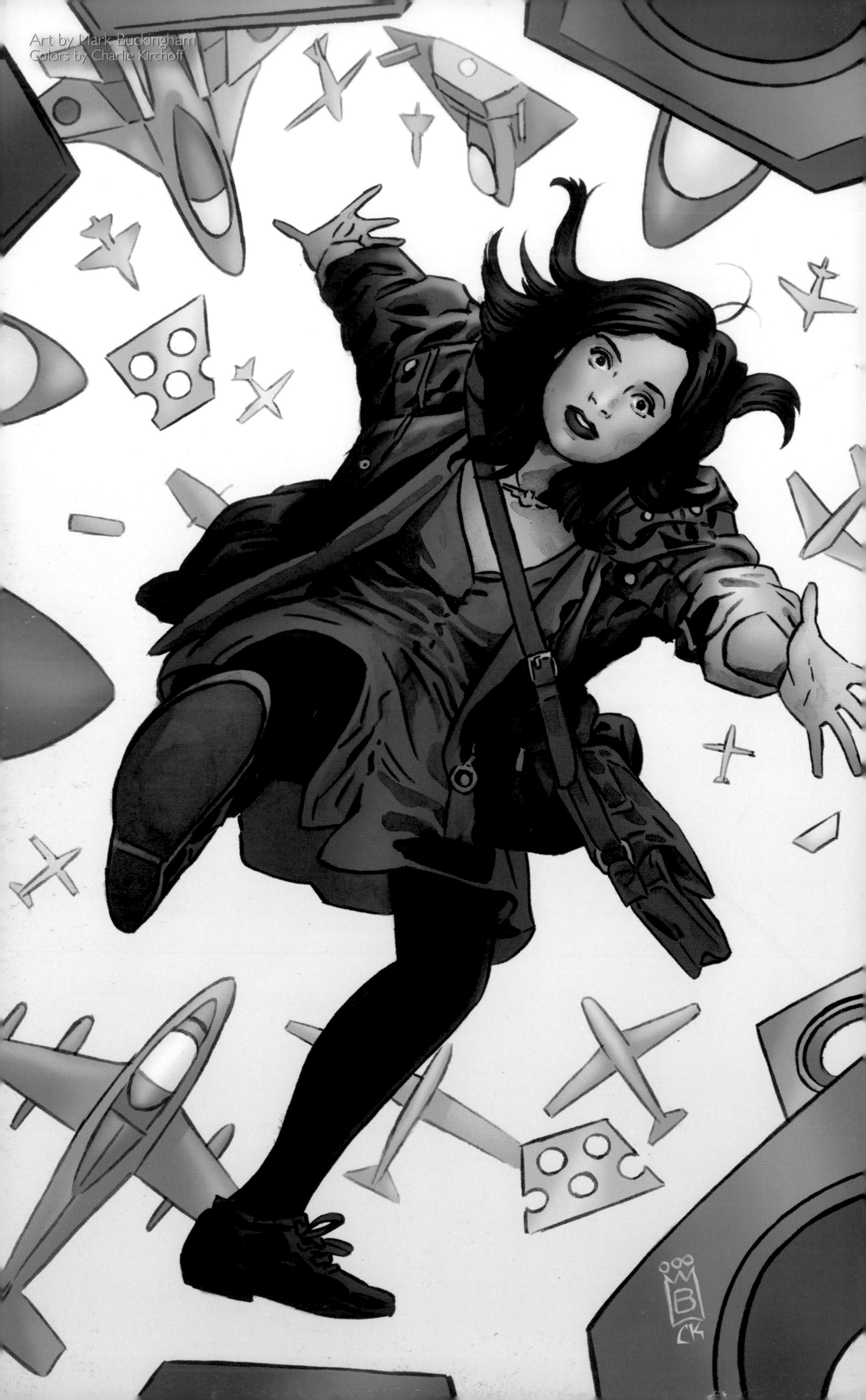

Art by Mark Buckingham
Colors by Charlie Kirchoff

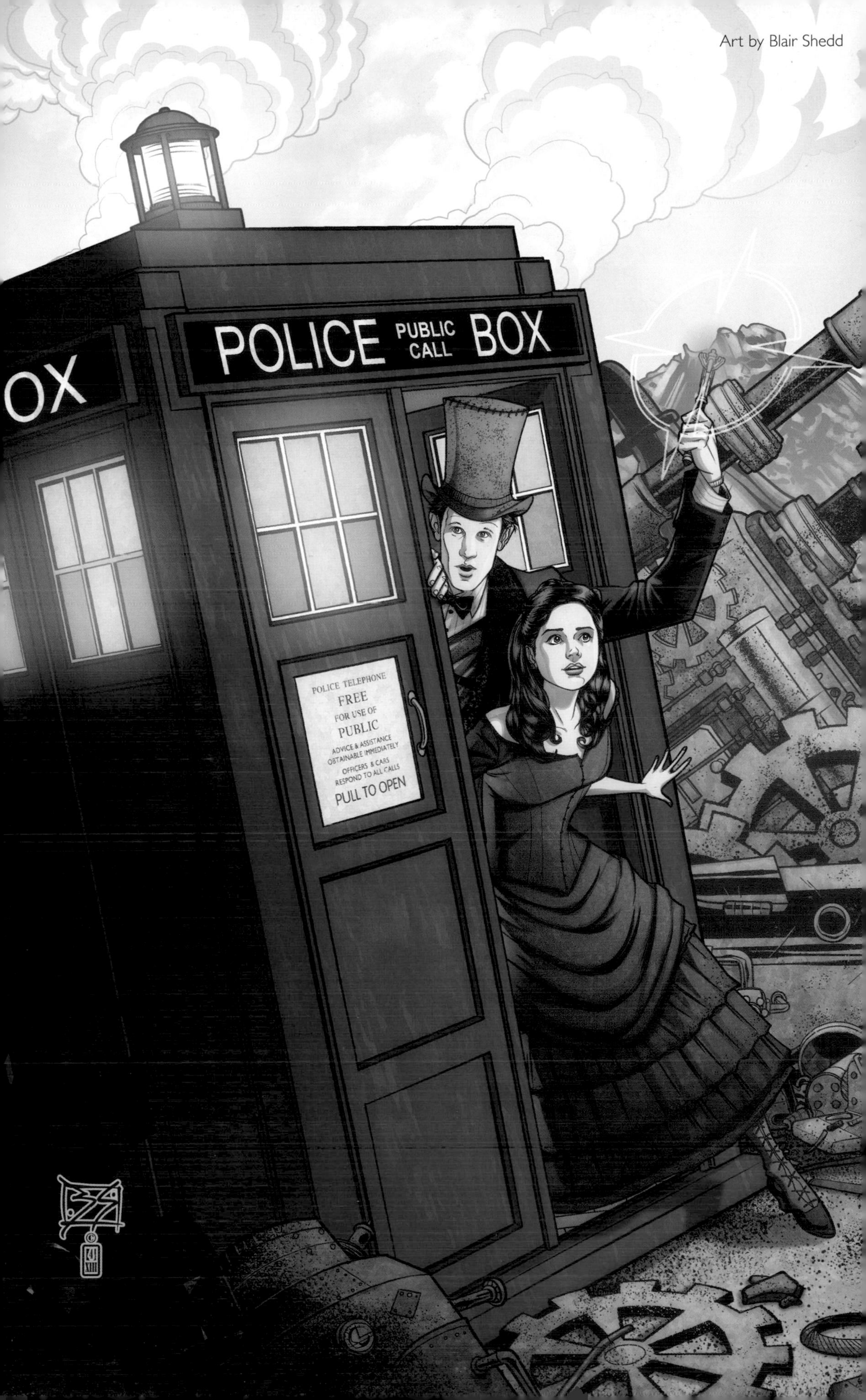
POLICE PUBLIC CALL BOX
OX
POLICE TELEPHONE
FREE
FOR USE OF
PUBLIC
ADVICE & ASSISTANCE
OBTAINABLE IMMEDIATELY
OFFICERS & CARS
RESPOND TO ALL CALLS
PULL TO OPEN

Art by Blair Shedd

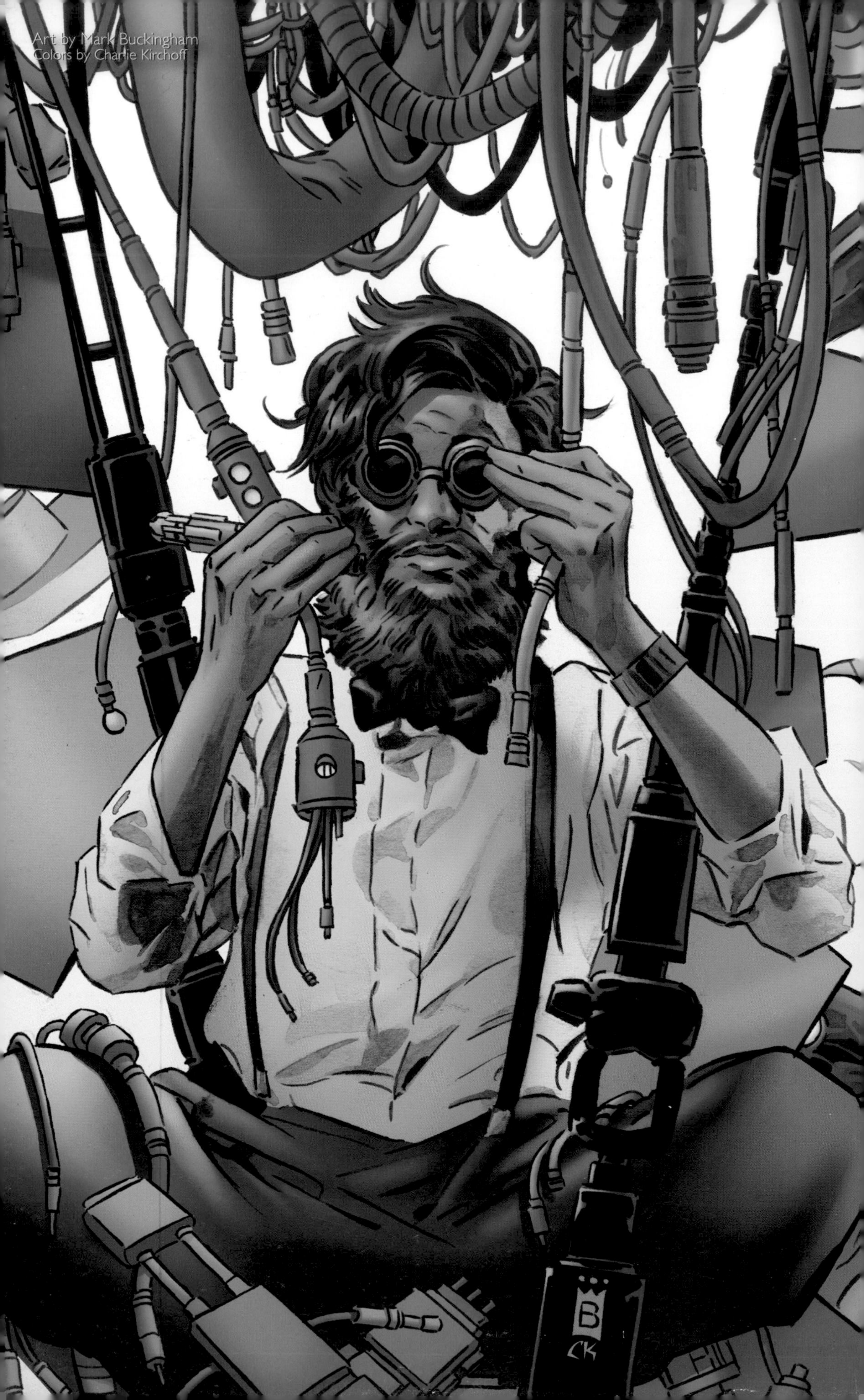

Art by Mark Buckingham
Colors by Charlie Kirchoff

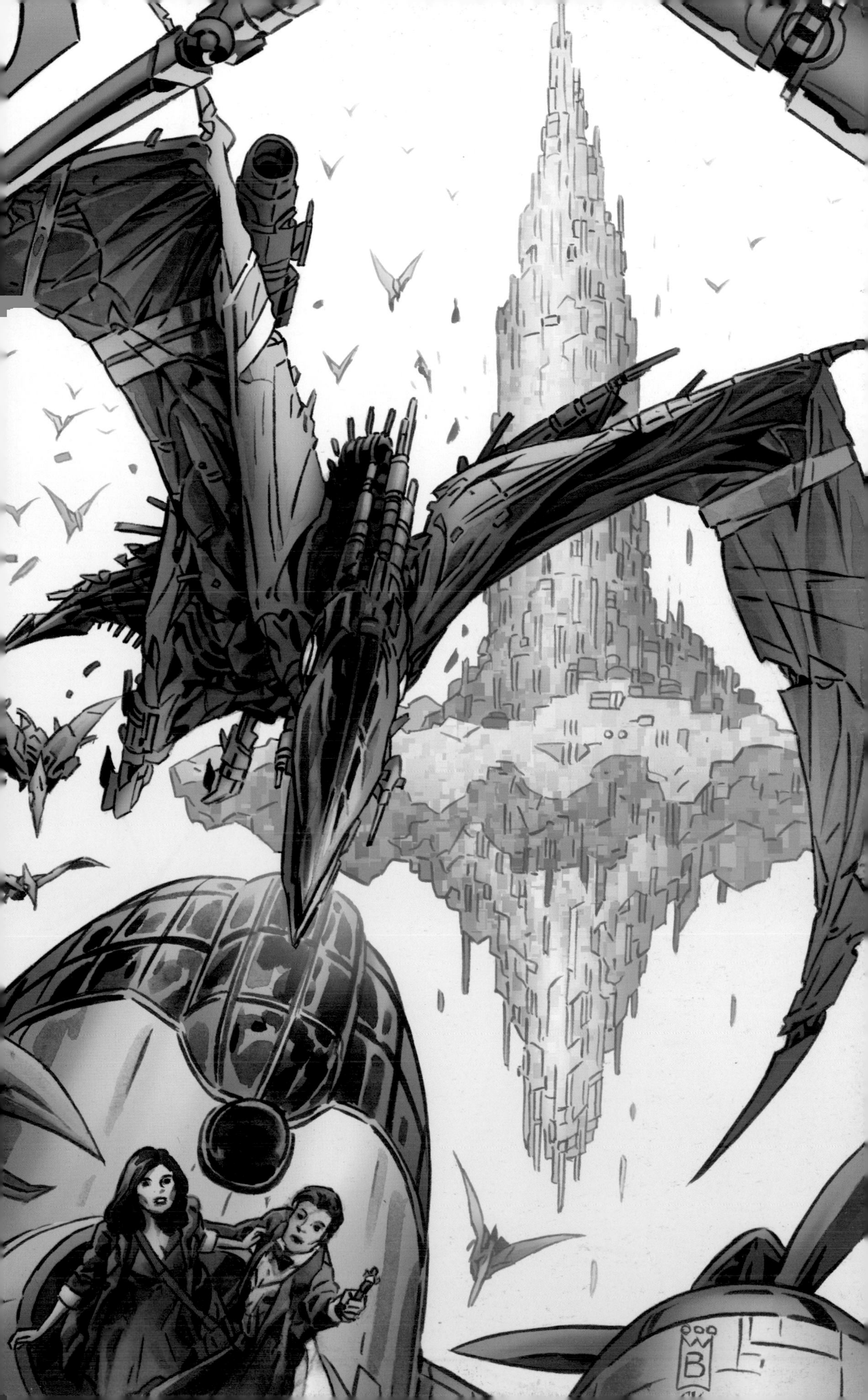

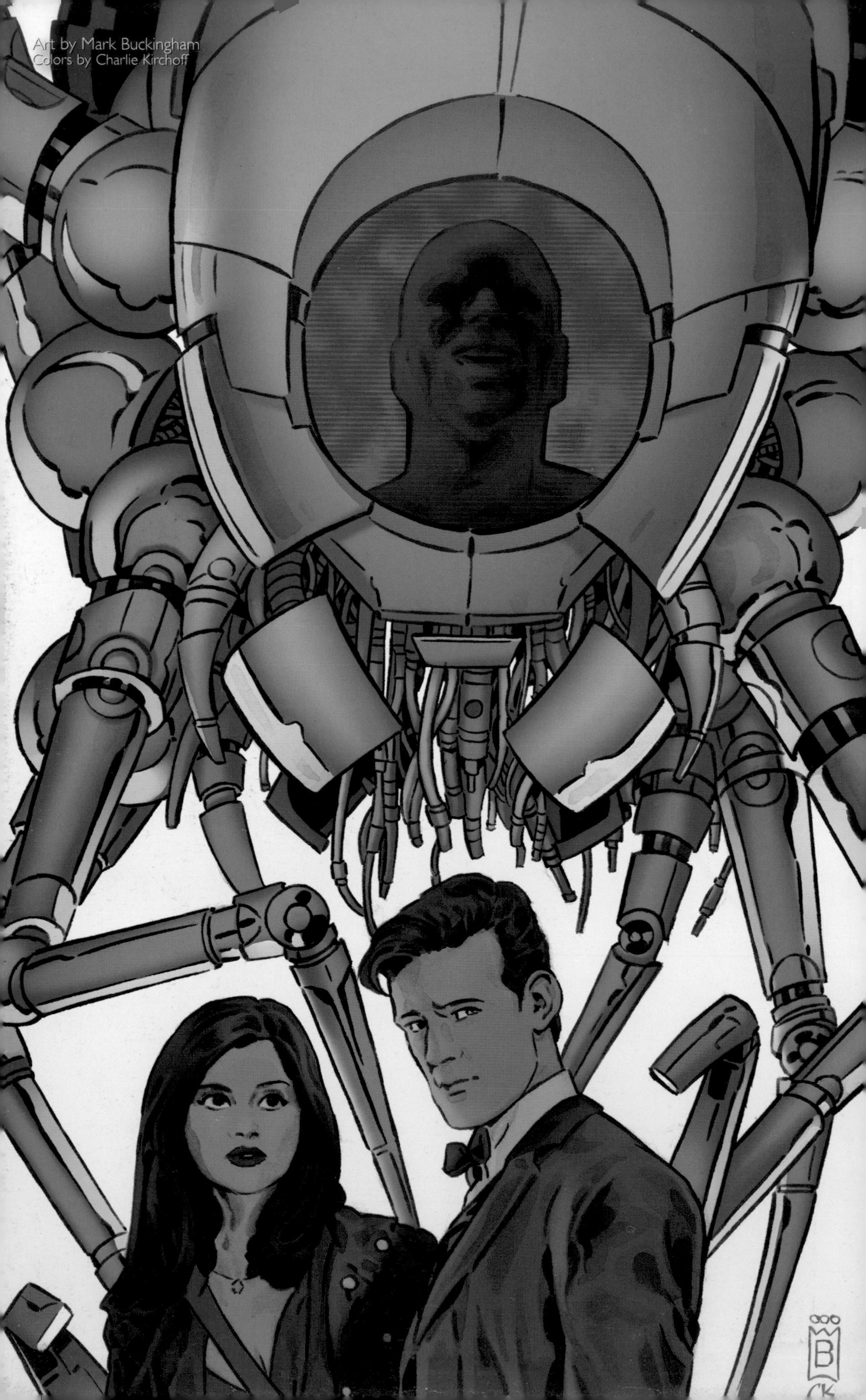

Art by Mark Buckingham
Colors by Charlie Kirchoff

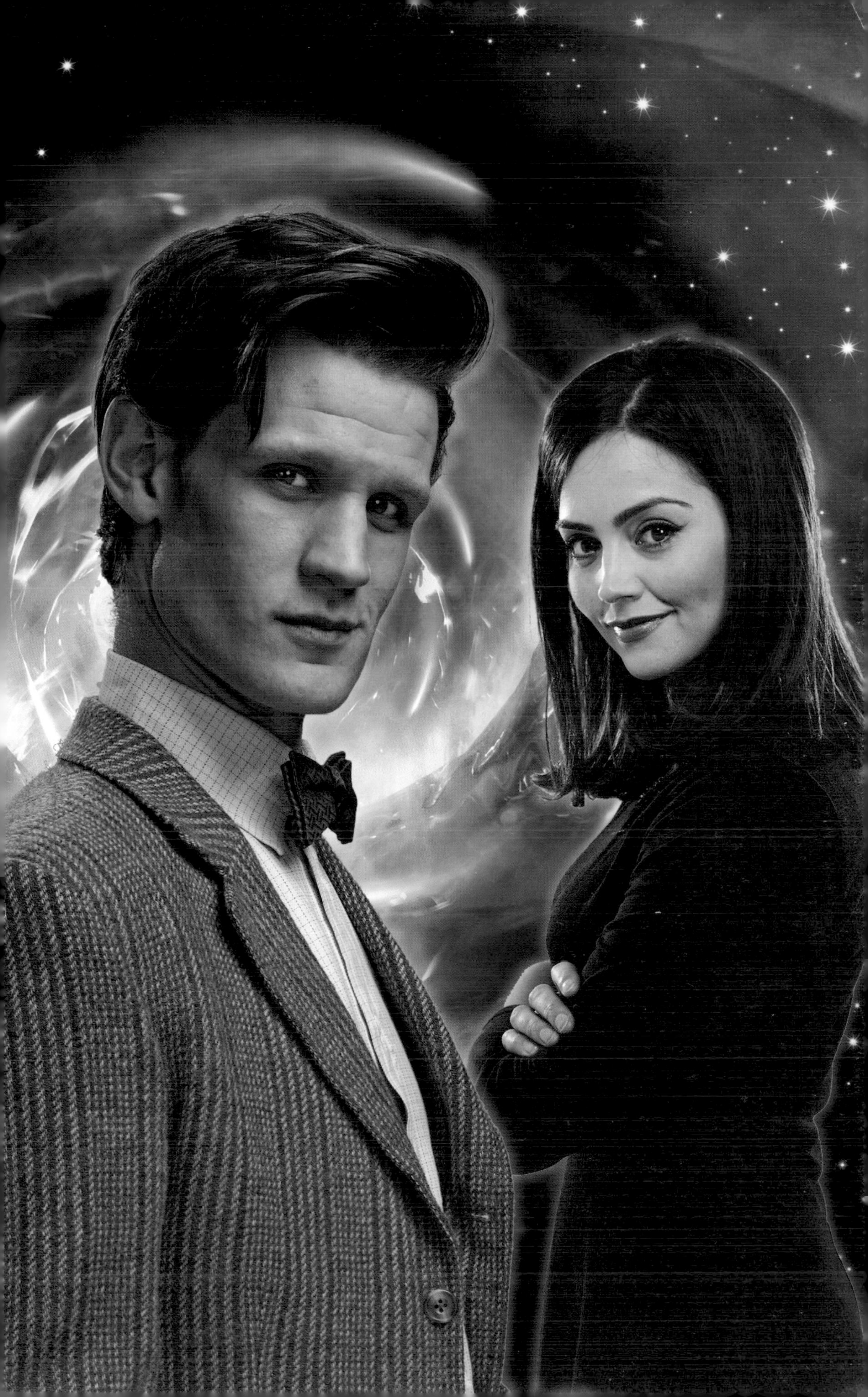

DOCTOR WHO

VOLUME 3: SKY JACKS!